Alfred's Kingdom

Wessex and the South 800–1500

Series editor: Dr Dennis Harding

History in the Landscape series

Alfred's Kingdom

Wessex and the South 800–1500

David A. Hinton

J.M. Dent & Sons Ltd, London

First published 1977
© David Hinton 1977
Made in Great Britain by
Wm. Clowes & Sons Ltd, Beccles
for J. M. Dent & Sons Ltd
Aldine House, Albemarle Street, London
This book is set in 11 on 12 pt Monophoto Garamond

ISBN 0 460 04289 0

British Library Cataloguing in Publication Data

Hinton, David Alban
    Alfred's Kingdom : Wessex and the South,
    800–1500. – (History in the landscape
    series).
    Bibl. – Index.
    ISBN 0 460 04289 0
    1. Title   2. Series
    309.1'422   HN383
    England – Social conditions
    Great Britain – Social conditions – To 1066
    Great Britain – Social conditions – Medieval

Contents

List of Plates

List of Figures

This book

Is dedicated to all the friends

Whom I stand to lose

For having written it.

Preface

This book attempts to survey the medieval development of the south of England, the heart-land of the Saxon kingdom of Wessex, as it is revealed by archaeological information. It is therefore primarily an economic and social history of a particular region. Many of the themes are relevant to other areas, but different geographical and historical factors mean that there was great variety within medieval England – of social structures, farming systems, methods of communication and available natural resources – so what applies to the south will not necessarily apply elsewhere. I have tried to bring out some of these differences, and further books in this series will explore different regions. One of them will seek to show how Roman Britain became Saxon England, and my theme begins in the eighth century, by which time Wessex had become recognizable as a formal kingdom and an administrative unit.

The history of England after Alfred's successes against the Danes (and I might as well confess immediately to an Alfredian bias, which will be apparent in the following chapters!) meant that Wessex quite rapidly ceased to be a meaningful unit. I have therefore dealt little with Somerset and west Dorset after the Norman Conquest, believing that they really then belong to different geographical systems – west Dorset to the south-west, Somerset to the Bristol Channel. I have included Oxfordshire, since I believe that that area, insofar as its trade was closely linked to South-ampton, can be seen as part of the south of England. But here too I must confess to bias: it would have been just as plausible to put Oxfordshire into a volume on the Midlands, or on London and the south-east. I have written about the areas that I know best, for I have spent much of my archaeological life in Oxford. I have also been able to draw on work that I have done recently in Hampshire and Dorset.

The manuscript of this book was written in 1975, and the typescript was completed at the end of March 1976. Its dedication is not entirely facetious. There may be those who will think that I have used information and ideas gained from their lectures or from their conversation, without acknowledgement. Certainly I have gained much from such sources, and for this I am grateful. Most of those whose work I have used are named at some point in the Bibliography, but there are some who are not, whom I wish to thank personally: in particular, David Brown and other former colleagues in the Ashmolean Museum and in Oxford, Patrick Wormald for his lectures on King Alfred, and Dennis Harding for his editing.

My contacts at Southampton have been many and fruitful: the Department of Archaeology is a friendly and stimulating place in which to work, thanks to both staff and students. The opportunity to read David Hill's doctoral thesis on the *burhs* and Derek Renn's on Angevin castles has been particularly valuable. The Department of Archaeology has also produced several BA dissertations which I have used, notably those by Fred Aldsworth on Saxon charters, Dominic Tweddle on Saxon wills, and Alan Vince, now a post-graduate student, on medieval pottery. The presence of Colin Platt in the Department of History is a constant boon. Conversation with Richard Hodges, and working with him at Wareham, have been profitable experiences.

I am grateful to those who have let me use their illustrations, which are separately acknowledged, and to Nick Bradford for his work on my own photographs. Finally I should thank Sue Davies for the use of her Rapidographs which she will now have to clean.

Acknowledgements for Illustrations

I am grateful to the following for permission to reproduce their copyright material: Ashmolean Museum – Figs 8, 11, 15, 16, 22; Plates xv, xxii, xxviii, xxix; Mr David Leigh – Plate viii; Oxford Archaeological Excavation Committee – Figs 6, 20, 33; Plates ii, ix; Mr Mark Robinson – Fig. 23; Mr Trevor Rowley – Fig. 27; Southampton Archaeological Research Committee – Plate i; Southampton University, Department of Archaeology – Plate iii; Winchester City Museum – Plate xiii; National Monuments Record – Plates v, vi, vii, x, xvi, xviii, xxi, xxiii; B. T. Batsford – Plate xx.

Chapter 1

Alfred's Inheritance

The south of England has some of the best land for mixed farming in northern Europe. Well-watered, naturally fertile, easily cleared for grazing or ploughing and with valuable tracts of woodland, most of it can support a large population and produce an agricultural surplus. Although there are barren stretches, notably the heathlands of Dorset and the New Forest, and although there used to be large tracts of forest – Selwood in the west, Wychwood in the north, Bere and Andredeswood in the east and Savernake in the centre – much of the country can be used for stock rearing and for grain crops. Most villages have a balance of soil types that permit all the basic farming activities, which reduced the risk of economic disaster from the failure of a particular crop. Only in the thirteenth and early fourteenth centuries, as more and more people attempted to live off a land whose surface area and soil fertility failed to grow as rapidly as the population that it had to support, was southern England's production inadequate.

Agriculture in the Middle Ages was of paramount importance, for most of the population lived and worked on the land, and those who lived in towns provided services which depended on agricultural products and prosperity. Although stone quarries were important by the eleventh century, although Domesday Book records three communities of potters and archaeology reveals others, and although salt-pans and fisheries gave coastal communities alternative occupations, most people in the south of England depended upon agriculture. The country's prosperity is difficult to measure in any meaningful way. Domesday Book gives a broad picture of conditions in 1066 and 1086, but even Domesday Book gives only a partial record, ignoring details in achieving overall assessments. Similarly, the kingdom of Wessex was 'assessed' at 100,000 hides of land in the seventh- or eighth-century Tribal Hidage list, but this figure cannot be turned into a financial equivalent. It means that the Wessex kingdom was expected to pay a very large sum to its Mercian overlord, but this sum may have been cripplingly large, chosen to keep Wessex in subjection, and may not have been a fair reflection of its wealth. Similarly, in the eleventh century, the quantities of silver that were levied to pay the notorious Danegeld cannot

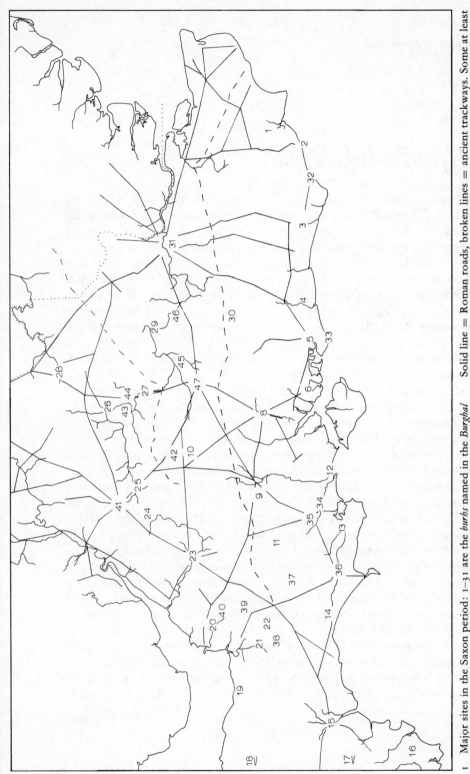

1 Major sites in the Saxon period: 1–31 are the *burhs* named in the *Burghal Hidage*; 32–46 are others known to have had a minster, or some sort of Saxon presence that was more, or may have been more, than just a 'village'. Some, such as Pevensey, a Roman fort (32), are sites which stand out as having had as much potential as Portchester (6), yet do not seem to have received the same use.

Solid line = Roman roads, broken lines = ancient trackways. Some at least of these were in regular use by the Saxons, others, e.g. the Winchester–Thames road, were apparently not major routes. Dotted line = boundary established by Alfred and Guthrum's Pact in 886.

be used to argue details of wealth distribution: they only show that England was rich enough to be made to pay enormous sums.

City Sites and Urban Origins

The archaeological evidence is like the documentary in that it reveals wealth but cannot be used for quantitative comparisons. This wealth is demonstrated spectacularly by the goods that passed in the eighth and ninth centuries through the port of Hamwic, the Saxon predecessor of Southampton, on the excellent natural harbour of the Solent, sheltered from storms by the Isle of Wight and with a unique double tide (7 on Fig. 1). The early port was on the west bank of the River Itchen. The coin evidence shows that its inhabitants had moved to the east bank of the River Test by the second half of the tenth century (Fig. 2). This shift in settlement meant that the original site became farmland, undeveloped until it was reincorporated into the town in the nineteenth century, and in consequence undisturbed by the medieval and post-medieval cellars, wells and rubbish pits which have obliterated much of the Saxon history of most towns. Unfortunately, even at Hamwic medieval ploughing and nineteenth-century brick-earth pits have destroyed the floor-levels of the houses and other buildings. Much of the evidence comes from the Saxon rubbish pits with which Hamwic abounds. Their contents are a remarkable tribute to the trade and to the wealth of the main harbour of the south of England, through which passed the exported surplus of its agricultural estates, and slaves taken in battle with rival kingdoms. It had been his encounter with English slaves in the market-place at Rome that had led Pope Gregory to send St Augustine and his mission to England in the late sixth century. Other crossings of the Channel were made voluntarily: many pilgrims travelled to Rome and other centres, suggesting regular ferry services. St Willibald is one who is known to have crossed from near Hamwic, in 721.

Buildings and gravel-surfaced streets, one with a wheel-rut still visible in it, have been found on Hamwic sites. Some street lines can be assumed, even where there are no surfaces left, from the absence of pits. The alignments of the streets suggest that they ran at right angles to a road along the river bank, forming a grid pattern. Such a regular grid is unlikely to have developed haphazardly, and it suggests that it was deliberately laid out by someone in authority. It was not all laid out at one time, however, for at least one street had earlier features below it. Nor is the grid a perfect chequer pattern, since at one point an excavation intended to locate an expected junction between two streets found a cemetery instead.

The size of Hamwic is difficult to measure, since its boundaries were not

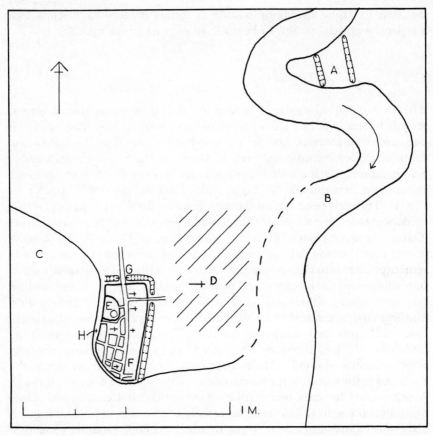

2 The Southampton peninsula: *A* – the Roman fort; *B* – River Itchen; *C* – River Test; *D* – St Mary's 'minster'; *E* – the castle; *F* – the Friary; *G* – the Bargate; *H* – the west walls. The shaded area shows the approximate area of Saxon Hamwic, east of the walled town.

defined by an enclosure ditch. The finds cover an area of over 30 hectares (75 acres), however. Its houses were built within large open plots probably surrounded by fences, not in end-to-end rows. Even in the most intensively occupied site in the south of England, there was plenty of open space in the streets. Of the harbour we are still ignorant. The precise line of the shore has not been found, nor any trace of warehouses, wharves or jetties. It has to be assumed that ships were beached on the shelving mud banks.

The people in Hamwic earned their living in various ways. Some were undoubtedly foreign merchants: *Frisii* from Dorestad and other Rhineland towns, and Franks from Quentovic and Rouen were probably most often seen. Their trade, if not their personal presence, is shown by the quantities of lava stone from Niedermendig in the Rhineland, and by the imported pottery and glass that are common in Hamwic rubbish pits. Less common are foreign coins. One very rare gold coin imitates a 'solidus' minted by the Emperor Louis the Pious (814–39) (Plate 1). Research into all these is trying to establish the precise source from which each product came, to see exactly how widespread were the trading contacts, many of which were presumably concerned with the import of wine. The northern coast of France and the Rhineland are assumed to have been the main districts, but the Seine basin was important too, not only because of Rouen but also because of the fair at St Denis, Paris. English traders at such fairs were not above disguising themselves as pilgrims to avoid tolls, which led to official complaints. Another complaint about English malpractice, also made by the Emperor Charlemagne to the Mercian King Offa, provides the earliest reference to one of England's greatest trades, in cloth.

The extent to which there was cloth and linen-making in Hamwic itself cannot be certain. No loom-emplacements have been found, but the cloth trade is demonstrated by the hundreds of pieces of equipment used in weaving: clay loom-weights, bone pins, spindle-whorls and 'pin-beaters' (Fig. 3). Such quantities of these are found that it becomes possible to think of specialist makers who concentrated on their manufacture for sale to weavers, not all of whom lived in the town. Such items are common-place on Saxon sites, for spinning and weaving were village industries, not just urban crafts.

Such was the demand for bone tools that large numbers of animals must have been slaughtered in Hamwic to provide the raw material. Enormous quantities of animal bone are found in the pits, and these too are being analysed. Cattle figure as prominently as sheep in the statistics, a reminder that the agricultural economy was not dominated by the demand for wool. Animals not only provided bones and meat but also skins that could be turned into leather, and parchment for books, for which monasteries created a large demand. Tanning requires special pits and gullies, and a tanners' quarter is now known in York, though not yet in Hamwic. That tanning took place can safely be inferred from the bones, however, and from a few finds of polishing-stones. The animals would arrive on the hoof for slaughter, and it would be uneconomic to ship the raw hides out for treatment elsewhere. This industry would lead to further demands for tools, though there is no evidence to suggest that the finished hides were turned into leather goods in Hamwic. One can assume shoe-makers and other leather-workers, but they were not necessarily supplying more than the local market. Much of the product was probably traded as hide out of Hamwic, inland or overseas, to be worked into shoes or whatever on arrival. Most medieval trade was never a matter of wholesaling finished goods to retailers.

The stench of the Hamwic slaughter-houses and tanneries must have been vile. Less objectionable, though often noisier and sometimes dangerous because of fire risk, were the various metal-working industries. A black-smith's furnace and forge, tapslag, and ores have been found. The black-smiths made such things as nails, the knives that everyone carried to cut their food and to defend themselves if threatened, horse-shoes, keys and tools. More skilled, perhaps, were the bronze-workers. Some of their small pottery crucibles have been found with copper deposits which show that they were used for melting the alloys that were poured into stone moulds – one for a ring survives – to produce the many different types of pin, the strap-tags and other small ornaments and objects that are common finds. Less common are lead products, although lead was an important English export, and neither silver nor gold is directly represented. There could have been glass-workers; although the 500 or more fragments of vessel glass found are probably all imports, the few beads could have been made on the spot. There is evidence of potters. Other trades are scarcely recognizable in the archaeological record: wood-working and carpentry, ship-building and house construction are revealed only through surviving rivets and nails, empty post-holes and occasional impressions in burnt daub debris.

The record of this community of craftsmen and merchants is therefore very partial, nor is it clear how the community functioned – who controlled its activities, how many people lived in it at any one time, whether its trade was cyclical or flowed evenly throughout the year, even the size of its anchorage and the site of its market. It was, however, the only place in the whole of southern England, except London and Canterbury, which was recognizably a town and which was on a par with such continental trading centres as Dorestad and Quentovic. Like them, but unlike London and Canterbury, it was a new site, not a Roman town reused. Similar new ports occur in Kent at such places as Fordwich and Sandwich, and in East Anglia at Ipswich and Norwich. Hamwic was the biggest, and the only one on the south coast. All these ports have the element *-wic* in their names and are close to royal centres, like Canterbury, or, in Hamwic's case, Winchester. Sites with established names which were also ports, like London and York, often had *-wic* added to their names in contemporary documents.

Hamwic may have been the first place in Wessex in which coins were minted, in the early eighth century (Plate 1). The moneyers' names on ninth-century pennies suggest that they may not have been natives of the kingdom, but came from far afield – the sort of people to be expected in a port, where there would be most demand for coins because that was where there would

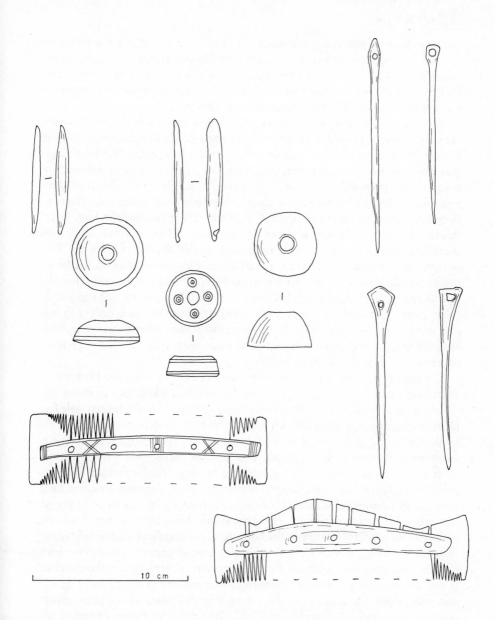

3 Saxon bone tools: top left – 'pin-beaters' (from Wareham); centre – spindle-whorls; right – needles; bottom – combs (from Hamwic).

be the most business transactions. It is not at all certain that the minting of *sceattas,* the eighth-century predecessors of the pennies, was closely super- vised by the crown, as was later coinage, so it would not necessarily have had to take place at a major royal centre. No trace of moneyers' activities has yet been found in Saxon Southampton, however.

The sceattas are very small coins, first struck in Kent in the late seventh century. Silver was used because gold had become very scarce in north-west Europe during the seventh century, when supplies from the Mediterranean were affected by the Arab conquests. They became increasingly debased by copper, and probably none were produced after about 750 because they were discredited. This may have affected Hamwic's trade, but such fluctua- tions are difficult to measure archaeologically. Over 200 sceattas have been found in the port, most of them of only two different types, and it is therefore assumed that they were struck in the Wessex kingdom. The designs of these two types are very similar to designs on sceattas found in the south Midlands, in the kingdom of Mercia, which suggests strongly that there were trading links between the inland kingdom and the south coast port. The trading community on the Solent was not only serving and exploiting Wessex. Was it in any real sense dependent on nearby Winchester, or was it an international mart with only the most general supervision from the Wessex kings?

The only place on the south coast which might have been like Hamwic is Wareham in Dorset (13 on Fig. 1). If Hamwic had a role as a port for the royal centre at Winchester, then Wareham might have had a similar role for Dorchester, another place known to have had a royal palace (36 on Fig. 1). Unlike Hamwic, there was Roman occupation at Wareham, but it was not a substantial Roman town. The place was to be developed later by King Alfred, but excavations (*h* on Fig. 4) have failed to throw further light on pre-Viking Wareham. It is at least clear that the port, if such it was, was on a very much smaller scale than Hamwic, and there are no traces at all yet of any urban life or crafts there. Indeed there may have been no wharf except perhaps a single jetty to supply the church, for Wareham was different from Hamwic in being a major ecclesiastical centre. Hamwic had at least one church, but probably with no function except to serve the townspeople. Wareham had a large 'minster' housing a community of nuns (*a* on Fig. 4), and was important enough to be a king's burial place in the early ninth century. A series of inscriptions with British, not Saxon, names and formulae date from the seventh to the ninth centuries – an interesting record that the British survived as a culturally distinct group within the Saxon kingdom.

Two ninth-century references might add to the picture of Wareham before Alfred's reign. It is then referred to as the *fierde* – the local assembly-

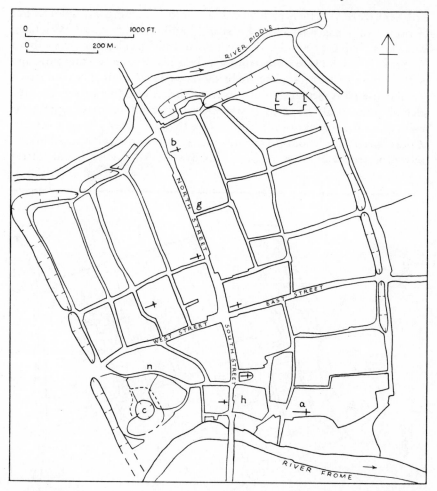

4 Wareham, Dorset: the ninth-century *burh* was surrounded on three sides by its Saxon banks, which still largely survive. The nucleus of the settlement was probably on the River Frome. *a* – the 'Minster' church of St Mary; *b* – the Saxon 'parish' church of St Martin; *c* – the Norman castle; *g* – site of 1974 excavation; *h* – site of abortive 1974 excavation; *l* – eighteenth-century bowling-green (long thought a Saxon earthwork!); *n* – site of 1975 excavation.

point for the army – and as 'a naturally very strong fortress'. This might imply some sort of defence-work, taking advantage of the peninsula of high ground between the Rivers Frome and Piddle. The documentary and ecclesiastical evidence about Wareham is suggestive, but archaeological evidence indicates that it was not a port and a town before the tenth century.

Recent work at Winchester (8 on Fig. 1) has been more informative, but in many ways has told a similar story. Unlike Hamwic and Wareham, Winchester had been a walled Roman town (Fig. 5). It has been the subject of ten years of intensive study from which its history is now emerging, and new concepts of Saxon society are being formed as a result. The evidence is that the town was virtually empty when a 'minster' was founded there in the seventh century, although there was probably a royal residence within the walls. Even the transfer of the bishop's see to Winchester, the enlargement of the church and the burials of most members of the royal household in it only produced very slow changes. Excavations at Lower Brook Street

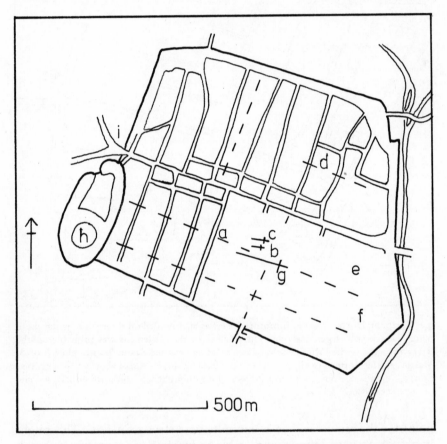

5 Winchester: the walls of *Venta Belgarum* provided the Saxon defences. Broken lines = known Roman street lines not reused. *a* – probable palace site; *b* – Old Minster; *c* – New Minster; *d* – Brook Street excavation site; *e* – Nunnaminster; *f* – Wolvesey Palace; *g* – Norman cathedral; *h* – Norman castle; *i* – West Gate.

(*d* on Fig. 5) have found late seventh-century burials, followed by a sequence of timber buildings forming a complex into which a stone building was added in the eighth or ninth centuries. This stone building was replaced by another, which in the tenth century was converted into a church. The excavator suggests that this complex may have been a small private estate, its owner drawn to Winchester by the royal and ecclesiastical centres. It is in marked contrast to Hamwic, where no stone buildings have either been found or inferred from rubble or mortar debris. Only a few fragments of window glass might hint at a structure of similar substance, but there is no proof that the glass was used in a Hamwic building: it might have been broken in transit. The stone building suggests a status difference, indicating a man of wealth at Winchester. The finds included two touch-stones for gold assaying, again a contrast to the base metal craftsmanship at Hamwic. Winchester however has produced very little pottery, no weaving implements and only one coin. All this suggests a very different kind of occupation from Hamwic's. The touch-stones show that the stone building was used by someone handling precious metals, perhaps a jeweller, perhaps even a moneyer. The possibility that Winchester was the site of the Wessex mint, not Hamwic, remains.

Of other places in the south of England that were later to become towns, the only one for which there is clear evidence of pre-Alfredian activity is Oxford (26 on Fig. 1), then in Mercia, not Wessex. Its history is not unlike Wareham's; it was not a Roman town, and a legendary history tells of a *monasterium* which may well date from the eighth century (*a* on Fig. 6). Until recently that was as far as the evidence went, but the recent discovery of a ninth-century burial has justified the claim that there was indeed a pre-Viking minster. Furthermore, excavation on the bank of the River Thames has produced, not actual occupation, but signs of human activity. Ignoring strong advice (from myself!) that the site was outside the medieval town and so not worth digging, the excavator not only found stratified sequences of early medieval occupation, but below them an artificial clay bank with eighth-century pottery in it. Being by the river (*b* on Fig. 6), this site was low-lying, and the earliest layers were below water-level, preserving lengths of waterlogged wattle fencing (Plate 11). The fencing had been used to retain the clay bank, and it has been dated by radiocarbon tests to the early ninth century. Clearly someone was already exploiting the river on the site of what was to become a city as famous as Winchester and Southampton.

This, then, is the effective summary of the positive archaeological record of the beginnings of urban life in the south. Other places have slight hints, but no more. Of these, the most interesting are the two Dorchesters. Dorchester-on-Thames was a small Roman town (44 on Fig. 1), and is one

MEDIEVAL OXFORD

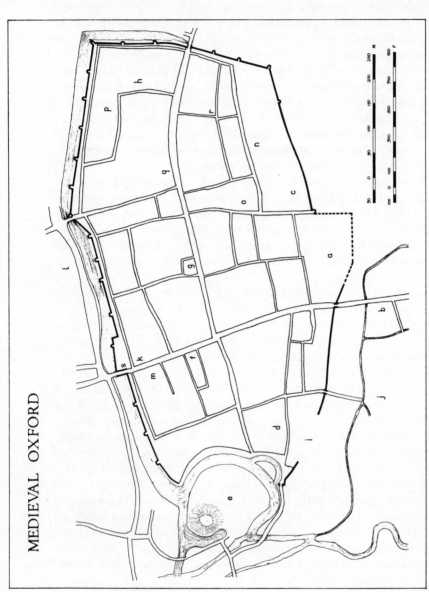

6 Oxford: the medieval ground-plan. *a* – St Frideswide's 'Minster'; *b* – St Aldate's excavation site; *c, d* –
sites of possible late ninth-/tenth-century defensive
ditch; *e* – Norman castle; *f* – site of 1954–5 Cornmarket
Street excavation; *g* – All Saints' church; *h* – St Peter's
church; *i* – site of Greyfriars; *j* – site of Blackfriars;
k – fifteenth-century shop; *l* – site of 1936 excavation;
m – site of 1970 Cornmarket Street excavation; *n* –
Merton College; *o* – Oriel College; *p* – New College;
q – All Souls College; *r* – Logic Lane, 1960 excavation;
s – St Michael's church.

of the few in which life has been shown to have continued. Certainly Saxon huts were built in it (Fig. 19, *b*), it may have been a royal centre in the seventh century, and it was a bishopric both then and again in the tenth century until just after the Norman Conquest. Despite these advantages it failed to become a town, its pottery sequence tails off in the ninth century and its latest coin-find is a penny dated to *c*. 865 – exactly the period which saw the emergence of Oxford. A road link from the Midlands to the port at Hamwic, which ignored the now-abandoned Roman town at Silchester (47 on Fig. 1), may account for this change in Thames crossing points.

Dorchester, Dorset, is a town which, despite many recent excavations, has not produced any direct archaeological evidence of itself (36 on Fig. 1). Like Winchester it was a major walled Roman town, and excavations in the cemetery at Poundbury immediately outside it have shown activity there at least into the sixth century. The cemetery site had become part of an agricultural settlement by the late Saxon period, however, so it did not have a continuous history. Nevertheless, Dorchester was a place of significance in the eighth century. Like Winchester it had some royal function: the king's reeve was there in 789 when the first Viking raid is recorded. Two eighth-century coins and a gold finger-ring have been found (Fig. 8), although the records of their find-spots are not very satisfactory. It seems that something was happening there – indeed its story may be like Winchester's without the bishop's minster, for the south-western see was placed at Sherborne (37 on Fig. 1). No structures like the stone and timber sequence at Winchester have been revealed, however. It was obviously an important place, but this importance did not necessarily mean that many people actually lived there.

Dorchester also gave its name to the shire, Dorset – the people 'dependent' upon it. Wessex was divided into shires at a very early stage in its history, and some of the kingdom's administration, such as the levies of the army, was arranged through the shires. Hampshire is named from Hamtun – a name used as an alternative for Hamwic – and it may be a sign of that place's relative importance in its area that it was selected, not Winchester. Wiltshire, however, was originally 'the people of the Wylye (river)', and Wilton, the centre of the area, may have been a later development; nothing is known of the place until the ninth century, when it emerges as a royal centre. Somerton, for Somerset, has no early history, and the shire was named Selwoodshire, after the forest, in some early sources. Similarly Berkshire appears to take its name from a wood, Berroc, located in the southern part of the Downs. It is far from clear how often the peoples of the shires met together, or whether they always met at the same place, and it is obviously wrong to think in terms of 'county towns' at this early period. Meetings were open-air assemblies, and required no permanent buildings or defences; consequently they required nothing that necessitated the development of a town to serve them.

'Up on lande'

So far as excavations show, therefore, Hamwic was the only place in Wessex which sustained any urban community of a type that would be recognized by modern standards. The lack of archaeological evidence in other towns demonstrates this lack of town life. In the countryside, however, the picture is different. There can be no doubt that throughout the region there were hundreds of thriving settlements. Nor is there much doubt that by the tenth century most of them were firmly established on or very close to the sites that they still occupy today, although their shallow-posted timber huts and houses have left hardly any trace that can be recognized by even the most skilful excavator, because they have been overlain and destroyed by the debris and activity of succeeding generations of villagers.

Most of the known Saxon settlements not below modern villages are located unexpectedly, often during excavation of sites originally selected to investigate earlier periods. Two recent cases are Old Down, Andover, Hants., where no one anticipated finding evidence of Saxon reuse of an Iron Age occupation site, and Ufton Nervet, Berks., an Iron Age and Roman site.

It has to be to abandoned sites that the archaeologist looks for his evidence of rural Saxon life, and it is difficult to be sure that such sites are representative. A site may have been abandoned because it was chosen badly by the first settlers, so that it never prospered. Its inhabitants might then have lived a more impoverished and depressed existence than their better placed neighbours. Other sites may have been different for legal or ownership reasons. One which is at present being excavated, Chalton in Hampshire, was a royal estate in the eleventh century, and could therefore have been different from other villages: special court sessions might have taken place there, for instance, giving it a function that was not directly agricultural and so giving it buildings and property arrangements different from those of exclusively farming settlements.

Chalton is a very exposed site, on the crest of a high chalk ridge (Plate III). The length of its occupation is uncertain, for it has produced very little pottery and only one object that can be closely dated, an enamelled escutcheon of the seventh century. The site had probably been abandoned at least by the ninth century, for it has no better made pottery of the type found not far away at Portchester, and which has been found in the fields around the surviving settlements down in the valleys.

The Chalton houses vary, but the type most commonly found on the site is a substantial rectangular building, post-built, divided internally by a cross-screen of posts that gives a small inner chamber taking up about a quarter of the space (Fig. 19, *a*). The main area was entered by doors opposite each other in the centre of the length of the wall. The post-holes suggest that some of the walls were of horizontal planks set between split logs, on a line just inside the principal upright posts. Some at least of these buildings stood within fenced enclosures, with lesser structures grouped around them. They conform closely to the image of house-building set out by King Alfred in his *Preface* to *St Augustine's Soliloquies*:

> Then I gathered for myself staves and props and bars, and handles for all the tools that I knew how to use, and crossbars and beams for all the structures I knew how to build . . . I advise each . . . to load his wagons with fair rods, so that he can plait many a fine wall, and put up many a peerless building, and build a fair enclosure with them.

Although the rectangular buildings are the most common at Chalton other timber structures have been found, and when the excavation of the entire site is complete it will be possible to see these different buildings, already numbering over sixty, in their physical context, and so to ask questions about their social functions. Other questions that may be asked concern lay-out of the site and the provision of a place of worship. Will a distinct church site be recognized and, if so, when was it established? Did the provision of a church become normal in the eighth century – if Chalton was still in use then? If the place was owned by the king, it might be expected to have acquired a church rather earlier than its non-royal neighbours, so that again its evidence could not be taken as typical. And where are the graves of those who used the Chalton site? No cemetery has yet been found.

It is difficult to know how far the evidence from sites such as Chalton, where the occupation has yet to be shown to have extended beyond the seventh century, can be used for village life in the eighth and ninth centuries. We do not know, for instance, if the most easily recognized of Saxon building types, the grub-hut, was still being constructed. This building was distinctive as it involved the digging of a cellar-pit, into which two or more posts were usually set (Fig. 19, *b*). Grub-huts are known from many sites: Chalton; Old Down; Ufton Nervet; Sutton Courtenay in the Thames Valley, where they were first recognized; further upstream at Eynsham; at Bourton-on-the-Water in Gloucestershire; as well as in East Anglia, the south-east and the Midlands. Just recently it has been realized that the floors of some of the cellar-pits were not living surfaces but had a wooden floor laid over them, and that the building was much bigger in area than the size of the cellar alone. The excavator of New Wintles, Eynsham, found that the filling of many of the pits was not compacted and trodden down but of rather fine dirt, which was the residue of the dust from the floor above that had fallen through cracks between the floor-boards. On the other hand, some of the earth floors in the grub-huts were certainly in everyday use: one at Dorchester-on-Thames had steps cut down into it and an oven on the floor. Such a structure need not have been a house: a shed for weaving was probably a common use, as the loom could be left in place overnight without being in the way. Some of the grub-huts might, however, have been considered adequate shelter for a slave. The Dorchester hut's oven suggests that it could be the first known example of a detached kitchen building, which was to be common in the Middle Ages.

There are still very many uncertainties, therefore, about the different types of Anglo-Saxon rural building. Of the rural economy it is equally difficult to generalize. Perhaps the most important thing to be established by recent work, both archaeologically and by reconsideration of documentary evidence, is that the countryside was much more fully exploited than used to be realized. This is not a realization confined to the Saxon period: it is clear that there was much more prehistoric and Roman settlement in valleys than used to be appreciated, and that it is wrong to say that heavier soils were avoided. Partly this reassessment has come from work by archaeologists on the routes of motorways, on which sites have been found in areas once thought to have been wasteland or woodland. The nine-mile length of the M40 through south Oxfordshire, for instance, produced fourteen sites of which two were quite unexpected Roman settlements, indicating extensive agriculture in the area in the Roman period. It is no longer sensible to suggest that these farms were totally abandoned in the fifth century. The buildings themselves were deserted, but the land would not have been. Although there were certainly large tracts of woodland, it is clear that very large areas of pasture and plough-land were maintained and cultivated. In much of England it seems likely that Roman estates survived as legal entities, even though they were supplying different markets and were usually being worked from different centres, not from the site of the villa. The evidence of this varies; the existence at the time of Domesday Book in 1086 of a particularly large land-holding at Lewknor, Oxon., became more interesting when we found a substantial Roman villa there, alongside the M40. Could the boundaries of the Roman farm have survived to become the boundaries of the medieval parish? This is suggested in parts of Wiltshire by the way that parish boundaries over-run the post-Roman Wansdyke, indicating that the earthwork was driven through the countryside like a modern motorway, leaving estates with land on both sides of it. Similarly it has been observed that parts of Hampshire have a distribution of one Roman villa per parish, as have the Chilterns.

It would be wrong to exaggerate and to suggest that all the land of pre-Viking England was intensively cultivated, for there were certainly wild places. The traveller had to carry a horn to blow in case he wandered off the track, to prove that he was not a furtive thief or outlaw. Woodland was exploited, as is shown in contemporary laws, both as a source of the rods, bars and beams that those who followed King Alfred's advice sought for their houses, and also as a food supply for pigs. Pannage was treated with as much respect in the laws as any cultivated crop. Pigs are valuable to a farmer because they allow him to utilize ground that cannot feed sheep and cattle; but they also act as useful ground clearance agents, their activities serving to prevent scrub and saplings from spreading. To a limited extent, therefore, the presence of large numbers of swine in a deposit of animal bones is an indication of the community's dependence on uncleared land, just as the more finicky sheep and cattle are more likely to indicate properly maintained pasture. It is thus another measure of the intensity of Anglo-Saxon agriculture that pig bones do not occur in very large quantities in the bone reports from most rural sites. These reports are often not yet completed, but preliminary results from, for example, New Wintles, show that cattle and sheep predominated. Nearby Cassington had more pigs than sheep, but more cattle than either. At Chalton, there seem to have been fewer cattle, but with deer and sheep appearing more than pigs. On the other hand, pigs were quite common in urban Hamwic: were they driven in for slaughter, or were they fattened in the back yards of the town on the household scraps? The pig is a usefully adaptable animal. Unfortunately the bone differences between sheep and goats are very slight, and they are very hard to separate in death, although not in life; an eighth-/ninth-century pit at Ufton Nervet contained a recognizable quantity of goat, however. The voracious appetite of the goat makes it unwelcome in a countryside cleared of its scrub. Twelfth-century documents from Glastonbury Abbey show that it was kept decreasingly, and it would be invaluable to have its record in archaeological deposits, as a guide to the extent of land clearance through the eras. The goat may never have been widely bred; it is the only animal to which no reference is made in King Ine's law code, and it is hardly ever mentioned in other documents, which suggests that its role in the agricultural economy was a minor one.

The balance of animal rearing is difficult enough to ascertain; the extent of cultivation of cereals and legume crops is even harder to estimate. Research is being pursued into this question but it is hampered by the fact that few seeds or grains survive, even in rubbish pits. At Hamwic, some grain has been recognized because it was oven-dried for storage, became carbonized and so had a better chance of survival. Unfortunately no one dried vegetables, so there is even less evidence about them, but various seeds have been recognized. Many are of plants like 'fat-hen' which can be eaten as a vegetable, but since they grow as weeds, their presence is not proof that they were deliberately grown or exploited. Similarly, nettles might have been grown for use in the tanning industry. Even grains have particular problems: at Wareham, we found a few in medieval rubbish pits, but it was possible that they had filtered down from the upper levels of the site, being carried into the lower deposits by root action. It was noticeable that the most grains were in the pit that had been the most penetrated by roots from the shrubs in the garden that covered the site in the nineteenth century.

The scale of the imports of lava querns to Hamwic is a measure of the quantity of grain grown, for it was by these querns that the grain was ground into flour. It is not yet known how common such querns will prove on village sites, for few have yet been recorded. The construction of a large mill complex attached to a royal estate on the Thames at Old Windsor (46 on Fig. 1) indicates large-scale cereal production.

On one site, Portchester Castle (6 on Fig. 1), furrows over the late Roman levels seem to indicate ploughing. Part of the interior of Winchester was also being ploughed some time before the tenth century when the fields were built over for the bishop's palace. Unfortunately the nature of the plough itself eludes us: no shares or coulters allow us to assess the strength of the implement, and whether it was iron-shod or wheeled. Estimating production remains largely a matter of assumption, and there is no way of knowing how much, if any, was grown as a deliberate surplus for market sale.

The only surplus which can be assumed is of wool, and perhaps of linen grown from flax. Spinning and weaving tools are found in large numbers: at Sutton Courtenay it was shown that one grub-hut had sheltered a loom, because a row of the loom-weights from it had fallen onto the floor. Combs, spindle-whorls and pins like those manufactured at Hamwic (Fig. 3) are found at Portchester, New Wintles, Sutton Courtenay and Dorchester; Chalton has produced only a couple of pins so far, another demonstration that that site may be different from others. Another site where implements have been prolific, including iron spikes from heckles used in carding wool or linen, is Shakenoak, Oxon. This site has been claimed as one which was continuously occupied from its Roman villa days until the eighth century. This claim has not stood up to critical examination, and it is more likely that it was reoccupied in the seventh century for a short while. The finds indicate considerable Saxon textile production from its flocks.

It is surely not over-estimating the potential of the Saxon economy to argue that the evidence of textile production indicates much more than weaving for home consumption alone, and that many of the looms were producing goods for sale. This market is attested by the finds from Hamwic, and from Charlemagne's letter. Although Hamwic shows that cattle-droving was also taking place, the evidence that is accumulating is that the Saxon looked to the cloth market to draw off the surplus of his extensive fields and pastures.

The Christian Presence

Bede's statement that St Martin's at Canterbury was a church built 'while the Romans were yet dwelling in the island' and that St Augustine was permitted to 'repair' churches has led to frequent speculation that Christian worship survived in Kent throughout the fifth and sixth centuries. This is a misreading of Bede, who certainly believed that St Martin's, in which the Christian queen Bertha worshipped, had been a Roman church, but he does not imply that it, or other churches, had remained in constant use. Excavations have not found anything to suggest that St Martin's is even a reused Roman building, only that much Roman material was reused in its construction. The only church in the English settlement area where archaeology even hints at continuity of use is a small church at Stone-by-Faversham, Kent where the foundations of a Roman building were certainly reused. That the Roman building was a *cella* is far from certain, but at least there are a few early Saxon sherds to hint that some sort of activity continued round the building.

Other churches in the English areas which are on, or close to, Roman buildings or sites have not produced any early Saxon material to justify a claim that they were Christian sites in the fifth and sixth centuries, nor is there any evidence that such Roman predecessors had Christian use. The location of a few churches on top of Roman buildings, as at Malmesbury and Wimborne, may not even mean that there was continuity of occupation on the settlement site. The processes of site change in the Saxon period prevent any claim of site continuity from the evidence of a church alone. The church at Widford in Oxfordshire, where the mosaic pavement of a Roman villa survives in situ below the chancel floor, is a special case, where there is nothing to suggest that the church is earlier than the thirteenth century. Roman occupation below a church need mean no more than that the area that had the best natural advantages for occupation in the Roman period was still the best area in the Saxon. Drainage and spring-lines attracted both the Roman and the Saxon land-owner, and it was usually the presence of the Saxon land-owner's house which led to the church being built alongside it. Occasionally there are other factors at work: the church at Knowlton, Dorset, is built inside a prehistoric ritual enclosure, perhaps to allay fears of evil spirits. A prominent position on a high point of land was frequently chosen for a village church – but often this will be found to be the best natural village centre in the area.

The possibility that some churches are on sites in Christian use in the fifth and sixth centuries still therefore depends on documentary rather than on direct archaeological evidence. St Albans provides the best English example of a Christian sequence such as can be seen in the Rhineland. The cemeteries of Roman towns were outside their walls. Burials of Christians, either third-century martyrs like St Alban, or fourth- and fifth-century 'saints', in such extra-mural cemeteries, meant that small shrines were put up, becoming in some cases so popular for pilgrims that a chapel was built with a priest to serve in it. A community might thus develop, eventually producing a full-scale church. Certainly the abbey at St Albans is on one of the extra-mural Roman cemeteries of Verulamium, and the establishment of a town at the abbey's gates in the late Saxon period meant that the old Roman centre was never reoccupied.

That St Alban's shrine was remembered and revered, to become the centre of the great medieval abbey, is an attractive hypothesis, particularly since it is known from documents that Verulamium was still a major centre in the fifth century, and archaeology has shown that there were people active in the Roman town well into the sixth. But direct evidence for the rest of the sequence is lacking, and it is dangerous to apply it to other places without substantial grounds. An obvious case where it might have been expected that an extra-mural cult-spot should become an early church centre is St Martin's, Canterbury, since it is known that it was a church by the end of the sixth century. Yet there is no Roman cemetery around it to justify such a claim, and the reasons for the choice of the site remain obscure. Such claims can easily be made on the flimsiest evidence: two urban churches in Cirencester (41 on Fig. 1) have been claimed as late Roman cemetery churches, when no cemeteries appear to surround them, and they occur only in late medieval documents. It is much more likely that they were medieval foundations, parish churches to serve a growing town population.

In the south of England, no cases of late Roman cemetery sites developing into the sites of Christian churches are known. Poundbury, the Roman cemetery outside Dorchester, Dorset, which continued to have some use into the sixth century, might well have produced such a case, but has not.

Of a different kind are the churches built by Irish Christians in the fifth, sixth and seventh centuries. Many of these saints are shadowy figures, church dedications to them and hagiographical lives usually being their only record. The contribution of a few is more certain. Maeldubh founded Malmesbury in Wiltshire (24 on Fig. 1), and there he trained Aldhelm, the first great Wessex bishop. Such men were not missionaries but sought isolation to achieve personal redemption by avoiding the world and its affairs; nevertheless they often attracted small bands of followers and a flourishing community might eventually grow from a small nucleus. The humble wooden cells, chapels and oratories of the founders then became overlain by grand stone churches, and the evidence of them is extremely difficult to find in an excavation. Glastonbury (39 on Fig. 1) had strong Irish links throughout its early history but its foundation remains uncertain: it is known that there were predecessors to King Ine's stone church of the late seventh century, but not that it was an Irish saint who began the community.

The rules that governed the lives of the Irish communities were not those of monasticism such as were formalized during the Middle Ages. The Irish saint's follower was not tied to him as a Benedictine monk was tied to his abbot, taking vows that gave the abbot paternal authority over him. The Irish had no fixed pattern of services and of labours, and they were free to leave their community to seek salvation elsewhere if they chose. Their buildings reflect their lives: an enclosure as a physical symbol of the exclusion of the outside world, and no set pattern within. A deep ditch attests such an enclosure at Glastonbury: presumably it had an internal bank.

The Mediterranean monasticism that St Augustine had known was more disciplined than the Irish. Few monasteries were established, however: Canterbury, perhaps, followed a regular rule, and so did Jarrow and Monkwearmouth in Northumbria. Such houses depend on great depth of devotion and endowments of wealth, and it may be that Christianity in the south was not so well established in the conscious lives of the people that monasticism of this sort could be maintained. Certainly we do not know what rules were applied in the seventh and eighth centuries, but the implication of King Alfred's failure to find monks for his foundation at Athelney at the end of the ninth century is that the principle of a full monastic life had never become established in Wessex, at least for men.

The organization of the early southern English houses therefore is uncertain, and probably varied according to the founder and to the zeal of the head of the community. Little is known of their physical appearance: King Ine's stone church at Glastonbury had a nave, side chapels (*porticus*), and presumably a chancel. It was small, the nave being less than 12 m

(40 ft) long, and was extended between the eighth and tenth centuries. Its position due east of the timber Old Church, and on the same axis, was deliberate, for it was not designed to replace the older building. It was presumably intended to create a line of separate oratories, similar to a line at St Augustine's, Canterbury.

So far as we know, Glastonbury was never raided by the Vikings. St Dunstan was educated there in the early tenth century, and he refers gratefully to the wealth of learned books that he found in its library. Recent excavations have located a small glass furnace which must belong to a period before the mid tenth century. What the rest of the monastery contained is far from clear: the line of oratories, and two very fine cross-shafts, belonged to the pre-Viking period, but how many of the oratories were standing at any one time is uncertain.

There may well have been numbers of Irish priests at Glastonbury, affecting the community's life and regulations. The glass furnace may owe something to their influence, for such craftsmanship is known from Irish monastic sites. It is not precluded by the regular Rule, but none has been found on an English monastic site, although it is known that there were glaziers, brought from Gaul, in eighth-century Northumbrian houses, and goldsmithing and silversmithing were practised in southern England by clerics – Dunstan himself was a craftsman.

King Ine's church at Glastonbury was small, but the church at Winchester which his predecessor Cenwalh had built, and which Ine considered sufficient for a bishop's *cathedra*, was not a lot larger, having a nave some 17 m (55 ft) long. It had a square-ended eastern annex, and *porticus,* presumably one on each side, and the main altar stood in the nave in front of the opening to the chancel. The north *porticus* contained a well, perhaps for use in baptisms, a ceremony performed only by bishops in the early church. At some time before the end of the tenth century a stone tower dedicated to St Martin was added to the Old Minster complex, a separate structure west of Cenwalh's church. In the ninth century, St Swithun was buried between the two and a cross was erected. The principle of an axis line may have been behind this arrangement, as at Canterbury and Glastonbury.

Another major church of which something is known from excavations is Abingdon, Berks. (43 on Fig. 1), where one of the greatest of England's medieval monasteries was founded by Hean in the late seventh century. Unfortunately the 1920s excavations are not easy to elucidate, and it is not certain if Saxon foundations below the Norman church were those of Hean's church or of some subsequent building. Around the chancel there may have been an external passage allowing pilgrims to view sacred relics kept in a crypt. Such an arrangement is known at the major Northamptonshire church at Brixworth, and at Cirencester, but not elsewhere in the south.

Hean's foundation was not the only community at Abingdon, for there was a nunnery nearby, traditionally established by his sister. Houses for women were at least as important as those for men in Saxon England – a reflection of the relatively high status accorded to women in society. Houses for women included the community at Wareham, Dorset. The church of Lady St Mary was regrettably destroyed in the nineteenth century, but was probably larger than those at Glastonbury and Winchester. It had a 17 m (55 ft) long nave, and prints and water-colours (Plate IV) show it as having had either a series of separate *porticus,* or a continuous aisle, on both sides of the nave, whereas Winchester had only single small *porticus.* The centre of the Wareham range was two storeys high, indicating an upper chapel. Since it is no longer extant, the date of the structure is uncertain: Asser's reference to it as a famous house, and its use for a royal burial, suggest a very substantial building. The pictures show continuous side aisles with the openings into the nave formed by an arcade pierced through the solid wall, not formed by a line of columns. This is the form of arcading known at the major pre-Viking churches at Brixworth and Wing, and perhaps at Cirencester, and is not certainly known in later churches. It seems on balance that a seventh- or eighth-century date is likely, especially since there is nothing in its later known history to suggest that it had much importance subsequently.

The existence of five British memorial stones at Wareham has been taken as evidence that there was some sort of pre-Saxon community on the site. The stones themselves can only be dated on the style of their lettering, but this does not indicate that they are early: a range between the later seventh and early ninth centuries seems likely, so that some if not all post-date the Saxon conquest of the area. They are not absolute proof of a *cella memoriae* on the spot, although the existence of such a shrine would explain why Britons still conscious of their ethnic identity should have sought burial at the place. There is no tradition of such a shrine, however, and no observations have been made in the church that might substantiate it.

The west wall of the nave at Wareham may still be partly Saxon. The other church with a good claim to have the earliest standing masonry in Wessex is Titchfield, Hampshire, where the lowest two stages of the tower (Plate V) may be a two-storey west porch of a type known in the north, as in the late seventh- or early eighth-century Monkwearmouth. The masonry is also like Monkwearmouth and the type of mortar used can be compared to that in Cenwalh's minster at Winchester. The wall is made of rubble, laid in courses, with generous use of Roman tile, and with a string-course – a projecting horizontal band – between the two storeys. The corners are strengthened with large stones, more carefully cut to shape – dressed – than the rubble. These 'quoins' are matched by the stones that form the arch over the west door. The Saxons did not understand masonry construction enough to cut the stones to form a fully load-bearing, keyed arch. Like the arcades at Wareham, the doorway was just an opening pierced through the wall, the stones being fitted together with blocking-pieces and mortar generously used to stop them slipping out. The stones were not freshly quarried, but were brought from the nearby Roman fort at Portchester. Such random assembly can be seen in the arches at other pre-Viking churches, like Brixworth. There is every reason to see Titchfield's porch as at least pre-Viking, and a good case has been made out for a late seventh-century date, and connections with Northumbria because of the travels of St Wilfrid.

Much more complete, though much more in dispute, is the church of St Lawrence at Bradford-on-Avon, Wilts. (Plate VI). Bradford was one of Aldhelm's foundations – Frome was the other – and there is certainly a surviving Saxon building there. It has a square chancel, a tiny chancel arch opening into a small nave from which opened two *porticus,* of which only the north survives. The west end has been rebuilt. Although it has often been claimed as Aldhelm's work, another strong possibility is that it was built by Shaftesbury Abbey after Bradford was presented to the nuns in 1001. Two carved flying angels over the chancel arch certainly belong to that period, and the decoration of arcading on the exterior is probably also a sign of a late date, with a strong comparison to the church at Milborne Port, Somerset. The arcading has been claimed as a later addition but the masonry does not substantiate this suggestion.

The record of church building in the south is not well known, therefore, either from archaeological or from documentary evidence. Nothing is known or can be inferred about the early work at such houses as Nursling, Wimborne, Waltham, St Frideswide's at Oxford, or even about episcopal seats such as Selsey, Sussex (which has probably been eroded away by the sea) (33 on Fig. 1), Dorchester, Oxfordshire, or Sherborne, Dorset. The picture is much less complete than it is for Northumbria, or Kent. It is therefore difficult to say confidently that relatively less money was spent in Wessex on church building and on maintaining ecclesiastical communities, but the direct evidence is certainly that this was the case. The lack of known ecclesiastical productions, such as manuscripts, plate and major sculptures, suggests a similar relative difference between Wessex and other kingdoms. On the other hand, at least some churches had big land holdings. The vast Chilcomb estate around Winchester given to the minster by Cenwalh ensured it a good income. The signs are, however, that money was less lavishly spent than elsewhere – and perhaps a lack of treasures in the churches meant that the Viking onslaught on Wessex was delayed until more fruitful and more accessible treasuries in other kingdoms had been plundered and exhausted.

Wealth and Commerce

The picture that emerges from recent work is of a prosperous rural economy, with a flourishing overseas trade through Hamwic. How was this trade operated in Wessex before it was disturbed and perhaps briefly destroyed by the Vikings? Hints in the laws indicate that the merchant was a rare visitor in the countryside – but frequent enough for his activities to require control and legislation. In Kent, probably a slightly more advanced economy, bargains had to be vouched for by the king's reeve or by reliable witnesses. The earliest Wessex laws, promulgated by King Ine in the late seventh century, similarly required witnesses for transactions made in the countryside and insisted that travellers should make their presence known by blowing horns. King Alfred made traders present their men to the king's reeve before setting out on a journey, so that it could be seen that they were not a band of brigands. The royal official who was killed by the first recorded Viking disturbance in 789 had ridden to the coast to find out the strangers' business. Clearly this was a regular part of his duties.

The itinerant merchant was a not unfamiliar figure, therefore. How he operated is uncertain, and it is not clear whether he was more likely to be a foreigner or a native. Hamwic shows plenty of foreign products, but it can be assumed that not all were brought by overseas merchants. Nor is it certain that the foreign merchants who did sail into Hamwic would themselves have led purchasing expeditions into the hinterland. They may have bought English goods in the port, relying on the natives to collect them from the villages, treating Hamwic almost as a trading fair like St Denis. Allied to this problem is the means of exchange. Were Frankish coins acceptable in England, in kingdoms which were not yet striking their own? If not, how were exchanges arranged in the seventh and early eighth centuries outside Kent and the London basin, before sceattas (Plate 1) were available elsewhere, and were coins used in the middle of the eighth century, before the reformed pennies were minted?

There are few finds of sceattas, or of the early pennies initiated by King Offa, in the south, except at Hamwic (Fig. 7). This makes the sceattas from Dorchester, Dorset, both of which are 'Southampton' types, seem particularly interesting if their provenance is reliable, but more important is that it

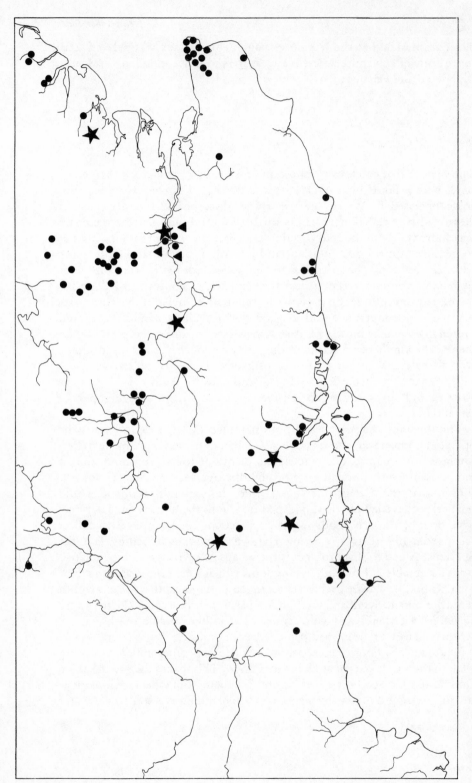

7 The distribution of coins (= spots) in southern England (NB those north of London indicate density, not precise location), and of gold objects (stars) and silver objects (triangles) attributable to the eighth century.

suggests the long survival of an almost non-monetary, barter, economy. This does not imply an impoverished economy, however, and it is worth noting that of the few gold and silver eighth-century objects such as finger-rings and sword-hilts, a large proportion is found in the non-monetary area. Clearly this was a wealthy region, even though it made little use of coin. The personal objects reveal reserves of private wealth, perhaps unmatched by that in other kingdoms (Fig. 8). Hamwic did not of course rely exclusively on its links with Mercia, even though the coin evidence indicates that its trade was more far-flung than might otherwise have been thought.

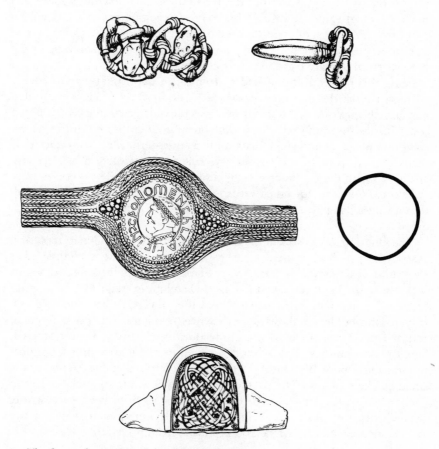

8   The fine craftsmanship of the eighth and ninth centuries is shown by the gold finger-rings from (top) Dorchester, Dorset, and (centre) Bossington, Hants., and the sword pommel (bottom) from Windsor, Berks. Drawn by Mrs P. Clarke.

Increased use of coin in Wessex during the ninth century is shown by hoards deposited at such places as Sevington in Wiltshire in the 850s, hidden in reaction to Viking raids. The Wessex kingdom had also expanded so that the mint at Canterbury came within its control and was used by King Ecgberht after 825. The Wessex kings probably also used the Kentish mint at Rochester, and briefly the London mint until the king of Mercia re-established his control over the town.

Although the largest numbers of coins are found in certain centres – over 200 sceattas have come from Hamwic – most of the spots on the distribution maps are stray finds in the countryside. It was essentially a rural economy that was being served. The spread of coinage is a reflection of increasing social sophistication, the recognition that a symbol-object can have an actual value. It argues also for the development of a recognized authority, whose symbol established the coin's validity. Coinage and statehood were not far apart in Wessex, at least so far as the minting of the pennies from the late eighth century is concerned.

Being a rural economy, it had a strength in depth that was to enable Alfred to resist the Scandinavian threat. The burning of Hamwic in 840 may have been a disaster, but Hamwic was the only economic centre which could be destroyed in such a way. The burning of crops and churches, the slaughter of slaves and stock, have only a short-term effect. Agriculture is quick to recover its former prosperity, unless the destruction is as systematic as William the Conqueror's deliberate devastation. The Vikings were different: they came for quick returns, and the damage that they inflicted, though agonizing to those affected, rarely caused permanent economic disaster.

The kingdom of Wessex in the early ninth century expanded its territory, eastwards into Kent, northwards to establish permanent control over Berkshire, and westwards into Devon. Stability came to the kingdom with a well-established and respected dynasty. Developing trade and developing recognition of government are shown by the coinage. Royal control of rich private land-holders is shown by insistence on the fulfilment of services in return for estates. Racial disharmony does not seem to have occurred. The British elements, such as those attested by the Wareham inscriptions, the descendants of the 'Jutes' in the Isle of Wight and the Meon valley, small pockets of non-Saxons indicated by a few names such as Exton (= the *tun* of the East Saxon folk), all seem to have been successfully welded into the wealthy and internally stable kingdom to which King Alfred succeeded in 871. His troubles came from his external foes.

Chapter 2

King Alfred the Great

There are few people in history who have both gained and retained the approbation of historians: Alfred of Wessex is one of them. Despite the discrediting of some of the popular myths about him, in particular the episode of the cakes, Alfred's achievements and ideals were such that he alone of English kings justifies being called 'the Great'.

Alfred's reputation has been gained largely because we know so much more about him than about any of his successors until after the Norman Conquest, partly from his own propaganda. The *Anglo-Saxon Chronicle*, for instance, was begun in his reign in imitation of similar Frankish *Annals,* and it was designed to emphasize the success of the Wessex dynasty, and of that dynasty's present incumbent in particular. Not only does it ignore most events outside Wessex, but it deliberately disguises matters that might not show the dynasty in an entirely favourable light. A similar slant is shown by Alfred's biographer, Asser. It is possible that Asser wrote to convince his fellow Welshmen of the merits of the king, to encourage them to give him their allegiance. The delicacy with which Asser treats Alfred's illness may be because the king had a more unsavoury reputation amongst his contemporaries than we have been allowed to know. Like the *Chronicle,* Asser's *Life* is closely based on Frankish models, particularly lives of Charlemagne and Louis the Pious.

It is worth stressing these Frankish influences, for Alfred's court and kingdom were culturally very much affected by the Carolingian empire. One of Alfred's closest advisers, John, came from a part of what is now Germany, and Grimbald, who may have been even more influential, was also a Frank. In many different ways, it can be seen that Frankish examples were the models on which major developments in England were based.

The substantial historical evidence about King Alfred's career can be illuminated by archaeology. The archaeology of a period for which there is documentary evidence is usually concerned with the economic and social aspects of that period, and with the everyday lives of those who lived in it. Only rarely can it contribute to political history, and only rarely can it throw light on the work of an individual whose name, if known at all, is more than an entry in a taxation roll. It can fairly be claimed that a study of the archaeology of the late ninth and early tenth centuries contributes to our knowledge of what a particular individual achieved.

To some extent, the archaeologist's contribution is to demonstrate that claims made for Alfred by Asser and the *Chronicle* are not mere exaggerations.

> What shall I say of the cities and towns which he restored, and of the others which he built, where before there had never been any? Or of the work in gold and silver, incomparably made under his direction? Or of the halls and royal chambers, wonderfully made of stone and wood by his command? Or of the royal residences, built of stone, moved from their former positions, and most beautifully set up in more fitting places by the king's command? (Asser).

Of these rhetorical questions, only the last deals with something on which archaeology has nothing to say – except to question whether Asser has not allowed over-enthusiasm to run ahead of him, for archaeology has in fact shown that although palaces were grand, there is little evidence of stone building, let alone of their being moved to new sites.

'The Cities and Towns'

The survival of documents is as haphazard as the survival of archaeological remains, and just as objects that do not find a place in a museum can be lost and forgotten, documents that are not in a safe depository can be destroyed by damp or fire. The depredations of the Vikings in the ninth century and again in the eleventh led to the destruction of many churches that housed archive collections, and losses by fire were endemic in the Middle Ages. The dissolution of many religious institutions in the sixteenth century led to the dispersal and frequently the negligent destruction of thousands of manuscripts. A further disaster occurred in 1731 when the greater part of the magnificent library formed by Sir Robert Cotton was burnt. Fortunately, diligent antiquarians had made copies of many of the Cotton manuscripts, so that some record of them survives. One manuscript which was burnt, but which had been copied, is a remarkable document known as the *Burghal Hidage,* the subject of several important recent studies.

The *Burghal Hidage* is a list of strong-points, and a statement of how many *hides* 'belonged' to each of them, with a table which shows that this assessment provided that the walls of each fort should have a fixed quota of one man from each hide, providing four men per $5\frac{1}{2}$ yards of wall (5.03 m). It was probably written soon after Alfred's reign, for it refers to Oxford and Buckingham which were not within Alfred's jurisdiction. Despite this, it probably shows a strategy initiated by King Alfred to provide a chain of fortresses round the borders of Wessex, with a few in the central areas, which meant that everyone was within 25 miles, and usually rather less, of a place of refuge to which he could take his family and some of his property when a Viking raiding-party was in the area. Although it is not an original scheme – a chain of forts set at 20 km distances along the coast on the opposite side of the Channel may have been the direct inspiration – it shows foresight in its planning and control in its execution that is a tribute to Alfred's government. The idea of fortresses was not new to Wessex, for their maintenance was one of the duties that invariably had to be under-taken by land-owners. The kingdom of Mercia is now known to have had sites surrounded by bank and ditch defences, and these too may have acted as models for the Wessex system. There is nothing to indicate that these forts were part of a planned overall system, however.

We know that this scheme was largely Alfred's because of what Asser tells us, not in praise of the system, but rather in condemnation of the slackness of those who failed to obey orders: 'I can speak of fortresses, which he commanded and which have not been begun, or which, being begun too late, have not been brought to a perfect end because the armies of the enemy broke in by land and sea.' Asser also records two forts being built in the Somerset marshes, from one of which, Athelney, the king began his great counter-attack against the Viking Guthrum in 878 (38 on Fig. 1). Similarly there was a fort at an unidentified site called Cynuit in Devon, in which a Saxon army took shelter, apparently behind some rather feeble defences, and proceeded to make a successful attack on the besieging Vikings. The Viking armies also used forts: they had one at Reading in 872, and in 876 they were in Cambridge, a Roman site where the walls survived; in 877 they moved to Wareham, presumably destroying the community of nuns there but not necessarily burning down the church, before going on to Exeter, another place with Roman walls to offer protection. The great Saxon victory of 878 culminated in a successful siege of the Vikings who had taken refuge in a fortress at Edington.

The Alfredian *burhs* are interesting archaeological sites. There are one or two in the list in the *Burghal Hidage* that have yet to be positively identified. *Eorpeburnan* is the first named, and nowhere called that is now known. A probable site is Castle Toll at Newendon, on the borders of Kent and Sussex (1 on Fig. 1). Excavations here have at any rate not disproved that a bank across a neck of land may be ninth century. The ditch was unfinished by its builders – and the *Chronicle* tells us that in 892 the Vikings successfully stormed a fort on the River Limen because it was incomplete and not properly defended.

After *Eorpeburnan,* the *Burghal Hidage* proceeds westwards along the coast. There is no doubt about the location of the next two places, Hastings (2) and Lewes (3), which have both become small towns, although the precise line of the latter's defences is not certain: the former was a Roman fort. Burpham (4) is probably a site like *Eorpeburnan,* a bank running between a marsh and a river to cut off a peninsula. Next is another Roman town, this time a former 'capital' – Chichester (5). Presumably the walls could easily be made serviceable, and the place was easier to defend than nearby Selsey, which was the bishop's seat. Recent excavations at Chichester have not proved that anyone was living there before the tenth century.

The next *burh* in the list is another Roman fort. This is Portchester (6), sited to command the important inlets that offer the best harbourage between the Solent and Thanet. The Roman walls still stood in the ninth century, and still stand, with alterations, today. This is another site on which there have been major recent excavations, which have shown that after at least the sixth century, some of the area inside the walls was being ploughed. Presumably there was a small community of farmers for whom the walls provided natural shelter. More intensive use began at an uncertain date: rectangular buildings were erected in the eighth or ninth century, but there is very little that was found associated with these structures to allow any more specific period to be hazarded for them. At some time in the Saxon period the gates were reconstructed. Portchester is the only *burh* in the list known not to have been on land owned by King Alfred: it was owned by the bishop of Winchester until 904, when it was exchanged between the bishop and Alfred's successor, Edward the Elder. The bishop might, however, have been responsible for making it defensive before the exchange. A letter to Bishop Waerferth of Worcester (889–99) written by Alfred's daughter and son-in-law when rulers of Mercia, gave that prelate authority that 'the borough at Worcester be built for the protection of all the people . . .'

After Portchester came Hamton (7). Here there is a curiosity in the list, for only 150 hides 'belonged' to the port, yet Hamwic was the most prosperous place in Wessex – or had been until the Danish raid in 840. The *Burghal Hidage* formula would provide only 150 men to defend a mere 188 m (206 yards) which is far too short to provide a circuit around the port of Hamwic. Nor have the excavations there shown any trace of a bank and ditch. The best explanation is that the Saxons again used a Roman fort, for there is one on a peninsula just up river from Hamwic (*A* on Fig. 2). The Roman wall that cut off this neck of land was 190 m (208 yards) long, almost exactly the right length for the assessment. It was therefore probably used by the Saxons: it is known to have survived reasonably intact until the sixteenth century. Furthermore, a few traces of Saxon use of the site have been found, notably a few post-Roman burials. There is a slight caveat to this identification: it could be that the *burh* was on the bank of the Test, the site that was to become the medieval port. Traces of an early ditch have been found, in which was possibly tenth-century pottery and a late tenth-century coin at the top of its fill. Although it is difficult to see how this could have been an effective defence if it was only 188 m (206 yards) long, it does raise a shadow of doubt about the Roman fort's reuse.

About Winchester (8) there is no doubt. The assessment is for 2400 hides, which gives a wall length of 3016 m (3300 yards), only 11 m (18 yards) less than the actual circuit round the Roman walls of 3027 m (3318 yards). Interestingly, a recent excavation produced an unexpected salient in the wall, which gave it a length even closer to the total in the *Burghal Hidage* than had previously been thought.

With Winchester the list has moved inland, and it stays inland for the next three sites. At Wilton (9) there is no evidence of the *burh's* physical appearance, nor of the precise lines of its defences, which presumably have been built over by the medieval market town. There is a hint in the documents that there was a minster there by the ninth century. *Cissanbyrig* (10) is probably a different kind of site, a reused Iron Age hill-fort. Such a place could quite easily have been put into a state of defence. The most likely hill-fort is Chisbury near Bedwyn, a royal estate, and has not been excavated. Shaftesbury (11) is a site that takes advantage of a spur of high ground: a bank of 877 m (960 yards) as provided by its 700 hides would be enough to secure it. Where this bank was is uncertain: it has been claimed that a slight ridge visible in gardens west of the site of the abbey is the last vestiges of it. If so, the abbey was outside the defences, which seems extraordinary. Asser tells us that Alfred founded a nunnery at Shaftesbury, where there may already have been a minster, probably in a derelict state, and that he had it built 'next to' the gate. An early eleventh-century inscription which no longer survives recorded that Alfred built the *urbs* in 880. This inscription might have been set over the gate.

The *Burghal Hidage* list next returns to the sea, to a site which had not been occupied before. This is now called Christchurch, but to the Saxons was Twyneham (12). A recent excavation showed that a bank and ditch there ran across the peninsula of land between the Rivers Stour and Avon. Another site within the town has produced some Roman tile and other debris but no Roman structures, and nothing at all that suggests any occupation before the tenth century.

Of the sites so far considered, only Portchester with its Roman walls has kept its defensive circuit complete. At Wareham (13) there are preserved the remarkably impressive banks with which three sides of the town were surrounded (Plate VII). Wareham, where there was already at least a minster, was described by Asser as the 'safest situation in the world, except on its western side where it is joined to the mainland'. The ridge of high ground between the River Frome and the broad stretch of swamp through which the River Piddle meandered, was an obvious strong-point (Fig. 4). The western bank was put into a state of defence as recently as 1940, as a barricade against tanks! As a result its outside ditch was lowered and its slope was made nearly vertical, which may have damaged it archaeologically, but gives a much better idea of its defensive potential, as it rears above a spectator standing in the ditch below. Here it can really be seen that a thin line of men with arrows, spears and stones would be a very effective deterrent.

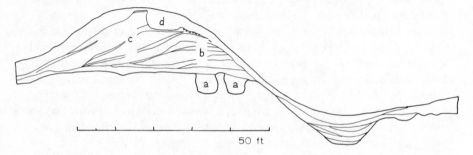

9   Section through the bank and ditch on the west side of Wareham (see Plate VII) (after RCHM): *a* – Iron Age pits; *b* – layers of first-phase bank; *c* – layers of second-phase bank; *d* – area of robbed-out stone wall.

A section was excavated in the 1950s through the west bank of Wareham, showing that it had three phases (Fig. 9). Iron Age pits were discovered in the soil below the rampart, and extensive Roman occupation somewhere nearby was shown by the large number of sherds found. The first phase of the bank could have been built at any time after the fourth century, the date of the latest pottery in it, so it cannot be absolutely certain that it was not already there by Alfred's period – it could have been thrown up by the British against the Saxons in the seventh century, for there are many British linear defences. There are no British parallels for the enclosure of a peninsula, however. Could it be that Alfred added a north and east bank to an existing west bank? Only further excavations could hope to establish this point, and it must be remembered that the chances of finding ninth-century pottery in a ninth-century bank are remote. If the site had not been occupied before the bank was built, there would be no pottery lying on the ground to get thrown up with the soil. Nor could it be proved that the bank was not constructed by the Vikings in 877, when they wintered in Wareham.

There is therefore an element of doubt about the west bank and its date. The changes made to it in the tenth or eleventh centuries, and again in the twelfth century, have obscured some of the details of its construction, and it was probably higher than the 3 m (9 ft) above the original ground surface, which was all that survived to be found in the excavation. An external ditch can be assumed, but later recutting had removed its sides. From this ditch layers of sand and gravel were thrown up to form the bank, which was probably fronted by a vertical pile of turves laced with timber.

It would have been possible to defend Wareham with the west bank alone, as no enemy was likely to be able to attack over the marshes on the north and east sides. It is perhaps a mark of Wareham's status that it was, nevertheless, given banks on those sides. No bank was built on the south, however, along the River Frome, nor did the assessment give coverage to this side. 1600 hides would give 2011 m (2200 yards), which is very close to the length of the three banks. Did it fall to the established *monasterium* to provide defenders along the bank of the river?

After Wareham, the next *burh* was *Brydian,* probably another reused Iron Age hill-fort, Bredy (14), which overlooks the mouth of the River Brit. Next comes Exeter (15), the third major Roman town. There was a minster in the town in the seventh century, but its later history is unknown. If it did still exist in 878, the community would certainly have been destroyed by the Viking party which moved in from Wareham that year. At Exeter, the assessment provides enough to man only a fraction of the walls, for no obvious reason.

The next Devonshire site is Halwell (16), and the *burh* could be either of the two Iron Age forts within the present parish. Walking round one of them recently when its centre was under plough revealed no pottery to solve the question. Halwell is the last site on the south coast, for the *Burghal Hidage* did not provide cover for Cornwall: the British kingdom of Dumnonia had been soundly defeated by Alfred's father King Aethelwulf, but had not been incorporated in Wessex. The frontier is marked by *Hlidan* probably but not certainly Lydford (17), a well-sited promontory guarding the access-route up the valley of the Lyd. It is the only *burh* where a long stretch of the walls has been excavated, showing that the bank was thrown up in sections, each about 25 m (80 ft) long.

The *Burghal Hidage* has now reached the north coastline, with Pilton (18), a fort covering the harbour of Barnstaple, just as the Roman fort site could have covered Hamwic. The inhospitable Devon coastline needed only one more defensive point – Watchet (19). The next in the list is another very small fort needing only a handful of men, Axbridge in Somerset (20), now well inland, but then on the edge of the marshes, and overlooking the navigable River Yeo. Further up this stream is Cheddar (40), where excavations have revealed that there was a palace, which Axbridge helped to protect.

Turning inland, the list next gives us Lyng (21), one of the two forts mentioned by Asser, and joined to Athelney by a causeway. It has been suggested that a predecessor of the present church was part of the defensive system, for the bank and ditch which cuts off the promontory passes under the church site. Lyng today is a small village, and the causeway still links it to Athelney (38), now marked by a single farm. These places rose above the marshes like islands. The fort used by Alfred in 878 may have been Athelney Tump, a detached hillock which has the same conical shape as Glastonbury Tor. Excavations here showed no trace of temporary occupation, but probably none would have survived the digging of foundations for the medieval church that now crowns the tump. Alfred might have felt safer on it with his 'small force' than on the larger but lower island on which he later built a monastery.

Nothing is known about Saxon Langport (22), another hill-top site. It is the last of the chain of small Devon and Somerset forts, for it is succeeded by Bath (23), a former Roman town. It is usually thought that Bath is being described in the Saxon poem *The Ruin*, although the poet may have been describing an imaginary Babylon. At any rate, the picture fits the ruined baths and fallen temples of *Acemannesceastre*:

> Wonderful is this wall of stone, wrecked by fate.
> The city buildings crumble, the bold works of the giants decay.
> Roofs have caved in, towers collapsed,
> Barred gates are gone, gateways have gaping mouths, hoar frost
> clings to mortar. (trans. K. Crossley-Holland)

Nevertheless, a minster was founded there in *c.* 675, although its history is unknown, and it was possible to put into repair 'The stone wall (which) encompassed all'.

Malmesbury (24) was chosen because of its site on a high promontory overlooking the River Avon. It is not known if the minster founded by Maeldubh still survived. There is no record of any Saxon use of the next site, Cricklade (25), but there is now some archaeological evidence of Roman occupation, possibly for a small Roman market which could have been a landing-point for Cirencester, to which Cricklade is joined by a Roman road. Cricklade's Saxon defences still partly survive, although much less visibly than Wareham's. They formed a complete rectangular circuit, so that there was a bank even along the river. There was an external ditch also, at least along the land sides. The bank was originally earth with a turf revetment along the front, later strengthened by a stone wall and rampart, as at Wareham. The top of the bank had been so worn down that there is no way of knowing its height, except that it was over 2 m (6 ft), its height at one point on the north side where an extension to St Mary's Church was built over it in the thirteenth century. Its full width was about 10 m (32 ft).

Because of copyist's errors, there is some doubt about the assessments of Cricklade and Oxford (26), the next *burh* in the list. The most recent editor prefers to give Cricklade 1500 hides, which would produce 1870 m (2046 yards), marginally short of the actual circuit of slightly less than 2102 m (2300 yards). This gives Oxford 1400 hides, a length of 1759 m (1925 yards), which is a circuit much shorter than the medieval walls (Fig. 6). It is probable that the original *burh* became too small, and so was later enlarged. This new interpretation has led to reconsideration of Oxford's defences, and already one possible line has been suggested by the location of a ditch under one of the college quadrangles (*c* on Fig. 6). Although it was some 3½ m (12 ft) deep, nothing was found in the fill of the ditch: this in itself hints at an early date, like the lack of Saxon finds in the Wareham bank. Another section of ditch at Oxford has been excavated recently in Church Street (*d*), its surviving depth being only some 1¼ m (4 ft). The upper fill of this included pottery that was earlier than might have been expected – eighth or ninth century. There were also some tenth-century sherds, however, so the earlier ones were residual. The ditch could well be the late ninth-century defence, having only had a short life before it was filled and built over. It could be even earlier, perhaps something to do with the people who constructed the clay bank down by the river. It is too far away from St Frideswide's to be connected with the eighth-century minster site there.

Another new site on a royal estate was Wallingford (27 on Fig. 1). As at Cricklade, a bank was thrown up to form a rectangular enclosure, the fourth side of which was the River Thames (Fig. 10). Wallingford has 2400 hides, giving a circuit of 3016 m (3300 yards). This figure must include the line along the river, unlike Wareham. The boundary probably crossed the river at one point, to cover the ford or bridge with a ditch and bank. The modern council boundary still follows the river except at that one point where it swings onto the opposite bank, and takes the line of a ditch which may well have been first dug as part of an out-work defence for the bridge-head. This bridge-head defence work has recently been shown to have Frankish models. Another clear example occurs later in the *Hidage* at Southwark.

The banks that survive at Wallingford are almost as impressive as Wareham's, but they are slightly less complete. Sections have been dug through them twice recently, once by an archaeologist, and once by the GPO! Fortunately the latter was observed by archaeologists, and a record

37

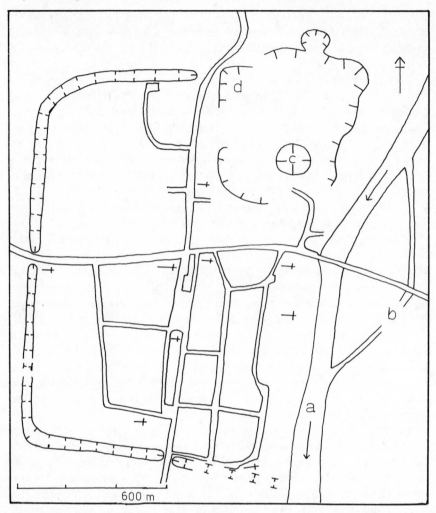

10 Wallingford, like Wareham a *burh* with surviving banks: *a* – River Thames; *b* – boundary ditch marking possible bridge-head defence; *c* – Norman castle; *d* – Saxon gateway and road, obliterated by thirteenth-century extension of castle.

made. As at Wareham and Cricklade there was more than one phase, the earliest bank containing only a single Roman sherd, so that again it could not be closely dated. Below it was an old ground surface that had been agricultural land before the bank was thrown up. The small area seen suggested that this bank was made of turves throughout, not just at its front. Unfortunately the whole of the front had been cut away, so that it could not be compared to the other section, dug across the northern bank. The first phase here was also of turves, in this case fronted with a timber revetment. It is worth noticing how the bank has 'moved' over the years. The original crest was at least $1\frac{1}{2}$ m (5 ft) further out than the present one: later erosion of the front and silting-up behind have caused the highest point of the bank to creep gradually backwards.

The *Burghal Hidage* list now jumps northwards to Buckingham (28). Like Oxford, this was not in the control of Wessex in Alfred's reign, and the *burh* was not built until 914 by Edward the Elder – he took Oxford in 911. The list then reverts to the Thames frontier, with a fort at *Sceaftesige*, probably an island now called Sashes (29). It then goes southwards to Eashing (30), and ends back at the Thames at Southwark (31), on the opposite bank from London, so that the two together acted as a double *burh* to block the river. London itself was 'honourably restored and made habitable' by Alfred in 886, but he 'handed it over to the care of his son-in-law Ethelred, ealdorman of the Mercians' (Asser). Clearly Alfred regarded it as part of Mercia, to be ruled separately from his Wessex government. This explains also the absence of any Kentish *burhs* in the list. Although Kent had no king of its own it was still regarded and administered as a separate kingdom, so places like Rochester and Canterbury are not included, although the former was one place where the burghal system is known to have operated successfully. In 884, Viking forces 'laid siege to . . . Rochester . . . and outside the gate built a strong fortress, and yet were unable to take that city, since the citizens valiantly defended themselves, until King Alfred, bearing help to them, came with a great army'.

The Vikings fled from Rochester without putting up a fight from their own temporary fort. The siege shows how the defensive system could work: safely encircled by their walls, the townsfolk held out until King Alfred came to their relief. A small defending force could hold out for some time in such circumstances, and Alfred had set up a system which provided him with an army constantly ready to meet such emergencies. The scheme worked perfectly in 884, but failed in 892 because the fort on the Limen was unfinished. It was to work again soon after Alfred's death when, in 904, a Viking force reached Cricklade but turned away, the inference being that the *burh* there had been completed and was defended against the attack. It could be argued that the encirclement of the Wessex kingdom by the chain of forts was started not long before 892, for otherwise the Limen fort would have been completed in time. The chain was substantially finished by, or soon after, Alfred's death in 899.

The system is interesting because the government foresight, planning and control that is claimed by Asser is visibly borne out by the forts themselves. No one who looks at the ramparts at Wareham or Wallingford can fail to be impressed by their scale, and by the concept that lies behind them. One aspect of that concept which is currently being discussed among archaeologists is the extent to which a defensive intention was matched by a commercial one. How far was the planning and lay-out of the defences matched by planning and lay-out of the interiors, with streets, churches, and property blocks? The evidence for this is strongest at Winchester, but the question is better discussed in the context of later developments. The main intention was obviously to provide refuges, to block rivers and to guard river crossings. Geographical distribution was a major factor; royal ownership, or at least a royal *vill* or palace nearby, was another, as was the presence of an extant or decayed minster, and occasionally of an important road. Only finally, perhaps, was there consideration of the potential of the site to grow as a town with a market and a permanent population.

It is worth noting some of the places that were not *burhs* in the *Burghal Hidage*. Some places that were to become of major importance were not included, and there may be a strong presumption therefore that their sites were not yet occupied. Of these, Bristol stands out: better placed than Bath to defend the entry to the River Avon, it would surely have been a better site if it had already had some nucleus of settlement. So far, none is known until the tenth or eleventh centuries – there are Saxon finds from below the mound of the Norman castle, but nothing that need be earlier than the date of Bristol's earliest recorded coin, which may be a penny of 979–85.

Most of the more obvious omissions are places where it is known that there was some sort of occupation. Dorchester-on-Thames (44) was probably excluded because Oxford had become the preferred crossing-point of the Thames. Dorchester, Dorset (36), despite its walls and its known use, was not on the coast and was not necessary on geographical grounds. Some of the places with minsters which might still have had small communities were Abingdon (43), Wimborne (34), Cirencester (41), Glastonbury (39) and Sherborne (37). The last, a bishop's seat, is perhaps especially curious, as it could so easily have replaced Shaftesbury. Why was Alfred so determined to found a nunnery for his daughter at the latter – and why should he not include the nunnery within the defences? If the church

11   A small fragment of silver from Cricklade, Wilts., showing a dragon-like creature in the ninth-century 'Trewhiddle' style. Drawn by Mrs P. Clarke. Length 1.0 cm.

really was outside the gate, it can hardly be said that Alfred ordered the *burh* to be established at Shaftesbury to protect the minster. Finally, why was there no provision for the Isle of Wight?

'The fourth part (of his wealth) he distributed among the minsters'

It is appropriate to deal next with Alfred's contribution to the church, and to church buildings, for many of the *burhs* were on existing minster sites, and most of the others were to have minsters within them. Documents do not let us know precisely when such churches were set up. A good example of this problem is Cricklade, where there are fragments of pilaster strips – projecting vertical bands of stone – high up in the wall of the south aisle above the nave arcade, which show that it was originally a Saxon church. Although they cannot be dated precisely, the pilaster strips at any rate establish a Saxon fabric as the predecessor of the present church, and it is certainly therefore the *mater ecclesia* (mother or 'minster' church, to serve a wide area around it, not just the townspeople) of an eleventh-century document.

That this was the site of the church from the earliest days of the *burh* is perhaps indicated by the discovery in the churchyard of a small ninth-century silver fragment from a garter-tag or drinking-horn mount, into which is cut a small dragon-like creature (Fig. 11). This may indicate that the churchyard was in use by the beginning of the tenth century, and thus that there was a church there from the earliest days of the *burh*.

In the other *burhs* in which there were not already minsters, there is even less evidence of the dates when churches were built, so although none of the *burhs* that became towns did not have a minster by the eleventh century, we cannot be sure if they were part of the original plan. This is not the case at Shaftesbury, site of Alfred's new nunnery, or at Athelney which, although it is not in the *Burghal Hidage,* is called a fort by Asser and was where Alfred founded a monastery. Architecturally, we know nothing of his nunnery at Shaftesbury, although in the future excavations may find its foundations. The community that he founded for men at Athelney is similarly unknown from excavations but there is an interesting description of it by the twelfth-century writer William of Malmesbury, who says that it had four *postes* (? = pillars) and four round *cancelli* (? = semi-circular chapels) leading out of the ambulatory. The significance of this is that it seems to indicate a radical difference between this church and such rectangular plans as the minster at Wareham or the cruciform Old Minster at Winchester. Instead it seems to indicate a church in which the nave formed the centre of the structure, with chapels leading off from each of its four sides so that on plan it may have looked rather like a four-leafed clover, or more probably a square with a semi-circular projection in the middle of each side. A description of the church at Abingdon may indicate something of this kind, though the date of the building being described is uncertain.

The church at Athelney was clearly extremely unusual in England, its radical plan being based on Carolingian models such as the ninth-century St Germigny-des-Près. As with the *burhs*, there is strong Frankish influence visible behind Alfred's minster. It is understandable why this should have been so, for the plan was probably suggested by Athelney's first abbot, John, who came from Saxony, and would have known such churches from his previous career. Alfred's venture was a sad fiasco, although he brought monks to it from overseas, because his own people were unwilling to take the vows.

No other churches are definitely Alfredian, although that at Deerhurst, Glos., was restored either in his reign or very soon after. There is no further record of how the money that Alfred devoted to the church was spent, except that some went to churches in other kingdoms. Asser also tells us that Alfred established a school, and his concern for education is shown by the works of scholarship which he caused to be translated and distributed. Much of this work was probably done at Winchester, by the community at the Old Minster, and one tangible relic of Alfred's concern for this house remains, a stone with a wall-painting on it (Fig. 12). It was discovered in 1966 in the foundation rubble of the New Minster, which was consecrated in 903, and the colours are too fresh to have been very old when buried. Since it is known that in order to build the New Minster Edward the Elder had to pull down the dormitory that Alfred had built for the Old Minster, the painted stone may well have come from that. The

12 Painting on stone found in 1966 in the foundations of the early tenth-century New Minster at Winchester. Length 58.6 cm.

excavator has cited German parallels for such decoration of domestic buildings, which again shows Frankish influences. It also has implications for Alfredian art patronage. Alfred's own influence can fairly be claimed as being behind his son's decision to build the magnificent New Minster, and his widow's foundation of Nunnaminster, also at Winchester. Such royal examples were to be followed in the next century by many of the Saxon nobility, although Alfred's own contemporaries had proved so reluctant to take monastic vows.

'The royal residences'

There is as yet little in the archaeological record to substantiate Asser's claims that Alfred built many palaces; there is none at all to suggest that he physically moved any to new sites, and there is no direct evidence of stone buildings that are specifically dated to this period. The site of the royal palace at Winchester has not been excavated. It may have been a stone building, since it is probable from the painted stone found in the 1966 excavation that stone was used at Alfred's command for domestic buildings at the Old Minster. Somewhere on the site of the palace at Old Windsor, Berks. (46 on Fig. 1), there was a stone building with the great luxury of glazed windows, for the debris from it was used to fill up a mill-stream. The excavations, which ended in 1958, have not been published but a preliminary report suggests that the stone building was destroyed by fire in the late ninth or early tenth century. The theory that this resulted from a Viking raid is the sort of speculation that is better not made until the evidence has been properly presented.

Another palace site (40 on Fig. 1) is at Cheddar, Somerset, which was an important royal residence from at least 941 when the *Witan,* the royal council, is known to have met there; but it is not included among the royal residences named by King Alfred in his will. Interpretation of this site is bedevilled by the lack of pottery from it that can be regarded as contemporary with the buildings (Fig. 13). The earliest datable object, apart from Roman material, is a coin of *c.* 845, and there is another coin of *c.* 870. Such coins are rare finds, and they are evidence that the site was in use in the ninth century. It is at any rate possible that the Long Hall found in the excavations was known to, if not built by, King Alfred. It is a timber building, 23 m (78 ft) in length, bow-sided, and 6½ m (20 ft) wide in the centre. It had opposed doors in the centre of the sides, like an enlarged version of some of the Chalton houses (Fig. 19, *a*), and a single door near one end. A burnt clay spread at one point could be the debris from the fire in an open hearth in the middle of the floor. Three posts across the interior

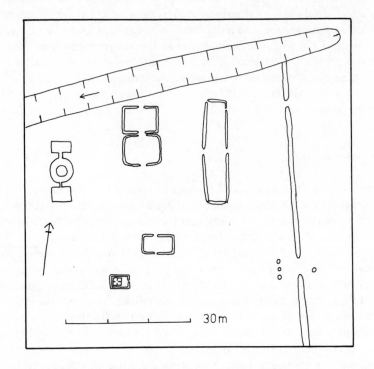

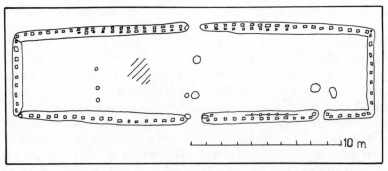

13 The Saxon palace site at Cheddar, Somerset, showing the complex as it may have been for a brief period in the early tenth century. The northern boundary was a ditch, the eastern a palisade with gate. The north-eastern building may have been a fowl-house; the southern was a privy.

The post-holes and trenches of the great bow-sided hall are shown enlarged in the lower picture. Shading = hearth area (after Rahtz).

may mark the line of a partition for an inner chamber, as was also seen on a smaller scale in the Chalton houses. Nearby was a smaller rectangular building, and there may have been others. The whole site had a ditch along at least one side, in which the coins were found.

The general impression of the Cheddar site is that it was like the one described in a passage in the *Anglo-Saxon Chronicle,* when in 786 King Cynewulf was surprised at his palace at Meretun, an unlocated site in Hampshire. He was in his mistress's bower at the time, clearly a building separate from the rest. Later there was a fight at the gate, indicating an enclosure around the complex. At Cheddar, later buildings at the palace included a structure that has been interpreted as a corn-mill, which would mean that agricultural processing took place there, as it had done at Old Windsor. An alternative interpretation of the Cheddar building is that it was a fowl-house, as in some Frankish monasteries.

A comparable site did not come into royal ownership until 904 – the *burh* at Portchester. The first series of timber buildings must have been constructed for the bishop of Winchester, the original owner. They cannot be dated precisely, and there is no way of knowing how many there were at any one time. The picture that emerges is of a complex of timber rectangular buildings, some of them perhaps to serve the garrison of the *burh*. None has had an industrial or agricultural use ascribed to it, but the excavations have only been in a small part of the total area of the fort.

It is not really possible to ascribe any of these sites to the direct intervention of King Alfred. Archaeologically, they can be shown to have been in use during his reign, and the Long Hall at Cheddar, impressive in its length, is the sort of building that might have sheltered his 'hearth-companions', and where in his court he would have 'carefully considered the judgements of almost his whole realm', as he travelled through his kingdom. There is a graphic description of this activity in a contemporary charter, which mentions that Alfred heard a law-suit 'while washing his hands within the chamber at Wardour'.

'The wayfaring men . . . from every nation'

Asser was not thinking specifically of merchants when he praised Alfred's generosity in giving gifts to travellers. We know of Irish monks and of a Scandinavian trader, Othere, who came to Alfred and were generously treated. Othere's travels clearly fascinated the king, who included an account of them in his preface to the translation of Orosius' *Universal History*, which shows that contacts with the Scandinavians were not all bellicose. Othere's boat had travelled as far north as Lapland.

It is not known if any English boats ventured beyond the Channel, but a recent find of this period illuminates knowledge of shipping and cargo-carrying potential. The vessel was found submerged in marshes near Graveney in Kent, and a radiocarbon date from her timbers suggests that she was built in *c.* AD 900, perhaps slightly earlier. She may not have been built in England, of course, but she must be representative of the sort of broad, open-decked vessel used for cross-Channel trade. Her bow had been lost, but she was originally about 14 m (45 ft) long, and 3 m (10 ft) wide in the centre. Like the earlier ship at Sutton Hoo, she had a keel, which had been repaired at least once, and her planking was sealed with tar and hair. Her cargo is uncertain: there was a fragment of a Rhenish Mayen quern-stone below her, and such stones were one of the major imports to Hamwic. There were also bits of Roman tile, and building-stone fragments, which she might have carried as ballast. Hops were detected by analysis of the seed evidence, and it is suggested that these came from the use of hop strands to make vegetable fibre ropes, for hops were not used for making beer until much later. No trace of oars or mast remained, but she probably had both. The impression is of a sturdy, sea-worthy vessel, not very fast, but able to carry quite a heavy cargo. The repairs suggest that she had a long life, which perhaps is a tribute to her reliability. There were probably many like her.

Alfred's Laws make little provision for trade, the only direct reference being that merchants should present their men before the royal reeve prior to setting out. A more practical concern for commerce was shown by his raising the weight of the pennies, to improve the standard of what had become a rather debased currency. This mark of effective government took the weight to twenty-four grains, perhaps to bring the coin weights into line with a fifteen-ounce:pound system and make the mercantile and monetary pounds comparable. He brought Mercia into the same framework by introducing the Wessex pound of 240 pennies there. He also minted the first known half-pence, perhaps to encourage the flow of small change, but the coins were minted for less than a century. One was found recently in excavations at Chichester. He added at least two places, Exeter and Gloucester, to the list of towns where there were mints in operation, and the earliest coins that have the Winchester and (forged) Oxford signatures struck on them also date from Alfred's reign. The quality of the designs on Alfred's coins are noticeably better than on those of his predecessors. One design that he used was a monogram, of London, that revived an early ninth-century coin style. This had been copied from Carolingian coins – which in turn had been copied from classical Byzantine issues. In this case, as elsewhere, Frankish influences can be seen, but some may have been transmitted at second hand. One import found in the

Winchester excavations is a silver Dirham minted in 898 in Samarkand. Its discovery shows that oriental objects could find their way to England, but this single example cannot be treated as evidence of trade, only of occasional, perhaps indirect, contacts.

The coinage shows that Alfred deliberately set out to revive the trade of his kingdom, after its disruption by the Viking raids. It is difficult to measure the success of the attempt, but the Graveney boat is a hint of it, as is the growth of town life in the following century.

'The craftsmen skilled in every earthly work'

Asser is emphatic about Alfred's role as an art patron. Clearly the king regarded craftsmanship as a reflection of his own dignity; the artistic splendours, and the gold and silver available to his smiths, were the measures by which he would be judged by others. How much do we know about these achievements of late ninth-century Wessex?

The direct record is slight. The painted stone from the 1966 Winchester excavation (Fig. 12), for instance, probably came from a building commissioned by King Alfred, but even with that object there is an element of doubt. It might for instance have been painted earlier, and kept its colours unfaded for a longer period than seems likely.

To be entirely rigorous – perhaps finicky would be the better word – there is only one thing other than coins in the art record that can absolutely be dated to Alfred's reign. This is a copy of King Alfred's translation of Pope Gregory's *Cura Pastoralis,* a copy of which the king sent to every bishop in his kingdom. The surviving book, as its Preface says, is the one that was sent to Waerferth, bishop of Worcester between 889 and 899, so that it must have been written between those dates. This is of course a record of Alfred's concern for the education of his clergy, but it is interesting artistically because it contains many initial letters which have been decorated by the scribe, who has turned them into little painted creatures or, in a few instances, into human heads or figures (Figs 14 and 17, *b*). Illumination of manuscripts was not new, and the idea had originally been borrowed from pagan, classical books by the Early Church, which gave the paintings in Christian books religious meanings, either as direct illustrations of Christ, the Apostles or biblical scenes, or as patterns that formed a Cross or some similar device. The full significance of such paintings and drawings to their creators is often not known. It may be that some of the little creatures and other patterns in the Alfredian manuscript had a symbolism which the scribe understood, although they appear to be merely decorative to us.

14   Decorated initial letters from the Alfredian *Cura Pastoralis,* dated to the 890s.

Compared to work that was done both earlier and later than that in the *Cura Pastoralis* (which is usually referred to by its library shelf number, Bodleian Hatton 20), the ornament is very simple, and although the animals are quite neatly drawn, the human faces look naïve. Standards had slipped a long way from what they had once been, but the significance of the decoration is that it was the first attempt to revive standards, an attempt that was to bear fruit in the next century. It is also interesting to look for the sources that were used by the illuminator. He was certainly using some manuscript painted in the Midlands or south of England about a hundred years earlier, for several that survive from the late eighth or early ninth centuries have little creatures forming their initials. One that is known to have been at Winchester by the middle of the tenth century, and was possibly owned by Queen Ealswith, was a Mercian book, with initials very like those in Hatton 20.

Although many English manuscripts survive from the pre-Viking period, there is none that was written or decorated in the Wessex kingdom. It is impossible to be certain, but it seems quite likely that Alfred was directly responsible for introducing the art of illumination to the original nucleus of his realm. All the earlier southern English works are ascribed to Canterbury. There was no tradition of such work in Wessex that Alfred could call on. It is always assumed that Hatton 20 was written at Winchester in the Old Minster, and certainly this house, so close to a royal palace, and which may already have been storing royal archives, is the most likely place; the only other possibilities are Glastonbury, and Canterbury itself. It is also possible that some of the people whom Alfred gathered to him 'from wherever he could, to assist his righteous intention' had been trained in the school at Canterbury. Asser tells us that many others were Mercians.

The painted stone that is almost certainly from one of Alfred's buildings at Winchester is relevant in this argument, for the design on it is part of a large composition and very similar in its details to earlier paintings. Some of these parallels are Carolingian, but one of the closest is a Canterbury gospel-book of the late eighth century, called the *Codex Aureus*. This manuscript had an exciting history for it was one of a collection looted by a Viking raiding-party who ransomed it. One of the Kentish ealdormen, named Alfred like his king, bought them back – a unique record of such a transaction – and restored them to Canterbury:

> In the name of our Lord Jesus Christ, I Ealdorman Alfred and Waerburh my wife obtained these books from the heathen army with our pure money, that was with pure gold, and this we did for the love of God and for the benefit of our souls and because we did not wish these holy books to remain longer in heathen possession.

It is an irony that the *Codex Aureus* is now preserved in the Royal Library at Stockholm, but its ransoming by Alfred shows graphically the high regard in which such works of art were held even by the laity, and how likely it is therefore that they would have been used as models.

Other parallels for the wall-painting are later in date. In particular, there is a manuscript with paintings done in Winchester in the second quarter of the tenth century. Two of these paintings show Christ being worshipped by Choirs of Angels, Prophets and Martyrs, shown as crowds of figures very like those on the wall-painting. This explains the nature of the whole scene on the wall of Alfred's building. Its inspiration may also have come from an earlier English source, in this case Last Judgement scenes from the north not the south. An alternative source is from such Carolingian works as the *Metz Sacramentary* and, with so many Frankish influences demonstrated in other areas of Alfred's work, this suggestion may seem preferable.

The problem of deciding which sources inspired the Saxon works of art is well illustrated by what is perhaps the single most famous object in England – the Alfred Jewel (Fig. 15). This takes its name from the inscription cut in gold letters around it: *Aelfred mec heht gewyrcan* ('Alfred ordered me to be made'). The grammatical construction of this inscription is Anglian rather than Saxon, another sign of the influence of the Mercians at Alfred's court. It is a constant frustration that the inscription does not give the title of the man who commissioned it. Alas, it does not actually state that it was made for *King* Alfred, and since we have already met another Alfred who was rich enough to have employed 'a cunning craftsman in gold and gems, when a leader bids him prepare a jewel in his honour' (*Exeter Book: Endowments of Men*), there will always be a tiny doubt in most minds about ascribing it too positively to the king himself.

It might be easier to be positive if we knew for certain the function of the Alfred Jewel. There is only one other object like it, named the Minster

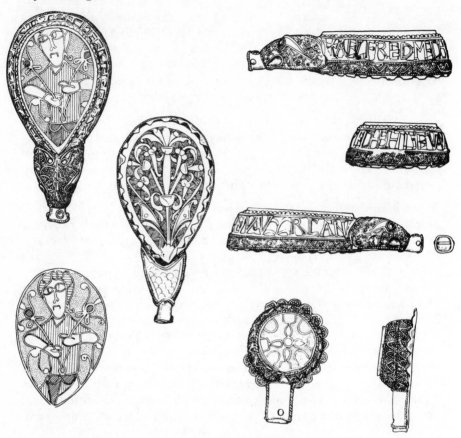

15   Drawings (by Mrs P. Clarke) of the Alfred and Minster Lovell Jewels, goldwork of the late ninth century. The figure and the cross are done in cloisonné enamel. Scale: $\frac{1}{1}$.

Lovell Jewel after its Oxfordshire find-spot (Fig. 15). Both have gold frames, decorated with gold filigree and granulation; both have cloisonné enamel settings (coloured glass set in panels between strips of gold), the Alfred Jewel showing a male figure holding two plants, the Minster Lovell Jewel showing a round-armed 'Anglian' cross (cf. Fig. 14, right); both have flat backs; and both have short open tubes with a rivet through the end, that must have held some short ivory or wooden rod. The Alfred Jewel also has a large piece of rock crystal covering the enamel, and a gold animal's head grasps the nozzle in its jaws.

Both jewels are best explained, until someone proposes a better explanation, as *aestels*; it is not certain what an *aestel* was, but we at least know that the Saxons knew, for King Alfred wrote in the Preface to his *Cura Pastoralis* that he was going to send an *aestel* worth 50 *mancuses* to each of his bishops, with the bishop's copy of the translation. A *mancus* was a sum of gold worth thirty pennies, and Alfred was therefore distributing very costly objects. The *aestel* may have been a book-marker, the most probable translation of the Latin word 'indicatorium' which a monk who probably understood Anglo-Saxon wrote above the word *aestel* in the thirteenth century.

There is a circular argument involved in the claim that the two jewels are very costly objects, that their flat backs and nozzles make them admirably suitable for book-markers, and that they are therefore two of the *aestels* made for King Alfred. Nevertheless it is difficult to think of any other purpose that the jewels could fulfil, and the connection with King Alfred is further strengthened by a recent identification of the figure on the Alfred Jewel as Christ personifying Wisdom, a concept frequently found in Alfred's writing; one of the basic tenets of his educative works was that by acquiring wisdom through learning a man could reach Christ. In the passage from the Preface to the *Soliloquies* quoted in Chapter One, Alfred is using his image of a man collecting timber from a wood as a metaphor for a man seeking to acquire wisdom.

The details of the two jewels show that stylistically their most probable date is in the second half of the ninth or the early tenth century. It is very difficult to be more precise about any object unless there is some other reason for its date – the date of the painted stone, for example, depends on the context of its find-spot, without which it would not be possible to say on the basis of its style that it is not a work of the first half of the tenth century. Of the Alfred Jewel, it can be said that it might have been made during Alfred's reign, but on stylistic grounds it cannot be positively ascribed to a single decade. It is only the inscription and the probability of its association with King Alfred, strengthened by its find-spot only four miles from his monastery at Athelney, which allow the narrower dating to be suggested.

There are one or two metalwork objects for which a date can be suggested other than on grounds of style. Occasionally hoards of treasure are found, and these may comprise both jewellery and coins. One such, from Sevington in Wiltshire, had various English pennies in it of which the last was minted in about 850. The hoard must have been hidden very soon after that date, so that the objects with it – a double-ended spoon, a fork or prong, and various bronze and silver strap-ends and scraps – must have been made before then. Another hoard from Trewhiddle in Cornwall was deposited before about 875, and had many silver objects with the coins, including a chalice, a plaited and knotted silver wire scourge, mounts from drinking horns or cups, strap-ends and other small ornaments. The decoration on these objects is divided into panels, each containing a plant or a fantastic animal in a very distinctive style that is known on many other ninth-century objects – the animal on the fragment from Cricklade, for instance, is in the Trewhiddle style (Fig. 11). The designs were made by cutting away the background and these sunken areas were then filled with niello, a sulphide which had to be heated gently to fuse it to the object. The niello is black, which provides a very effective background to the polished silver, the creatures and plants of the design standing out clearly.

There are two objects in the Trewhiddle style which can be closely dated because of inscriptions on them. Both are gold finger-rings. One has on it the name *Aethelwulf rex,* King Aethelwulf being Alfred's father, and king from 828 to 858, between which dates the ring was presumably made. The main design shows two birds at a fountain, an early Christian Tree-of-Life motif. The other has its inscription, *Aethelswyth regina,* on the inside of the ring, not as part of the main design, which shows the Lamb of God. Aethelswyth was Alfred's sister, and was queen of Mercia between 853 and 888. These two finger-rings were probably not worn by the monarchs whose names are on them, but were gifts and rewards donated by them for faithful service. In the Germanic tradition, the handing-out of treasure, particularly weapons and rings, was a lord's principal means of rewarding his men and binding them to him. The poem written to celebrate the Battle of Brunanburh in 937 describes the victor as:

> Athelstan the King, ruler of earls
> And ring-giver to men.

It is interesting that King Alfred's magnanimity in distributing largesse was praised by Asser because 'it is written, the Lord loveth a cheerful giver'. The old pagan code was being given a Christian gloss. Tangible examples of Alfred's generosity were the *aestels,* gifts from the king to his faithful bishops. Asser records the goldsmiths' work which Alfred bestowed on Guthrum and his men in 878 at their christening ceremony, perhaps as a sign that in accepting his gifts they were accepting his overlordship, the Germanic equivalent to their acknowledgement of it through their acceptance of Christianity. Alfred also stood as god-father to Guthrum, which seems to have been a long-standing demonstration of overlordship, practised also by the Franks. Part of the significance of the gift of a fragment from the True Cross sent to Alfred by the Pope perhaps lay in symbolizing a special relationship between them.

Other favourite treasures were brooches, worn by both men and women. They were usually slightly concave discs, some being very big. One of the finest, the Fuller brooch, has five male figures as the central part of its design, representing the Five Senses. Hearing, for example, is cupping his

I Coins from the Saxon *mercimonium* at Hamwic: top left – obverse of a 'Southampton sceatta', an example of the earliest coinage minted in the Wessex kingdom; top right – reverse of the same sceatta, showing a bird turned into an almost abstract pattern; bottom left – a penny minted for the king of Wessex in the early ninth century; bottom right – a rare gold coin, an import minted for the Frankish king Louis the Pious, 814–39. All about twice actual size.

II The ninth-century wattle fence on the St Aldate's site, Oxford.

III High-level photograph of excavations in progress at Chalton, Hants. Various buildings and enclosures are clearly revealed by posts or trenches cut into the chalk sub-soil. See also *a* on Fig. 19.

IV A late eighteenth-century print of Lady St Mary, Wareham. The nave, and the side aisle with its two-storey *porticus* were Saxon, probably pre-Viking.

NORTH VIEW of St MARY'S CHURCH in WAREHAM.

This Plate is most gratefully Inscribed to the Donor Mrs Turner, Relict of George Turner Esq of Penleigh, in Wiltshire, by the Author.

v The west porch at Titchfield, Hants. This is certainly a Saxon structure and may well be pre-Viking. The contrast between the large stone quoins and door surround, and the rubble of the rest of the wall, is typical. The band of flint and the larger stones above are later additions, as of course is the steeple. It has been suggested that the stones were brought by the Saxons from the nearby Roman fort at Portchester.

vi St Lawrence's chapel, Bradford-on-Avon, Wilts. The date is a matter of dispute, but the eleventh century now seems most likely. The triangular scar shows where the south *porticus* originally projected.

vii The west bank of the Saxon *burh* defences at Wareham survive in a remarkably intact condition. A trace of the ditch on the outside of the bank can be seen on the left, but most of the ditch has been filled.

VIII The stone cross-shaft at Codford, Wilts.; perhaps late ninth century. The dancing figure is juggling with a branch above his head.

IX A succession of tenth- and eleventh-century gravel street surfaces, revealed in excavations in Oxford on the site of the Norman castle.

X The eleventh-century tower of St Michael's church, Oxford, stood by the north gate of the town, and was clearly useable as part of the defences. Compare the quoins and rubble wall to Titchfield (Plate V). Each belfry window has a central baluster shaft supporting a 'through-stone' which goes through the full thickness of the wall, a crude way of strengthening it at the weak points caused by the openings. The dressed stone quoins at ground level are not original, nor is the parapet at the top.

xi   The eleventh-century church of St Martin stood beside the north gate at Wareham. It is original except for the seventeenth-century porch, the windows and the rebuilt west wall, and is the best surviving example of a small Saxon urban 'parish' church.

xii   Breamore, Hants. Apart from the south porch on the left, and the east wall of the chancel, the structure of this church is late Saxon. The windows and doors visible are later; the belfry tower probably reproduces the original diminishing pyramidal arrangement; the quoins and pilaster strips are large dressed stones contrasting with the rubble flint walls. The south *porticus* is substantially lower and narrower than a transept.

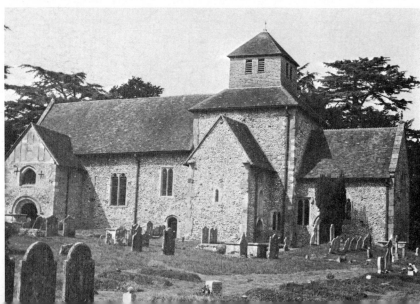

ear and running towards the sound that he has heard (Fig. 17, *c*). There is no hint in the surviving literature to show where the idea for this portrayal of the Senses was taken from, nor do any of the manuscript paintings have figures in them like those on the brooch.

Swords were also highly prized, and some of the hilts were given very elaborate silver, or occasionally gold, ornament. Many are decorated with Trewhiddle-style ornament, the finest being one found in the bed of the river at Abingdon, Oxon. (Fig. 16). This has animals' heads modelled on its pommel, perhaps in reference to the 'horney-beaked raven and the eagle' which would descend to devour what the sword would leave behind it on the battle-field. Below the pommel is a curved guard, and there is another at the base of the hilt. Both the guards have strips of silver set into them on both sides, with panels of elaborate plant and animal designs; some of the latter are superbly ferocious, winged dragons, biting at their own bodies. The upper guard has four panels that have a very different theme, for they show the symbols of the Four Evangelists. They fortified the Christian Saxon warrior as he went out to do battle with the invading pagan Vikings.

These objects cannot be dated within precise limits, and it cannot be proved that they were made at a workshop that was under royal patronage. Nevertheless there are hints that this might have been so: the birds on the King Aethelwulf ring are very like the Eagle on the Abingdon sword, there are leaf designs on the sword like some on the Fuller brooch and the Alfred Jewel, and the use of elaborate symbolism may be the hall-mark of a single production centre. These are only hints, however, and no more. To go further and to suggest that the workshop that produced the Alfred and Minster Lovell jewels, and perhaps the rest, was at Winchester, is not borne out by the finds from the recent excavations, only two strap-ends providing a comparison. The presence of a man dealing with gold in pre-Alfredian Winchester has, however, been shown in the Lower Brook Street excavations, so jewellers may have established themselves there. Two objects, a strap-end and a garter-tag, found at Portchester, are closer to a design on the Alfred Jewel – and Portchester was the bishop of Winchester's property until 904, so that a connection is not unreasonable. The manuscript Hatton 20 has two initials decorated with designs very like the cloisonné enamel cross on the Minster Lovell jewel (Fig. 14, right; Fig. 15), and the same book contains a little male figure comparable to the Man symbol on the Abingdon sword. These links are suggestive, but far from conclusive.

The Man symbol and the Hatton 20 figure both wear shoes which are not unlike those worn by a curious but delightful dancing figure on a stone cross-shaft at Codford St Peter, Wilts (Plate VIII). So difficult is the dating of sculpture that such distant parallels as these may sometimes be

16 The Abingdon sword (drawn by Mrs P. Clarke). This is dated to the late ninth or early tenth century. Silver strips inlaid into the iron are engraved with small panels of ornament: Panels 3 and 5 show two of the four symbols of the Evangelists, the Man of Matthew and the Eagle of John. About three-quarters actual size.

useful. In this case, though, a better parallel is a Canterbury manuscript, painted in about 735, which has dancing figures in front of King David (Fig. 17). They wear costume like the Codford dancer, and are in a similar pose. The cross need not be of such an early date, however, for it could be like Hatton 20, or the Winchester wall-painting, in which work done a century or more earlier was the source of inspiration in the late ninth or early tenth century. The leaf ornament on the sides of the cross-shaft would seem to fit the later period.

If the Codford cross really does belong to the Alfredian period, or just after, it points to a new direction in Wessex sculpture. Unlike Northumbria and Mercia, Wessex in the seventh and eighth centuries had

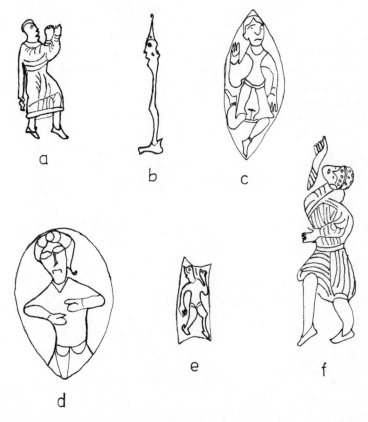

17 A selection of dancers and other figures: *a* – from an eighth-century Canterbury manuscript; *b* – from Hatton 20, 890s; *c* – Hearing, on the Fuller brooch; *d* – perhaps the young Christ, on the Alfred Jewel; *e* – St Matthew's symbol, on the Abingdon sword; *f* – the dancer on the Codford cross. All actual size, except *f*, reduced from about 3 ft high.

produced no magnificent carved cross-shafts with elaborate iconography
and scenes from biblical texts, except for two shafts at Glastonbury,
destroyed in the eighteenth century. Even Kent can show only some fragments from Reculver, now at Canterbury. Such carvings as have survived
in Wessex are usually of rather unskilfully executed interlaced biting snake
patterns (Fig. 18), magnified versions of the sort of designs which appear
on the Abingdon sword (Fig. 16). Interlaced snake patterns were popular
on coins and other objects in the eighth and ninth centuries (Fig. 8), and
probably it is to those years that many of the shafts belong. It has been said
that the elaborate one at Ramsbury, Wilts., must have been carved after 909
when the bishop's see there was established, but this is hardly a criterion for
there would have been some sort of settlement in Ramsbury before then.
Another point is the comparison of the biting heads on the shafts to
manuscript initials like those in Hatton 20 and later paintings. The sculptural
series may have extended well into the tenth century. It is not, however,
influenced by Scandinavian styles. Not until at least the tenth century were
Wessex artists prepared to come to terms with the invaders' art forms, and
any earlier contacts were in the opposite direction, so far as the south of
England is concerned.

Other sculptures to be seriously considered are some panels at Bradford-
on-Avon, with geometrical and plain interlace patterns, and in the church at
Britford, Wilts., where a series of panels are set in the jambs of the arches of
the *porticus*. These are plants and flowers, neatly cut but not very lively.
There are Italian parallels for them, as there are for one of the shafts at

18 Simplified drawings of various ribbon-interlace creatures carved on stone cross-
shafts of the eighth to tenth centuries. Compare similar patterns on contemporary metalwork, Figs 8, 16. Left – Ramsbury, Wilts.; centre – Colerne, Wilts.; right – Glastonbury,
Somerset.

Ramsbury. Britford was a royal manor in the ninth century, and the church might well have been built as a chapel for the palace, which would explain its elaborate decoration. The jambs could, of course, have been added long after the initial foundation of the church.

From this survey of the various art forms of the ninth century, the general picture that emerges is that in the ecclesiastical arts, manuscript paintings and sculpture, Wessex had little of interest until Alfred's period and the work then done at Winchester, shown by Hatton 20 and the wall-painting. Both these show strongly the influence of earlier work, especially the paintings done at Canterbury in the eighth and early ninth centuries, some of which in their turn had been influenced by Carolingian works. To this list can perhaps be added the Codford cross. These were the beginnings of an art movement that was to be one of the finest flowerings of European culture. With metalwork, the story is slightly different. Wessex had many eighth- and ninth-century smiths, and the Alfred and Minster Lovell jewels and their contemporaries were a revival of an established craft; only the use of cloisonné enamel was new. Furthermore, the achievements of Alfred's jewellers were to be pursued in different directions. The surviving personal ornaments of the tenth and eleventh centuries are mostly less sumptuous, less beautiful and less interesting. Skilled metalworking was lavished on church treasures, instead.

Physical survivals are a testimony to Alfred's patronage, although not everyone agrees exactly which objects can be referred to as 'Alfredian'. The consciousness of earlier traditions that is shown by the use of the Canterbury works as models, and the commissioning of gold and silver objects to demonstrate the king's magnanimity, are echoed in Alfred's writings, for instance in his lament in the *Cura Pastoralis* that there were now no scholarly priests in the realm as there had once been, so that it had become the royal duty to revive the former standards, as it had been the great Charlemagne's in the Frankish kingdom. This deliberate policy of the revival of what was thought once to have flourished was the motive behind the patronage, and it is in revival rather than in original creativity that the key to an understanding of the Alfredian renaissance is to be sought. Similarly the king fostered vernacular literature, the old books of Saxon poetry whose traditions he was anxious that his subjects should know and understand.

'The oft-mentioned Alfred'

King Alfred's reign saw successful resistance to the Vikings, the preservation of the Wessex kingdom and a renaissance of Saxon culture. The historical records about it are informative, and the archaeological records support them. It can be shown that there were developments in the late ninth century, like the paintings, the burghal system or the coinage, which can be directly attributed to the king or to the king's government. Other developments, such as the rebuilding of churches, may have depended partly on the king and partly on his contemporaries and immediate successors, some at least inspired by him.

All this is important for its own sake, but it makes a particular impact because of what was to follow. The late Saxon culture that saw thriving scholarship, famous monasteries, splendid artistic works and a growing economy, can be seen to have resulted from Alfred's success, and the use made of it by his son and grandson. If the Viking menace had revived in the first half of the tenth century, and had over-run Wessex, Alfred's reign would be a dimly understood episode, a temporary and irrelevant interlude. It is because the foundations that he laid were built upon that we remember him and can try to understand him. It is the ultimate tribute to him that his successors proved how surely he had laid those foundations.

It is rarely that archaeology can study an individual. We have seen the difficulties of attributing a site or an object or a building to a date as precise as that of one man's lifetime, and particularly of attributing it to the motivation of one individual. Perhaps the attempt should not be made, for it may obscure the more general truth that the period as a whole can be seen to mark new directions. How far new directions can be truly the work of a single person is a question that neither the documentary historian nor the archaeologist can fully answer. The particular interest for the archaeologist is that it is in this period that the most satisfactory correlations of all the different material evidence can be made. In no other period does the decoration of the manuscripts interact so closely with that of the metalwork and the sculpture; in no other are the design sources so eclectic and so interesting to trace; in no other can the construction of a fort like Cricklade be illuminated by a tiny scrap of ornamental silver, or the poetry brought to life by a gold finger-ring; in no other can a warrior be seen to be fighting for his faith because of the symbols that he carries on his sword; and in no other do the material and documentary evidence complete and complement each other so satisfyingly.

Chapter 3

The Growth of Towns

During the Saxon period, the structure of society changed from being essentially tribal and customary to being effectively class-based and codified. Of the three loyalties that a man might owe – to his kin, to his lord and to his king – the first ceased to be legally predominant, and the balance between the second and the third was not finally fought out until the end of the Middle Ages. The Germanic traditions of society were challenged by growing concepts of kingship and 'statehood', and by growing sophistication of governmental and economic systems. A major role of archaeology is the study of the physical manifestations of economic development, and the growth and decay of towns is one of the important indicators of the balance and scale of commercial life, its profitability, and its place in the growth of new systems of administration.

It is easier to justify the study of archaeology in the earlier periods of the Middle Ages than in the later, not only because the less that is known from documents the more welcome is even the most minute piece of evidence, but because the archaeologist can often say when occupation on a certain site began, although he may not be able to say very much about the activity that went on thereafter. An excavator who finds tenth-century pottery sherds in a rubbish pit can claim that they were being used locally, and that activity on that site had therefore begun by that date, even if the rubbish pit also contained fourteenth-century material. It may not be possible to say when occupation on the site ended: it might be that a fifteenth-century building above that fourteenth-century pit had been bulldozed away without trace, leaving the pit as the latest archaeologically recognizable feature.

Planning Problems

Much attention has been paid recently to the archaeology of towns, and the study of their growth and early development. The programme of ten years' research at Winchester has set an example that has stimulated similarly intensive work in the south at Chichester, Oxford and Southampton, and in a less intensive way at very many others. All pre-Conquest towns have had some form of archaeological excavation within them in the last decade, except for a few small ones like Shaftesbury, Dorset.

The focus of much of this research has also been stimulated by the work at Winchester. It has been realized through excavation and documents that the street lay-out of that city was largely established at the end of the ninth century (Fig. 5), and this has led to a review of other towns' topographies to see if similar patterns can be identified. One purpose of such investigation is to attempt to decide if there is a regularity in the street patterns that would suggest, not random and piecemeal development, but the control of development along lines predetermined by a central authority, a problem already seen in deciding the significance of the lay-out of Hamwic.

At Winchester, the *burh* defences used the line of the Roman walls, and it was therefore likely that the Roman gate positions would also be used. The principal road through the town is the one that links the West and East Gates. It is the main shopping street in the modern town, the High Street; an Anglo-Saxon charter shows that it was already called *ceap straet* by the early tenth century – Cheap Street means 'market street'. Its line was predetermined by the position of the gates, so it served both the Roman and the medieval towns. The reopened north and south entrances also affected the internal lay-out, and the need for access to the town walls produced another street, an intra-mural service road. Like the High Street, this road has for long stretches remained in constant use, and has preserved the same line since it was laid down, although the walls have gone. The date of its construction is known from excavations under the castle inserted into the town in the Norman period, which ignored and disrupted the existing street pattern. Below the castle was found a series of six road surfaces, each made of stone cobbles. As traffic wore away the centre of the road, a temporary improvement was made by throwing old wooden hurdles into it. The next stage was a complete recobbling, so that the level of the road gradually built up. The great good fortune of the excavation was to find two coins associated with the second of the surfaces: one was the late ninth-century Arabic dirham mentioned in the last chapter, the other was an early tenth-century English penny. It is unlikely that the latter at least was of any great age when lost, and even the most conservative and sceptical critic would allow that the street must have been in use by the end of the first half of the tenth century.

The evidence from Winchester therefore shows that streets were being regularly surfaced in the tenth century, which is a considerable testimony to the town's government – many small towns had no proper street paving even in the nineteenth century. There is no direct evidence from documents to show who was the governing force, but it was presumably the king's reeve, who was also probably responsible for maintaining the walls. The important status of the reeve is shown by the *Anglo-Saxon Chronicle,* which thought the death of the reeves at Winchester in 896 and at Bath in 906 worth recording. It was to the king's reeves that Alfred's laws demanded that merchants should present themselves; the Dorchester reeve was on official business when slain by Vikings in 789; as a royal official, the reeve enjoyed the king's special protection, the *mund-bryce.* Later laws affirmed his role in regulating urban and trading life.

All this shows that there must have been a royal official in Winchester who could and did exercise authority over the physical development of the town. It may reasonably be thought, therefore, that it would also have been he who was responsible for the other feature of that development which the recent excavations have clarified, the proliferation of side streets in the late ninth and early tenth centuries. Winchester seems to have been physically transformed, over a fairly brief period. The relatively empty town of the eighth century, which had a church, a palace, and at least one major tenement, in Lower Brook Street, but a small population, had become quite crowded by the early tenth century, to the extent that when King Edward the Elder wished to build the New Minster between the Old Minster and High Street, he had to buy out many property-holders already in possession. Physical change is shown by what happened to the Lower Brook Street tenement, where the boundaries were so altered that a road was built right across it. These changes seem to indicate a major influx of population, and a realignment of any existing roads, except for the spinal High Street, which may have been made narrower. The way that this realignment was imposed on the town is suggested by the regular pattern that the roads follow. Each leads off from the High Street at a precise right angle, and runs straight backwards to the wall. A grid pattern was established, which is so well spaced and regular that it would seem to have been decreed by a central authority. The new plan ignored all Roman roads except those dictated by the gates; although in part predetermined by the Roman lay-out, and Roman in appearance because of its regularity, it was in fact new, an act of deliberate creation.

The evidence from Winchester is, therefore, that it developed in the late ninth and early tenth centuries into a place that was recognizably a town, with an urban life and character previously seen in the south only at Hamwic. Winchester is exceptional because of the amount of excavation that has taken place there, and because of the amount of surviving documentary evidence about it. It is also exceptional in its role: it was being deliberately set up, like Charlemagne's Aachen, to be the principal royal and ecclesiastical centre of Wessex. The concept of a capital city had not yet evolved in Europe, but Winchester had most of the attributes of a functioning state capital by the eleventh century, and this followed logically from what happened to it under Alfred and Edward the Elder. It was to be challenged, and eventually outstripped, by Edward the Confessor's Westminster, but his predecessors clearly looked to Winchester.

It is important to stress that Winchester was exceptional in its function as well as in the amount of surviving evidence about it, because of the difficulties of using Winchester as a case study on which to model ideas about the development of other towns. The Roman defences were a predetermining factor at Winchester, and they were a factor which operated in other refurbished Roman towns, like Chichester, Dorchester, Exeter or Bath, where the walls and gates affected the spinal and intra-mural streets. Also like Winchester, it is known that the other streets did not respect the Roman ones. Similarly, the decision to give rectangular defences with central entrances to such *burhs* as Wareham and Wallingford would have led to similar spinal and intra-mural streets. What is lacking in all these other towns is knowledge of the chronology of the rest of the internal development.

One of the towns with a clear-cut grid pattern is Wareham (Fig. 4), where there was probably no east gate out on to the marshes, so that originally there were probably just north and west gates, and a southern river crossing. A T-junction would result if a street were to be built into the centre from each access point, and such streets indeed exist. It would be unreasonable to argue that these are not features that date from the construction of the *burh* banks, and are a primary consequence of the planning of the defences. It does not follow, however, that the rest of the streets were laid out at the same time. Since it is logical to divide urban plots into squares or rectangles, as each owner will want a portion of street frontage for access and to further the interests of his business, the subdivision of the town may result in a rectangular grid pattern – as can be seen clearly in the northern half of Wareham – with secondary streets set at right angles to the primary streets, no matter when they are laid out. So a road that does not appear until quite late in the town's history will still be likely to conform to the grid. The most north-easterly side street at Wareham is an example of this. Since a recent excavation (*g* on Fig. 4) showed that it overlies a twelfth-century pit, it cannot have existed until well into the Middle Ages, yet superficially it looks like part of a Saxon grid pattern.

At Oxford (Fig. 6), the *burh* defences and gates would also have dictated the axial roads inside. A section through the west street where it was overlain by the Norman castle – a similar situation to that at Winchester – produced no less than eighteen road surfaces, each a thin spread of gravel (Plate ix). A single sherd of pottery from the lowest surface is of a type that was very common in the tenth and eleventh centuries. One of the side streets which was also covered by the post-Conquest castle was sectioned at the same time. It had eight surfaces, again with pottery earlier than the twelfth century. This street overlay the Church Street ditch. If the ditch was previously part of the defences, the street would be later in date than the *burh* lay-out, and so not part of any original plan for the town, but a later modification.

The 'new' port site at Southampton provides a similar case, for excavations have shown that a street that might have been part of a late Saxon lay-out did not in fact exist until the early thirteenth century. A grid pattern cannot be used as evidence of a unified town plan unless the dates of its streets can be proved from archaeological or documentary sources.

Even if this particular aspect of the Winchester research can only be applied with great caution in other towns, many of the other lessons learnt there are highly relevant. Although the town grew rapidly, there were still open spaces within it at the end of the tenth century. It was then that the new bishop's palace of Wolvesey was built over fields that had not been developed, but which had been under plough, for the plough-scars were recognized in the underlying levels. The physical appearance of such towns can still be seen at the new *burh* of Wallingford (Fig. 10), where there are still such large areas of open ground within the enclosure of the defences that even at the height of the town's medieval prosperity, pressure on space was not so demanding that the open ground was built over, probably partly because the burgesses had valuable grazing rights on it. Such pressures show in tenth-century Winchester by the type of houses that were being built in Lower Brook Street, some of which were designed to take full advantage of the commercial benefits offered by the street. Their foundations show that they were built all along the frontage, which meant that this was used to its maximum commercial effect, not for space-wasting functions like garden enclosures. A measure of a town's commercial life is the use that it makes of its frontages, for the busier the town, the more valuable is access to its streets.

In this development, Winchester may also be exceptional, but there is not the range of evidence elsewhere to compare with it. A more typical example may come from the Oxford castle site, which has recently produced traces of a late Saxon building, unfortunately in a very incomplete state. Rectangular, with post-holes for its timbers, it had a cellar that was at least a metre deep (Fig. 19, *c*). As there were several occupation layers above it, it must have been taken down a long time before the whole site was sealed by the castle. The pottery with it also suggests a date that could be early in the tenth century. Cellar buildings occurred in the countryside in the earlier Saxon period, although none is known with such a neat rectangular outline. Generally in the Middle Ages, cellars are a feature of town houses, a reflection of pressures that cause buildings to make maximum use of surface space. In unrestricted areas it is easier to grow sideways than upwards or downwards. The Oxford building hints, therefore, at the development of a specifically urban house type. It is also placed very close to the junction of the two streets, although this may not be very significant, since it is possible that it had been demolished before the secondary street was laid down.

This is the first coherent building plan published from any of the late Saxon towns in the south; although Oxford had already produced other examples of cellars, these were without the post-holes round them. Some of the cellars were very deep and almost circular, and may have been used as latrine pits. Others were shallower and rectangular, and are more likely to have been ordinary cellars, for storage. The evidence of these comes from a site excavated in 1954–5 in Cornmarket Street, Oxford's north–south principal commercial street and the equivalent to Winchester's High Street (*f* on Fig. 6).

Although the general line of Cornmarket has been maintained through the centuries, its exact width has varied. The Saxon pits, from both sides of the road, show that in the earlier period its boundaries were several metres to the east of the present shop fronts. On the west side, pits extend at least $2\frac{1}{2}$ m (8 ft) under the present pavement; on the opposite side, there are no pits in the 7 m (21 ft) behind the modern shop fronts. Until re-arrangement in the twelfth century, the street was not on quite the same line as today. A similar process at Winchester could account for the slight difference between the line of the High Street and the Roman road line. Only excavation can demonstrate this positively.

Oxford's topography has been illuminated further by a recent excavation within All Saints' church (*g* on Fig. 6). The technique of digging inside churches was developed on the continent, and has now been applied in England with valuable results. Despite later graves and vaults, archaeological evidence survived to give a coherent history of the site, which stood alongside the town's east–west street. It did not become ecclesiastical until quite late in its life. At first it was an open yard (Fig. 20). Quantities of charred grain on the ground surface provided enough material for a radiocarbon date to be obtained, which was AD 880–90 ± 80 years. This yard was later subdivided by a timber fence running at right angles to the road; the radiocarbon date for the latest fence was AD 970 ± 80. On one side of this fence was a deep rectangular cellar pit, also set at a right angle to the street. A coin of Edward the Confessor in its fill suggests that the stone building which succeeded it did not pre-date the mid eleventh century. The sequence shows that successively more intensive use was made of the site, presumably as its commercial value grew in the expanding late Saxon town.

The stone building was apparently not built as a church, but was converted into one later.

Another site which has illustrated the expansion of a *burh* into a town is in Wareham, alongside the north–south road, near the north gate (*g* on Fig. 4). Excavations showed that there had been no buildings and no activity other than agricultural on the site before the construction of the Alfredian *burh* enclosure. Thereafter there were various phases of occupation, and a pottery sequence extending to the fourteenth century. A tiny fragment of a silver coin dated to between 899 and 975 is the evidence that activity began in the tenth century.

Exactly what was happening on the Wareham site was never certain. Although post-holes in the sand suggested buildings set well back from the street, no coherent plans were revealed. Storage pits and wells were found, and a complex of ditches draining into at least one clay-lined cistern. The deepest ditch ran parallel to the street, and its uneroded sides and the lack of a silt layer on its bottom indicated that it was timber-lined. It was probably therefore too elaborate for drainage, nor would drainage explain the clay-lined cistern. The complex indicated some activity that required the use, and thus the storing, of a lot of water. The washing of textiles or hides is the most likely explanation, and two bone tools were found that were probably used for weaving (Fig. 3). A blacksmith's forge is another possibility since slag was found, but the gullies and cistern seemed more elaborate than a forge would require. The general picture was of a large enclosure alongside the street being used for some industrial purpose, without buildings along the frontage. The activity in this part of the town shows that Wareham was expanding, but that this site was not as valuable commercially as those investigated in Oxford or Winchester. A rubbish pit found when the contractors were digging a sewage connection pipe into the road showed that the Saxon street front was well to the south of the present one. It may be that the opposite side was also on a slightly different line, as at Oxford, or it may be simply that the original street was much narrower than the modern one. It is another example of a road that has the same general but not the same precise line as its Saxon predecessor.

The topographical information supplied by excavations in Winchester, Oxford and Wareham is not matched by results from elsewhere in the south. Chichester is beginning to produce some late Saxon evidence; Bath, Christchurch, Dorchester, Cricklade and Wilton have had sites that might have been productive, but were not; and no sites in the centres of such towns as Malmesbury and Wallingford have been attempted. The evidence is therefore very incomplete, but what we have so far indicates substantial development at least in certain places in the tenth and eleventh centuries.

It is an irony, therefore, to return to the biggest site in pre-Viking Wessex and find that there is no evidence that it was getting any bigger, or developing at a similar speed. The port at Hamwic was ravaged in 840 by a Viking raid, and the extent of its recovery from that disaster is difficult to measure. It may still have been quite large, at least until the 870s, as the number of coins found seems to show. The number then falls off rapidly: virtually none is later than the reign of Athelstan (925–39). At least by the middle of the tenth century, the port had all but abandoned its site by the River Itchen, and had moved a few hundred yards to the west, onto higher ground by the bank of the River Test (Fig. 2). Unfortunately it is even more difficult to gauge the size of its new site than its old one, which is very roughly delimited by the areas in which Saxon pits have been found. The occupation debris on the new site has been so extensively disturbed by the succeeding millennium that it is almost impossible for archaeologists to recognize it. Despite the move to the new site, the 'minster' in the old Hamwic remained the 'mother church' of medieval Southampton, its rights passing to St Denys Priory in the twelfth century.

The new port was not given a new name. As in the past, some of the coins minted there bore the name Hamtun, others Hamwic. It is not certain if these coins come from one and the same mint, or if two different sites were involved. It could be that there was minting within the walls of the old Roman fort if this was the Alfredian *burh*. Significant of the town's decline in status is that all minting at Hamtun seems to have stopped after about 1025. There is little excavated tenth-century evidence, apart from a coin and probably the pottery found in a recently located ditch, which further investigation may prove to have been the original enclosure of the new town. The new site's internal topography appears quite simply to have been a north–south road; it is not certain how far along this road the occupation extended, though it probably went well to the north of the later medieval town wall, and did not initially make use of the southern shore. Nor is it certain if there were any side roads. Like Oxford's Church Street ditch, the Southampton ditch was clearly not required by the eleventh century, since the coin and the pottery show that it was filled up by then.

Only more positive evidence about the date and function of the new port's ditch will clarify matters. It does seem that there was an absolute decline, however, for Domesday Book records only 76 (or 79 – the statement is ambivalent) royal tenants there in 1066, a figure which may ignore large numbers of non-royal tenants, but which does not suggest a big port even so. The reasons for the change of site are not clear. Security may have been one: the old port was very vulnerable to raids and the new site, on a ridge of higher land, was perhaps more defensible. Nevertheless, it is recorded as having succumbed to the renewed Viking raids of the late tenth and early eleventh centuries. Another suggested reason for the shift is the use of bigger boats in the period, shown by such vessels as those raised from Scandinavian fjords. Possibly the old harbour silted up through some shift in the current. The overall decline of Southampton has been seen as the result of competition from other ports such as Chichester and Wareham, and industrial competition from the newly thriving Winchester, which also became a much more important mint. This would be more convincing if it applied to a period of static economic growth. The evidence is, however, of a very prosperous period in the hundred years after King Alfred had quelled the first phase of Viking raids. Another possibility is a change in trading balance, overseas trade being conducted less by foreign merchants than by natives. If the old Hamwic had been dominated by foreigners, this could have affected its role in the new pattern of commerce. The apparent decline remains a problem, but the town was still important enough to be the one from which the shire took its name. It was increasingly referred to as Southampton to distinguish it from Northampton, which was also a shire town.

One place which might have outstripped Southampton as a trading station was Portchester, less well sited for internal communications, but with stout Roman walls to protect it, and a harbour which was probably quite deep enough for all types of shipping until the twelfth century. Portchester provides a good example of the difficulties of interpreting archaeological evidence when there are no documents to act as guides. The fort was obtained by the king in 904, and it was a *burh*. Neither surviving coins nor documents indicate that it was a mint or a market, however, and in Domesday Book it is treated as an ordinary village, without any urban characteristics. Excavations have shown an elaborate picture inside the *burh*, which the king may have retained in his ownership, although he disposed of most of the rest of the Portchester estate. A complex of timber buildings, including large aisled halls (*d* on Fig. 19), and at least one square stone tower have been found. These buildings are not like the Oxford hut, or most of those from town sites elsewhere like London or Thetford, nor has any street lay-out been observed. The quantity of pottery indicates extensive use of the site, however, and objects like crucibles and bone tools show industrial activity. It would not be possible from the excavated evidence to argue, for instance, that it was functioning in a different way from Wareham, but the documents show that it was clearly not regarded as a town by the Saxons.

Another topographical aspect of towns that excavations can demonstrate is the development of suburbs. It is a mark of the importance of Winchester that it was already expanding beyond its walls in the eleventh century, and excavations are clarifying this process. The extra-mural growth was partly because of Winchester's ecclesiastical complex, which

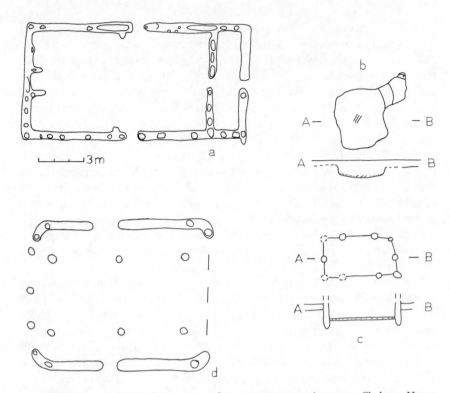

19　Four Saxon timber-built structures from recent excavations: *a* – Chalton, Hants. (after Addyman), a rectangular two-unit 'hall-house'; *b* – Dorchester, Oxon. (after Frere), a 'grub-hut' sunk into the ground, with steps leading down into it, and a hearth; *c* – the cellar building at Oxford (after Hassall); *d* – the aisled 'hall' at Portchester, Hants. (after Cunliffe). All to same scale.

denied more than a quarter of the town to secular development. Oxford, however, which had no such major ecclesiastical presence, also had to expand beyond the area enclosed by the *burh* defences. The walls of the medieval town include a very substantial area on the east side which was probably added to the original circuit as a result of the sort of tenth-century development seen at the All Saints' church site. This addition was certainly made before the Conquest, as it includes a St Peter's church (*h* on Fig. 6) that is treated as intra-mural by Domesday Book, and stands within the present defensive enclosure. An excavation between the spinal east–west road and the south wall (*r* on Fig. 6) showed that the side streets were not laid down before the early twelfth century, but substantial late Saxon occupation nearby was shown by large rubbish pits containing quantities of pottery, and a fine bone weaving tool. Extra-mural development has been proved by excavation on the south road out of the town, overlying the site where eighth-century occupation was found. The Church Street ditch was filled in, presumably because its space was needed.

There is physical evidence that the encircling defences of many towns were changed. The earthen banks with timber revetments and palisades at Wareham were strengthened at some time in the tenth or eleventh centuries by a stone wall along the crest of the rampart (Fig. 9). Construction involved the labour of carting large quantities of river-loam to widen the back of the bank, as well as building the wall itself from limestone, flint, and mortar, quantities of which survived as builders' debris. Since the footings were 2 m (7 ft) wide, set on a mortar raft in which the impression remained although the actual stones had been removed, the wall was very substantial and probably quite high. Its width would have allowed a wall-walk along the top, perhaps protected by a parapet, but there was also a path on the bank itself, which was piled up to a height of $1\frac{1}{2}$ m (4–5 ft) behind the wall. The excavators could see that the path was concave, trodden away in the middle by frequent use. A line of stones on the front of the bank probably helped to prevent its erosion.

Other *burhs* which had their defences changed from timber to stone include Wallingford, Lydford, Oxford and Cricklade. At the last, the wall was some $1\frac{1}{2}$ m (4 ft) wide, and its construction with mortar and limestone with rubble, and an outer line against erosion, was very similar to the arrangement at Wareham. A comparable construction is the wall at South Cadbury, an Iron Age hill-fort which is known to have been a mint site in *c.* 1010, and where excavations have shown that the perimeter was re-fortified and a stone gate-way built. The South Cadbury 'emergency mint' was a revival of the Alfredian policy of providing *burhs* for shelter against Viking raids. Were the other *burhs* refortified at that period? Do the stone walls signify by their uniformity a deliberate act of state by a single monarch? Or is it wrong to see the construction of all of them as having taken place in a short time-span, when in fact it might have been a more drawn-out and random development?

It might be thought that Ethelred was too weak a ruler to be able to instigate a coherent refortification policy during the second great period of Viking attack. The *Anglo-Saxon Chronicle* gives a picture of near-anarchical conditions, incompetence and treachery. 'Exeter was stormed on account of the French *ceorl* Hugh, whom the queen had appointed as her reeve, and the Danish army destroyed the borough completely'; 'when (the Danes) were in the east, the English army was kept in the west, and when they were in the south, our army was in the north . . . Finally there was no leader who would collect an army, but each fled as best he could, and in the end no shire would even help the next.' The evidence of South Cadbury presents a different picture, however, for there, probably through the local ealdorman, not only a stone defence and gate were constructed, but work even began on a building interpreted as a church. If it could be done in an isolated spot in south Somerset, it could be done for the populous towns. The importance of having such protection was acknowledged; Wallingford succumbed and was burnt in 1006, and the Vikings returned unmolested to their ships: 'The people of Winchester could see that army, proud and undaunted, when they went past their gate to the sea, after fetching themselves food and treasures for more than fifty miles from the sea.' But at least on that occasion the Wintonians were safe behind their walls.

The archaeological evidence therefore shows the maintenance and strengthening of town defences, and the documentary sources demonstrate the need for the work to be carried out, in a time of crisis in the late tenth and early eleventh centuries. But the archaeological dating evidence is not sufficiently exact to prove that the physical changes were a response to a specific threat at a specific period. The evidence at Wareham, for instance, is that the wall was built after the first phase timber rampart, and before a third phase of reconstruction when the outer ditch was recut and the bank enlarged. Pottery in this last phase was medieval, of the twelfth or thirteenth centuries. In the second phase, the pottery was so sparse and so characterless that it could not be closely dated, and a precise date cannot, therefore, be ascribed to the building of the stone wall from the archaeological evidence.

The difficulty of dating archaeological sites has to be stressed because it is always tempting to ascribe physical changes to known political, economic or social changes. The subject would be sterile if the attempt were not made, but attractive hypotheses may be misleading. To see the refortification work as stimulated by the Viking raids is one explanation of the physical evidence; to see it as the policy of a powerful ruler more concerned about his personal prestige is another. One king who might have promoted such a policy is Athelstan (925–39), revered by his contemporaries but only imperfectly known to us because of the accidents of documentary survival.

The only direct record that we have of Athelstan's concern for the defences of individual towns in the south comes from William of Malmesbury, the twelfth-century writer. Athelstan built towers and walls at Exeter – presumably repairing the Roman circuit – and also 'cleansed' the town of its British inhabitants, who until then had lived there under their own laws. This is the only direct evidence of new work on fortifications by Athelstan, and the implication is that it was set in train because of problems caused by the British in the neighbourhood, a particular cause which would not have been applicable outside the far south–west. Athelstan's Law Code does, however, include a stipulation that 'every borough is to be repaired by a fortnight after Rogation Days'.

Merchants, Mints and Markets

Athelstan's law code also indicates his concern for the trading communities of his kingdom and the regulation of its coinage. Royal interest in trade can be seen to become increasingly sophisticated. King Ine had laid down regulations for travellers and traders making purchases in the countryside – the implication being that trade in recognized centres was supervised by the king's reeve, as in Kent. King Alfred had not been more specific, except in requiring that traders' servants should be guaranteed. King Edward introduced a new concept: all transactions were to be conducted in a *port* – a recognized market centre, not necessarily a *burh* in its Burghal Hidage sense of an official fortress. King Athelstan's Grately Decrees were more practical, in that they began by allowing small transactions in the countryside: 'No goods over 20 pence are to be bought outside a town, but they are to be bought there in the witness of the town-reeve . . .'

Athelstan's code next proceeded to legislate about the minting of coins. 'There is to be one coinage over all the king's dominion, and no one is to mint money except in a *port*.' This was followed by a list of the towns where there were to be moneyers: 7 in Canterbury, 8 in London, 3 in Rochester, 6 in Winchester, 2 each in Lewes, Southampton, Wareham, Exeter and Shaftesbury, one in Hastings, Chichester and Dorchester; 'otherwise in the other *burhs*, one'. It is not known how much of this was new, and how much it put into writing what was already the practice. Close governmental control of the coinage is apparent from the eighth century onwards, since few foreign coins are found except on the coast. In this respect, therefore, the first part of the Grately Decree on coinage was a formal statement of a well-established practice. It did, however, mark an official change in the system of licensing the Archbishop of Canterbury to mint his own coinage – a practice which had already ceased in the previous reign when the venerable Archbishop Plegmund died. Although some ecclesiastical magnates were still licensed, the coins did not bear designs different from those on the royal issues, and they had to conform in weight. It is not stated in the Decrees that new mints were being set up, and that the number of moneyers in operation was being increased, but that is the implication. One thing which is clear is that the government was taking strong measures against improper practices by the licensed moneyers, and illegal counterfeiting: a convicted moneyer was to have his hand cut off, a punishment borrowed from Frankish practice. An unlicensed forger was to suffer an even worse fate.

The archaeological evidence of monetary control comes from the coins themselves: no mint sites have been recognized in excavations, and none of the dies used in striking has survived – which, like the absence of foreign coin, is itself a tribute to the government, since the old dies were presumably destroyed when the new ones were issued. Such issues were frequent, if the numbers of surviving coins of each design are a reflection of the length of time that they were in circulation. After King Edgar's reform, *c.* 973–5, issues were probably at six-yearly intervals, though even then there are uncertainties, and issues were three-yearly after Cnut's reign. This *renovatio monetae* was both a source of revenue to the government, and a means of ensuring its control of the currency.

It was not until Edgar's reform that coins had to carry the name of the mint at which they were struck, as well as the king's and the moneyer's, although some had in fact done so. So there are many coins whose mint-source is uncertain, and even after the reform, there are mint names so abbreviated that it is not certain where they were issued – is *Brygin* on a 979–85 coin Bristol or Bridgnorth? In that case, the coin die is the same as, or very similar to, one also used at Shaftesbury, which would indicate a west country moneyer, and make Bristol more probable than Bridgnorth. Such 'die-links' are important evidence in doubtful cases.

Vast quantities of tenth- and eleventh-century English coins come from graves and hoards in Scandinavia, because of the Danegeld payments. They are representative of the wealth of England, and more specifically of the output of each mint and of each moneyer, and so of their relative importance in coin issues. London's predominant position is reflected in the volume of coins minted there, just as it is by Athelstan's provision of eight moneyers for it. Winchester's importance in the south is marked by its six moneyers. There are also large hoards of coins from England itself, often the loot of Viking raiding parties, but presumably sometimes the property of travelling merchants. These hoards are not restricted to coins from individual mints, but may come from all over England. They suggest large-scale trading throughout the country, and that commerce was not internally restricted to particular regions.

The hoards may in some respects be misleading in the picture that they show of the wide geographical circulation of coins. They must have been the loot of pirates or the property of rich men, often of rich traders, and so are not representative of the real circulation of coins. This might be described as the area within which took place transactions involving exchange of goods or services for coins of a particular mint during the currency of a particular issue. What would be useful to know, in other words, is whether a farmer going to market at Wareham would be more likely to receive a Wareham-minted penny for his produce than a Winchester- or London-minted one. These everyday transactions are more difficult to reconstruct than those of the long-distance trader. Numismatists are at present producing a series of catalogues of the coins in various museum and other collections, and when these *Sylloges* are complete it may be possible to work out circulation areas.

This possibility is hampered because so few coins have known find-spots. It is very rare for a stray coin to be accurately recorded. More often, it passes into the hands of a dealer, whose interest is in its value to collectors, not in its provenance. Hoards of coins are often divided up among the finders, scattered and lost. The number of coins known is vast; the number in Scandinavia is high; but the number of provenanced coins in England that do not come from mercantile hoards is very low. I have yet to find a record of a single pre-Conquest Wareham penny not from a hoard. Bath-minted coins come from nearby Cheddar, from Tewkesbury, some fifty miles away, and Newchurch (Kent), apart from hoards at Cuerdale (Lancs.), Rome, Chester, Wedmore (Somerset), London, Chancton (Sussex) and Sedlescombe (Sussex). Two of the three stray finds, which are likely to represent trading networks, are geographically closer to their mint site than any of the hoard finds, except Wedmore. Another case is the man who was hanged near Stockbridge in Hampshire soon after 1065, with a linen roll under his arm in which were six pennies. All came from Winchester. Here perhaps was an ordinary man with the sort of coins that were ordinarily in his pocket, issued at the nearest mint.

The possibilities of this sort of study are important because of what they might reveal about each town's trading hinterland. The trading effectiveness of a town would depend upon the size and wealth of the area around it for whose products it was the market, and the importance of individual centres might be partly at least reflected in the area in which its coins predominated. Similarly coin distributions might reveal whether land or river communications were more important in deciding who made use of particular towns and markets.

That markets were not necessarily in towns, or in mint centres, is shown by Domesday Book, which records many places that had markets – often valuable ones – but no other known urban features. Some of these might be on royal estates, like Bampton in Oxfordshire, others might be attached to important churches, like the 'ten traders outside the monastery gates' at Abingdon, on the Thames. Such are Domesday's vagaries that it does not record markets at places which certainly had them, because the figures did not need to be individually itemized in the total assessment for each estate. Nor does Domesday indicate that there were trading fairs in Saxon

England except for one in Cornwall and one in Suffolk. Such assemblies were a profitable and important part of trading life in the Norman and later periods, but there is little evidence that they existed earlier and none that they were attached as might have been a natural development to the open-air assemblies of the hundred and shire courts. Although these were often sited at isolated places, they were nearly always easily accessible by a good road.

The documents reveal other facets of developing urban centres. Borough courts were to meet thrice-yearly, in a law code of King Edgar. Many towns had associations called *frith-gilds* or *cnihtengilds,* associations of men answerable to the reeve for their members' good behaviour, some of which had specific law-keeping duties. Knowledge of these gilds – which did not necessarily function like the later trade guilds – is dependent on chance survivals. They are known to have existed in London, Cambridge and Exeter, and even in small places like Abbotsbury in Dorset and Bedwyn in Wiltshire. Some of these gilds were colleges of priests, however, not of merchants.

Bedwyn is an interesting town, for it is an example of a site which seems to have developed in the tenth century, partly at least because the nearby hill-fort of Chisbury was probably one of the *burhs* of the *Burghal Hidage.* The fort itself was too difficult of access to be useful for trade, so a shift was made to a more convenient site. It was stimulated because it was on a large royal estate, and was used as a collecting centre for the payment of tax. It was a mint, although a small one. The present village has a triangular market-place, although this may not be the site of the Saxon market, but a development of the twelfth or thirteenth century. A recent excavation alongside a street that might have been of Saxon origin failed to find any traces of occupation. The date of a ditch on the edge of the site is not certain.

Another Wiltshire *burh* on which archaeology has yet to throw much light is Wilton, the *tun* on which the people of the Wylye valley were 'dependent' by the eighth century. Its defences have not been fully located, and it may be that some reliance was always placed on the nearby hill-fort, Old Sarum. That is the implication of a *Chronicle* entry for 1003, that the Danes raided Wilton, but passed by Old Sarum. The minters from Wilton operated at Old Sarum in the eleventh century, but no trace of this occupation has been found. It was presumably an 'emergency mint' like South Cadbury, but was not abandoned. A Norman castle was built within the hill-fort, the amalgamated sees of Ramsbury and Sherborne were centred on it in 1057, and a new cathedral was established – the only English example of a hill-top castle and cathedral. The town that developed to serve these establishments was not on the plateau, but on the sides of the hill.

Excavations have not shown whether this town had a coherent lay-out; although various streets are known, it has not been possible to get a plan of the site, or to locate the 'core' of its settlement area. The hope would be that some day it might be possible to see if Old Sarum had a small town deliberately laid out at a single operation, or if it grew piecemeal. The site has been damaged by pipe-lines, recent housing estates and farming activities, but is still perhaps the most promising of a small group of places in which the tenth or eleventh centuries probably saw economic developments, which could have been deliberately planned by their owners. Taunton is known from documents, Abingdon had its 'ten traders at the abbey gates', Romsey and Shaftesbury may have been stimulated by their nunneries, and all have market-places in their present topography. Were these features Saxon, or do they result from replanning in the twelfth or thirteenth centuries?

Somerset and Wiltshire had several small places like Bedwyn which were dignified as late Saxon *burhs* because of royal patronage. In terms of size, and in terms of the archaeological evidence that they have produced, the defences that they display, or their surviving churches, there is nothing to separate them from many other settlements. Axbridge, Langport, Amesbury, Calne, Chippenham, Tilshead and Warminster were all places with some mark of burghal status – a mint, or burgesses recorded in Domesday Book. There seems no reason why certain counties had these small *burhs* and others not. Bampton, a royal estate, would have been an obvious choice in Oxfordshire, or Andover in Hampshire, where charters were signed by Edgar and by Ethelred, near the big royal estate at Tarrant. Are these differences between regions significant? Was society organized differently in them? Was trade conducted under different regulations? Such things are not revealed in the documents, nor yet by archaeology.

The documents do, however, reveal another aspect of the growth of town life and of trade, in the purchase of property in towns attested by occasional charters. The example of Abingdon Abbey's acquisition in 1008 of a *haga* (an enclosure) in Cricklade may show that the abbey was attracted to the town's trading potential, and bought a small estate there to serve as a base for its operation. It has been suggested that this property survives as the present Abingdon Court Farm, in the north-east corner of the town, around which traces of a bank and ditch suggest a property boundary. Here presumably stock could be kept, and a house for the abbot's agent. The estate at Eynsham transferred to his newly founded monastery there in the early eleventh century by Aethelmaer 'the fat' included as an adjunct a *curia* in Oxford. The tenth-century bishops of Winchester bought privileges from the king that were intended to make Taunton a profitable market town. The scheme worked, for Domesday Book records 64 burgesses there, paying an average of 6*d.* each to the bishop, and a market worth 50*s.* The street lay-out at Taunton with its triangular market-place could date from this period, but there is no archaeological evidence about this. Further afield, the bishop of London bequeathed 'the estate at Waldringfield and my messuage in Ipswich, which I bought', to his nephew. Clearly he had purchased a property in the town to improve the marketing potential of his agricultural property, and the two went naturally together as a single unit.

Such purchases illustrate the development of trading centres and appreciation of the profits to be accrued. This was not new, for charters reveal the same thing in pre-Viking London and Canterbury. Unfortunately charters that deal with towns are very few, and it is not possible to see any patterns in the purchasing process except that it happened, and its happening partly explains a system revealed in Domesday Book, in which many burgesses 'belong' to a rural manor. Presumably many estates found it profitable to maintain an agent's house in the nearest market centre, and were taxed accordingly. Whether some of these 'contributory' places had had a connection with their centre since it was established as a *burh*, and had some particular responsibility for upkeep of the defences, is not at all clear. Athelstan's decree that the *burhs* were to be maintained is sadly inexplicit about how this was to be effected, and so another piece of potential evidence about town/country inter-relationship is missing. What is clear is that it was the responsibility of the local earl by the mid eleventh century, and he was entitled to every third penny of revenue from the town to pay for its upkeep. For Oxford, Domesday records the existence of *mansiones murales*, suggesting that the expense of upkeep may have fallen on particular properties in the town.

Profit and Prayer

Did the earl's third penny also pay for the building of the stone churches that survive beside the gates of Oxford and Wareham? Clearly these could have been part of the defensive system. At Oxford, the tower has a vulnerable window on the ground floor, but this could be blocked in emergencies, and the solid stone structure would be effective as a citadel, despite its ecclesiastical function – which is shown partly by its later use and partly by its belfry with original openings (Plate x; *s* on Fig. 6). It has a door on the second storey, which either led out to a wooden observation balcony, or onto a wooden wall-walk over the gate. At Wareham, the late tenth- or early eleventh-century church is less obviously defensive, although it is by the north gate (Plate xi; *b* on Fig. 4). It does not show any sign of having had a tower, and its simple and small nave and chancel suggest ordinary parish use. This is borne out by the recent excavation only a few metres away in North Street, which indicated the expansion of occupation in the area at exactly that period. It has been suggested that Cricklade had a similarly placed 'gate' church, marked by the presence there now of a thirteenth-century chapel, but this has been challenged because the bank would probably have been wider and have overlain the chapel site in the Saxon period. Nevertheless, the present church may have had a Saxon predecessor, as may the church at Lyng. Other 'gate' churches are known.

Cricklade's 'minster' church has already been discussed, and the evidence from the South Cadbury excavation has emphasized that such a building was considered an important part of a *burh*. Wareham, of course, already had a minster – St Mary's near the river – but the church by the gate shows that small urban churches to serve local residents were coming into demand. Wareham's St Martin's is the only one to survive in the south, but there is documentary evidence for them elsewhere – Oxford's St Peter's has already been mentioned, and there is now evidence from excavations.

The stone building of the mid eleventh century excavated in Oxford became All Saints' church at quite a late stage in its history, though the precise date has yet to be established. Winchester had four intra-mural and four extra-mural churches by the time of the *Winton Survey* of *c.* 1110. Only three Winchester churches were known to be of pre-1066 date until excavations were carried out, and this work has increased the known number to seven. At St Mary's the sequence is not unlike All Saints', Oxford, in that an originally secular stone building seems to have been converted into a church, in this case with the addition of a semi-circular apse. The date of conversion is probably earlier than at All Saints', but neither site has dating evidence available yet, nor is there a date so far for the first establishment of St Pancras' in Winchester, which had no secular origins, but was purpose-built with a nave and small square-ended chancel.

It is instructive to compare the internal lengths and widths (in metres) of the naves of these early urban churches, as a crude indication of the size of congregation expected to use them:

	Length	Width
Oxford, All Saints':	7	6
Wareham, St Martin's:	9 (min.)	5
Winchester, St Mary's:	6.40	5.40
Winchester, St Pancras':	10	6.30

The floor area of all of them was very limited (even compared with the minsters described in Chapter One) and even allowing that there were no pews, the only benches being round the walls for the old and infirm ('the weakest go to the wall'), the numbers of worshippers were small. Churches were intended to serve only a very local population. The evidence hints that they might have been built by the district's landlord – who else could have afforded a stone building? – and that his motive was profit at least as much as piety. By coercing his tenants into using his new church, whose construction was probably not an enormous outlay, especially in the conversion cases, and whose costs were upkeep and hire of priest, he could divert compulsory alms to his own use. How much he could divert seems to have depended on the strength of opposition shown by the established minster to this infringement on its rights and income. The churches show that such schemes were considered worthwhile, however.

Like the development of suburbs, the churches are a sign of at least modest urban prosperity. On what was this prosperity based? Everyday life inside a town may never be fully revealed, but at least it is now possible to argue a case against the picture created from documentary evidence by Professor Stephenson in the 1930s, that the townsman was doing agricultural work – stock-tending, ploughing and reaping in the fields all day – like his village contemporaries. Certainly every town would have contained some labourers whose job was to watch the grazing flocks, do the milking and feeding, and tend the horses. The fields within the towns were, as Wallingford still shows, big areas, too valuable to be left as waste land, and each town also had fields round it. Oxford's outlying Port Meadow was held *communiter* at the Domesday survey. The towns were more than large villages, however. A moneyer's presence would help to stimulate a market by drawing people into the town to have their coins reminted. In the *burhs*, garrison and defence maintenance duty, however it worked in detail, would bring in numbers of outsiders to be fed and lodged, and they would probably bring produce with them to sell. There is no direct evidence of such things as market stalls, but specialist traders are shown at Winchester in the early street names like Tanner and Fleshmonger Streets.

Archaeologically, the picture is still very incomplete. Building trades must have flourished; in the ports, there must have been shipwrights; the remains of iron slag show smithies. Crucibles – small clay containers with thick deposits of metal alloys sticking to them – and a stone mould for casting ingots show metal-workers' activity in Oxford. Wareham's gully complex may show tanning, but there is nothing to match the contemporary evidence from York. Nor is there any evidence that pottery was being made in the southern towns, except Exeter, as it was in nearly all the Danelaw centres. More positive is evidence of textile working: again this may explain the Wareham gullies, but more definite is the large number of objects from Oxford, Winchester and Wareham. Baked clay bun-shaped loom-weights, bone spindle-whorls, thread-pickers and 'pin-beaters' (Fig. 3) would all have been used in cloth production.

All these activities were not necessarily particular to towns rather than villages, however. Textile weaving is attested in the countryside by large numbers of finds, and only the bronze-working might be argued as being a solely urban occupation. The evidence from both towns and villages is far too incomplete to argue for specialization, except of course in the case of coin minting. It would have been the scale rather than the type of activity that would have marked the difference between a town and a village, so there is no absolute criterion by which archaeological evidence can distinguish between the status of these types of settlement, in the way that documentary evidence of mints, courts, reeves and burgesses can suggest legal distinctions.

It may become possible to establish archaeological criteria as more evidence becomes available and it may well be that archaeological criteria are more meaningful than legal ones in deciding how places were considered by contemporaries. Legal evidence makes no distinction between Winchester and Bedwyn, but physically they were very different. The activity and bustle in the streets of the big town would have been more noticeably different from the usually somnolent market-place of the small *port,* than the *port* from the village street. Some townspeople lived in different types of house: townsfolk's daily lives were more bound up with trade and exchange. It is these aspects of society that archaeology can investigate and illuminate.

Certainly town life was growing, although many places suffered setbacks from the renewed Viking raids. The immediate effects of the Norman Conquest were also unwelcome. Domesday Book reveals many reduced tax assessments between 1066 and 1086, and records numbers of 'waste', unoccupied tenements. Many of these were accounted for by the new castles: in Oxford and Winchester, the physical effects of these have been shown. Towns like Wareham, which lost almost half its houses, must have taken a long time to recover. Most, however, had become sufficiently well-established that they surmounted the temporary disruption, to flourish again in the twelfth century.

Chapter 4

The Medieval Church

Gothick melancholia in the eighteenth century and the High Church movement in the nineteenth both meant that the medieval church was studied for the lessons, spiritual and architectural, which it could provide. This led many students into antiquarianism, and medieval archaeology can be said to have been born in – and sometimes stifled by – ecclesiology. The most notable work was perhaps that of Thomas Rickman in the 1820s, whose *Attempt to Discriminate the Styles of Architecture in England* established what amounts to the first archaeological typology. The principle that artifacts can be arranged in chronological order by their stylistic features may be called the basis of the discipline of archaeology. The difficulty that remains of course is that not all objects will change in the same way at the same time in every place. Because the 'Perpendicular' style was used at Gloucester Cathedral in the 1330s is no reason to assume that it was immediately adopted by all English masons. New styles and ideas had to spread by diffusion, as men trained in one place went to work in another and took their ideas with them, or as patrons and craftsmen on pilgrimages, crusades and other journeys saw new ideas and copied them.

The process of diffusion works most quickly in the most costly and prestigious works of art. Rich patrons are generally aware of the latest new styles, and will not be content with anything else. Abbots and bishops wanted their churches to be finer than those of their contemporaries and would pay high wages to master masons and carpenters, who might therefore work anywhere in the country. The masters would train local men. Since a mason taught to cut the moulding of an arch to a design by William Wynford for New College, Oxford, in the 1380s might not leave Oxfordshire at the end of the contract, similar mouldings would appear in local churches which subsequently commissioned work from him. He might have a working life of twenty or thirty years, and might train apprentices in his ways, so that a debased but recognizable form of Wynford's mouldings might still be being worked half a century later. Conversely, a man might be flexible: a recent study of Thomas Wolvey, an early fifteenth-century mason, shows that he was far from wedded to a particular design.

The typology of mouldings is one of the many considerations by which the different parts of a church are dated. Such evidence is more precise than in most archaeological studies, but is still subject to provisos, not only the craftsman's individuality but also the amount of surviving evidence. A mid fifteenth-century arcade may show that an aisle was added to an existing nave at that time; but recent excavations like those at Winchester and Oxford have shown how the history of a church that considers only the visible standing evidence gives a very incomplete account.

The Buildings

The Old Minster at Winchester is one church where recent excavations have revealed how the ground plan was enlarged and remodelled over the years. This church was described by several tenth-century writers, and excavations have borne out the complexities of the building that they outlined. To Cenwalh's seventh-century church a screen was added at the west end, against which a series of small chapels was built. In the 970s, the originally free-standing St Martin's Tower was joined to Cenwalh's nave, enclosing the open-air tomb of St Swithun. In the 980s, the east end was lengthened, over and beyond Cenwalh's chancel, and a crypt was added, as were *porticus* to its sides. Further *porticus* were added at the west end. The very elaborate western structure probably made the Old Minster similar to Carolingian churches, such as Charlemagne's Aachen, providing a chamber at first-floor level in which was placed a throne for the king or the bishop. There was a similar arrangement in the church at Sherborne, a bishop's seat until 1075. A choir would also use the first floor of a west end for responsions in the litany, creating the effect of a choir of angels for those below. Despite its elaboration, the Old Minster was a small structure: the whole would have fitted into the nave of the Norman abbey which replaced it. Its main role was perhaps to serve as the chapel for the royal palace.

The Old Minster was probably inconveniently small for most functions, but reverence for Cenwalh's church may have led to reluctance simply to rebuild it on a larger scale. This would explain why the New Minster was founded by Edward in *c.* 904, literally abutting it, largely to be the church for the rapidly expanding population of Winchester. This church has yet to be fully excavated; apparently it was much wider than the Old Minster, having either aisles or flanking *porticus*. It cannot have been more than 77 m (250 ft) long altogether, however, since excavations east of it have revealed the south range of what may prove to be a cloister, built in the

Saxon period but altered and enlarged in the Norman. This may one day provide a coherent picture of a Saxon claustral arrangement. It may be linked to a series of buildings to the north, which partly overlie a timber oval oratory – a reminder that even the greatest houses were not exclusively stone-built.

The two minsters at Winchester were among the churches that were 'reformed' in the second half of the tenth century, the zealous Bishop Ethelwold instituting a fully monastic life there based on the Benedictine model developed in the French abbey at Cluny. Similar reforms were carried out at Abingdon, and a pious and prosperous era saw several new foundations of various sizes – Cerne, Eynsham, Abbotsbury. Other established houses where rules probably tightened, if not drastically, include Muchelney in Somerset, where foundations of a small Saxon church are visible, and Romsey, where excavation (in 1975) revealed the north *porticus* of a very substantial Saxon church, with big reused Roman stones in its footings; an apsidal chancel can still be seen below the crossing floor of the present church, and a nineteenth-century report indicates that there was a matching *porticus* on the south side. Internal administrative changes at a monastery did not necessarily mean physical changes, however, and the Romsey church may not belong to the Reform period.

The churches described so far were major ones – the cathedrals and the great abbeys. Only at Sherborne does anything now survive above ground level, the west wall with a small side door, and part of the north side. The plan of the present church has a crossing which is wider than the nave and the chancel. This may well 'fossilize' a Saxon crossing tower's foundations.

An eleventh-century code set out four categories of church, the great churches being the first. The second category were the minsters, some of which, like Cricklade, survive at least in part. This category is less easy to define. Minsters resulted from the early church system of aiming to provide a small corporate body of priests to serve a wide area, rather than to have a priest in each parish. The *mater ecclesia* at Cricklade was a minster of this kind, the 'mother-church' to its area, and one such was provided in every *burh*. Others were in rural places. The only urban one of which much survives is at Milborne Port (*port* here being the Saxon word for market, as in Edward the Elder's laws) in Somerset, a fine building with external decoration and a cruciform plan, the crossing being wider than the nave and chancel, as at Sherborne.

By the end of the tenth century, the priests serving a minster were living very different lives from monks in the reformed monasteries; they had their parochial function, they could own private property and they could be married. Attempts to introduce new regulations for priests to serve cathedrals were made at Exeter and Wells, but these were not sufficiently successful to justify the system in the twelfth century. Most of the priests' houses were then converted to Augustinian Canonries, living a life little different from ordinary monks except that they continued to serve some local churches: among these were St Frideswide's, Oxford; St Denys, Southampton; Dorchester-on-Thames; Cirencester; and Christchurch (Twyneham), a *burh* with a large minster recorded in Domesday. One or two remained as colleges of priests, serving a few local churches. One such was Wimborne, Dorset, where the plan of the splendid twelfth-century church is thought to perpetuate that of a Saxon predecessor, because the width of the crossing is greater than of the nave and chancel, as at Milborne Port. The foundations of a structure found in excavations at South Cadbury, in the early eleventh-century *burh*, had this plan, and so it may have been a minster.

Minsters were not confined to towns: it may be that each hundred district had a minster. The surviving names of Dorset indicate a large number of them – Yetminster, Charminster, and one of them, Sturminster, retained ecclesiastical jurisdiction over a wide area for some time. The names are more occasional in other counties, and the system may have lasted longer in Dorset than elsewhere, but Oxfordshire has its Minster Lovell, Wiltshire its Warminster, for instance. Among churches that can be taken as minsters is Breamore, Hants., where Saxon nave, *porticus* and chancel largely survive (Plate xii). It was a large parish with two dependent chapels in the Middle Ages, there was a house of Augustinian canons there, and it had been a royal estate, all of which are pointers to minster status in the past. Breamore church became an ordinary parish church, since the twelfth-century Augustinian house was on a different site, and it was presumably big enough to serve this reduced function despite an expanding population, so did not need to be much altered. Langford, Oxon., is another royal estate church that may have served a wide area, and has remained as a substantially Saxon – and very fine – building.

The difficulty of recognizing churches that used to be minsters, from documents and from surviving structures, is brought out in a problem that has arisen at Potterne in Wiltshire. It has been claimed that a site in the village which produced a series of slots and post-holes can be interpreted as the foundations of a timber 'baptistery', and that the church was moved to its present site in the twelfth century. Potterne was a large estate with several dependent settlements in the eleventh century, and shared the hundredal name of its district with another settlement. It was owned by the bishop of Salisbury, and a priest is specifically mentioned there in Domesday, with a substantial holding. The 'baptistery' church seems too small to have served a large village, with a status in the area that suggests that it may once have been the site of a 'mother-church'. The present church is on a ridge of high ground, a more typical church position than that of the 'baptistery' church. Although its present structure has nothing earlier than the thirteenth century it has a cruciform plan, which can sometimes be an indication of a Saxon foundation. It may be that the 'upper' church was the minster, the 'baptistery' church merely a dependent chapel, abandoned in the twelfth century. Two things could prove the point – either excavation inside the 'upper' church if a new heating system is put in, or an intensive search for pottery evidence throughout the area, to see where the original settlement nucleus lay.

The case of Potterne is exceptional, and the large number of village churches with surviving Saxon features is proof that few if any moved site at least after the tenth or eleventh century. Saxon features that are distinctive include round-headed door and window openings, the latter often double-splayed, or with a central baluster shaft on which rests a massive stone going right through the thickness of the wall (Fig. 19). Such through-stones were frequently used for door and window openings, and massive stones were often similarly used in quoins at corners. Plinths, pilaster strips and string-courses are found, such projections often indicating that rubble walls would not have been visible, but were intended to be plastered over (Plate xii). In plan, a nave and square-ended rather than apsidal chancel was usual. There are no cases of aisles in lesser churches, only of side chapels, the *porticus*, square-ended in surviving examples, though semi-circular ones were found at the Old Minster. These generally differ from Norman transepts because they are not a structural part of the church. They are entered by doors rather than full-width openings, and are usually both narrower and less tall than the nave (Plate xii). Their use was for burials and side altars, often with relics. A few Saxon churches, such as Milborne Port, do have true transepts. Where there were towers they were either at the west end or over the central crossing, and the upper storeys might well be of timber, not stone. A timber steeple can be made to look very impressive, and their use is not a sign of poverty in a church. Unfortunately, no timber towers have survived so their appearance has to be guessed from Scandinavian parallels and from manuscript drawings, which suggest a tiered construction of diminishing pyramids. The medieval crossing-tower at Breamore (Plate xii) may follow the lines of a Saxon predecessor of this type.

Most rural minsters ended up as parish churches, like Breamore, though some managed to maintain their rights over dependent villages for long into the Middle Ages. Most were lowered into the third Saxon category, a church with a graveyard. These often replaced the outdoor preaching crosses set up 'in the early days of the church' in the south; the crosses that survive, like those at Codford (Plate VIII) and Ramsbury (Fig. 18), or the one from East Stour, Dorset, now in the British Museum, may all be memorial, not preaching, crosses. The parish system formalized during the tenth century, and there was a consequent increase in village and small urban churches. The physical changes that even small churches underwent is graphically illustrated by the excavations in Winchester at the Lower Brook Street site (Fig. 5).

St Mary's, Winchester probably began life in the pre-Viking period as a small rectangular secular stone building, converted in the Late Saxon period by the addition of a semi-circular apse; at the same time, the east end of the floor of the nave was raised, forming a step. Soon afterwards, the south door into the nave was blocked. Next the nave was extended eastwards over the apse, a new south door was opened and a new square-ended chancel was built; then the north wall and door of the nave were rebuilt; finally the south door was blocked again. In addition to these major changes, there is evidence from post-holes and from wear on the floor that the altar position was changed; that a rood screen was put up; and that the font was moved from a small pit at the west end to the centre of the nave. These changes all happened to the church in some 250–300 years. In its subsequent 250–300 years, there were twelve further phases, some minor such as the reblocking of the south door, some involving major extension and rebuilding.

The blocking and unblocking of the south door of St Mary's is a curious feature, that might be expected to result from a special connection to the property next door, for whereas there was a lane on the north side, giving public access, on the south there was a private tenement. Yet this does not seem to have been a house suitable for the owner of the church, so that he could treat it as his private chapel, nor was it the priest's house. Instead it seems usually to have been an industrial property – a yard or workshops – not used domestically at all. The door remains unexplained, but its problem illustrates the dangers of providing explanations from partial evidence.

The excavator of St Mary's realized the potential that it gave not only for seeing the changes effected on a small urban church, but also for trying to see the causes of these changes – response to changes in church services, in ownership, and in frequency of use. Another church in Lower Brook Street, St Pancras, has also been excavated, in the hope of seeing similar patterns. Both churches were abandoned in the late Middle Ages, when population reduction made many urban churches redundant, and parishes were amalgamated. The general picture at St Pancras, of many alterations, is the same, but not the details of the evolution. A small two-celled church, with nave and tiny square chancel, was enlarged by the addition of side chapels and the extension of the nave westwards. The chancel was extended. The side chapels were replaced by larger ones, but the north one was soon taken down, so that a lane could run alongside the nave wall. The south chapel was extended eastwards. Then the lane was diverted to form a dog-leg around a new north aisle, and the north wall of the nave therefore needed an arcade. The west wall was strengthened, perhaps for a bell-cote. A south aisle was added later. The church was then demolished. Had it remained, its standing structure would have given no hint of the size, date or layout of the original church, nor of the changes that it had undergone.

The other urban church that has been excavated recently for which a plan is available is All Saints' in Oxford (Fig. 20). It had remained a church for longer than those in Winchester, for it did not become redundant until the 1970s. The medieval building was only known from seventeenth-century prints and descriptions, for it fell down in 1699. Much of it had been robbed out by footings for its successor, and by graves. Consequently only four phases were recognized after the conversion of a secular stone building

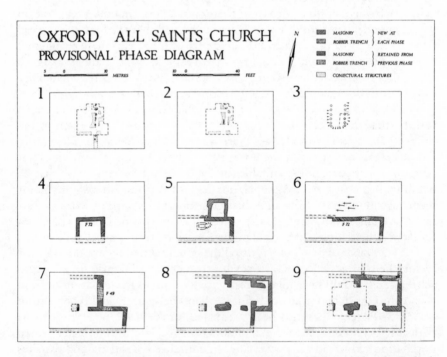

20 The excavator's interpretation of the development of All Saints' church, Oxford, from a ninth-century open yard divided by a line of fencing (Phase 1) to a timber building with a cellar (Phase 3 – compare *d* on Fig. 19), replaced by a stone structure (Phase 4), partly demolished by a furnace (Phase 5). Part of the Phase 4 building was used as the chancel of the first church on the site (Phase 6), to which a north aisle was added (Phase 7); later alterations included extending first the aisle (Phase 8), and then the chancel (Phase 9).

to ecclesiastical use, but these four refer only to the north side and east end, for the rest is lost. Clearly it underwent as many structural changes as the Winchester churches.

There have been fewer excavations of rural churches to set alongside the urban record, but work at Wharram Percy, Yorks., has shown that no fewer alterations need be expected. There is nothing yet to compare to the Wharram Percy evidence from the south, although investigation is now (1977) in progress in a church at Little Somborne, Hants. At Waterperry, Oxon., no structural evidence was found under the nave – perhaps showing that its walls were Saxon, at least at foundation level. Finds included a tenth- or eleventh-century sherd to justify this claim. A similar blank, without even the sherd, has so far been drawn at Stubbington, Hants. There is as yet no rural evidence of the kind seen in two of the urban excavations, that churches might have been converted from secular buildings.

One result of these excavations has been the demonstration that the altar in most churches was not at the extreme east end, but stood in front of the chancel arch at the east end of the nave; in some of the bigger churches, a life-size rood sculpture above the arch acted as a backdrop. The altar's location meant that much of the service was taken with the priest standing in the nave, close to his congregation, a physical reflection of the social standing of many of the clergy in the smaller churches. Hired by the church's owner, the priest was often low-born and not a man of rank. Throughout the Middle Ages, Chaucer's 'poor priest of a town' ('town' in the medieval sense of 'settlement') was a common figure.

It is not always clear if the Saxon urban churches fitted into the third category of the eleventh-century code, for although they may have had a parish, they did not necessarily have a graveyard. Normally this would be because the mother-church was careful not to lose the prerogative of burial, since it would have entailed a major loss of revenue. Only late in the life of St Mary's in Winchester were there burials in it, when the New Minster ceded its rights. Many such urban churches were the equivalent of the fourth category, the field-church without a graveyard. In this category also would go the private chapels which contemporary codes indicated as appropriate for a thegn to have attached to his residence. The Saxon square stone foundations at Portchester may be the base of a tower for a *burh* chapel, and has graves around it – presumably specially licensed. The number of field-churches increased after the eleventh century, at least in the countryside, as new parishes were not created. This did not prevent the building of places of worship, to serve as chapels for the increasing number of hamlets that developed as dependent settlements. These did not have burial or baptismal rites, and attendance at the parish church was compulsory on major feast days, guaranteeing that the central church should retain a major part of the parish income, and incidentally tending to maintain its role as the physical nub of its area.

The distribution map of Saxon churches shows that there were many small village churches, but the survivals are not evenly spread across the country (Fig. 21). This is partly because of the shorter life that a timber church is likely to have, and because the expenses of stone hauling reduce the likelihood of stone churches in areas deficient in suitable quarries. The chalklands not surprisingly have fewer Saxon churches than the Upper Thames Valley with its ready access to Cotswold limestone. The existence of a number of stone churches in an area may show that it was a prosperous one, but their lack may not necessarily show the opposite. Often, however, it does. The Dorset chalklands were not far from a limestone belt, but the wealth surplus of the estates was not enough to produce stone churches. The heathlands are a void, and the creation of the New Forest is unlikely to have been the sole cause of this. The record of Domesday Book is more often borne out than contradicted by church distribution. Although it is clear that there were many Saxon stone churches, it is still true that there are many more Norman ones. The intensification of building is a reflection of Norman pride, but also of the expanding economy, just as the survival of old churches often shows that relative poverty prevented them from being completely replaced, rather than merely altered.

Church building can be a general guide to an area's prosperity, but not an absolute one. Although income was a major motive of their Saxon owners, churches were also built for reasons of prestige – and even of piety! If an owner worshipped in the church himself, he might care for it more than if he lived far afield. It would be interesting to study the chancels of medieval churches, which became the part of the building that was the responsibility of the holder of the living, to see if any general differences can be detected between those maintained by ecclesiastical houses, by the crown or by individuals. Naves, which were the communal responsibility of the parish, perhaps generally received more attention. Frequently churches benefited from the donations of individuals: the famous Cotswold wool-churches are one result, and some churches benefited from the profits made in war by their local magnates. Certainly the relative poverty of medieval Dorset is shown by the small scale of its churches, but precise measurements, like the quantity of stone used in each church in each century, might reveal more precise fluctuations – if such things could be calculated.

The stone used in surviving churches and sculptures is evidence of quarrying as a major industry from the Saxon period onwards. Stone from the limestone belts was taken long distances overland so that oolites,

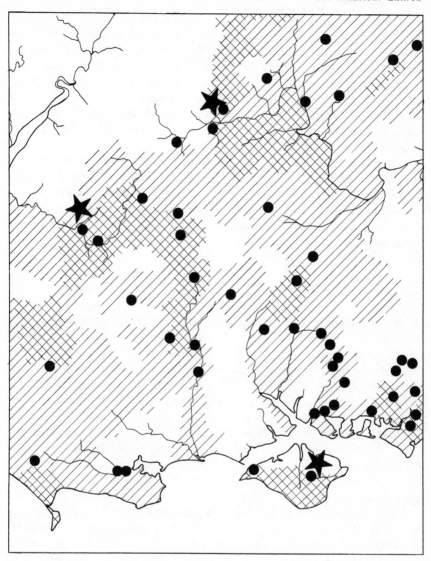

21 Distribution of churches (= spots) with some surviving Anglo-Saxon structural features (after Taylor and Taylor), plotted onto population density as revealed at Domesday (after Darby *et al.*). Blank areas = sparse population; oblique lines = medium density; chequered areas = high density. Major quarries are starred (after Jope). (NB map does not include Gloucestershire or Winchester.)

probably from the Box area in the south Cotswolds, are found widely in Wiltshire and occasionally in Hampshire in Saxon churches, and stone from the central Cotswolds around Taynton is found throughout the Upper Thames Valley. The Isle of Wight's Quarr was worth taking to the mainland, and can be found in east Hampshire and along the Sussex coast. The development of the quarrying industry can be studied in this way throughout the Middle Ages. Purbeck marble from Dorset, for example, was used in buildings and for making mortars from the late twelfth century, being taken as far away as Worcester Cathedral, whereas the county's Portland limestone was hardly exploited until the fourteenth, being used then at Exeter and London but not becoming a major industry until later. A thorough study of Oxford's medieval buildings has shown increasing use of the fine limestones in preference to the rougher products of local quarries. Prestige was the motive which caused patrons to spend large sums on stones from distant sources.

The Dependent Arts

That a church existed in a particular village in the late Saxon period may sometimes be suggested not by the surviving fabric, but by a piece of sculpture retained and incorporated in the later building. Sculptures can of course be easily moved, and the presence of, for instance, a tiny rood in the west tower at Alresford, Hants., or a sun-dial at St Michael, Winchester, does not absolutely prove that there were Saxon predecessors of the present churches. There are however remarkably few sculptures of this kind, intended to be built into the fabric of the building, which are not in churches that have surviving structural evidence of the Saxon period. Of free-standing crosses, like the Codford or Ramsbury ones, there are very many more examples, but they directly prove only that there was a graveyard, not necessarily that there was a church on the site.

The dating of Saxon sculptures is difficult and where stylistic comparisons are made, they are primarily to the larger body of surviving manuscript drawings and paintings. The art of decorating books, fostered at Winchester by King Alfred, developed there during the tenth century. The range of initials formed of little animals and figures seen in the *Cura Pastoralis* (Fig. 14) was extended and elaborated, and the practice of having whole-page illustrations was reintroduced. One of the first is a picture of the Birth of Christ, a very close copy of Byzantine work. It was painted at the Old Minster, into a psalter that had not been written there but had been given to the house by King Athelstan. He had acquired it from abroad, for its text was written at a Carolingian house in the ninth century. It is interesting to see the importance attached to such manuscripts; King Athelstan in particular is known to have valued them as gifts and many books were presented to him, by the Emperor Otto I, for instance. It was not considered improper to embellish these works, despite their age, for to do so was an act of reverence.

The psalter with the scene of the Nativity had two other pictures added to it at the Old Minster, both showing Christ surrounded by saints and choirs of angels. These pictures have been tellingly compared to the figures on the stone from the Old Minster dormitory painted in Alfred's reign (Fig. 12), and the two designs may have come from the same source, some book in the Minster library that had been painted many years before and was considered an appropriate model. The model for a picture might well be an old manuscript, not necessarily an English one, but from a distant part of Europe. Various traditions – earlier English work, Carolingian manuscripts, east Mediterranean works – can be recognized in tenth-century Winchester, the different sources being intermixed eventually to create an original art form in southern England, whose products were in their turn disseminated throughout Europe. The 'Winchester style' is particularly associated with the reforming Bishop Ethelwold, for the illumination of manuscripts was one of the tasks suitable for monks. The reform both increased the number of brethren, and reduced their duties, so that there was an increasing output of manuscripts, some undecorated, some with a few elaborated initials, some with outline drawings perhaps enlivened with a few strokes of coloured brushwork, some with fully-painted pages.

One of the first products of the 'reformed' New Minster was a scene showing King Edgar presenting its new charter to Christ, who is seated in heaven supported by flying angels. It was painted soon after 966, but already had most of the stylistic features of the 'Winchester School'. The concept of the presentation scene was not new – King Athelstan had become the first English king of whom a painted portrait survives, in a scene showing him presenting a book to St Cuthbert – and was another of the many ideas taken from Carolingian works. The juxtaposition of King Edgar with Christ and his angels, and with St Peter and the Virgin Mary, the two figures standing beside him, can be seen as part of a deliberate policy to enhance the status of the king, suggesting that he ruled through God's grace and had a divine role. This theocratic policy strengthened the power of the king, for who dares to challenge the lord's anointed? It also strengthened the church, whose magnates could look to a special place as the king's advisers, since they were the interpreters of God's will. It is not a coincidence that Edgar was the first English king to have a coronation, a ceremony which hints that the king is ordained by God through His ministers. Edgar was crowned at the age of thirty-one, the canonical coming of age. It is inconsistent that the ceremony should have taken place at Bath, at a relatively minor church, and not at Winchester. The Old Minster excavations have shown that that church was small for a state occasion, but the New Minster was available. The construction of the Old Minster west-work shown by the excavations also hints at church policy towards the elevation of the kingship, physically expressed by the throne looking down upon the people below.

One of the church leaders was of course Ethelwold who, as bishop of Winchester, was responsible for some of the rebuilding of the Old Minster and particularly for the incorporation of Swithun's tomb within the body of the church and the setting up of a great shrine in 971. This was paid for by the king, and reputedly contained 300 lbs. of gold, studded with gems. It may have been to mark the translation of Swithun's tomb that the bishop ordered one of the monks to create the most sumptuous and famous of all the Winchester manuscripts, *The Benedictional of St Ethelwold,* to contain the prayers read by the bishop from the altar on the major Feasts. The colophon with which the monk ended his book states the motives that led to such productions:

> A bishop, the great Ethelwold, ordered a certain monk subject to him to write the present book . . . He commanded also to be made in the book many frames well adorned and filled with various figures decorated with numerous beautiful colours and with gold . . . To the great father who ordered this book to be written may God grant an eternal kingdom above. Let all who look upon this book pray always that . . . I may abide in heaven. Godeman, the scribe, earnestly asks this. (trans. F. Wormald)

Such a book was an act of devotion by its patron and by its artist, for the admiration of posterity, who would marvel at the wealth of the former who supplied the expensive materials – the parchment, the pigments and the gold for the gold leaf that was liberally used – and the skill of the latter in their application. It is interesting that in this case Godeman was clearly both painter and writer; often a book might go through several different hands, even left incomplete, perhaps to be finished in a different style many years later.

New monastic foundations were initially staffed by brethren from established houses, until their own were trained. This was one way in which the 'Winchester School's' ideas spread, as well as by the exchange of works of art. There are hints that some of these exchanges were commercial; in his will written in 1013, Ethelred's son Aethelstan included in his bequests 'the drinking-horn which I bought from the Old Minster'. Some of the brethren engaged in the lowlier task of metal-working were perhaps able to augment their house's income.

Unfortunately nothing like Athelstan's drinking-horn has survived, nor have any of the treasures that adorned the great churches, many of which were despoiled by the second wave of Viking raids, and then again by William the Conqueror, whose carts were filled with the candlesticks, crosses and chalices sadly listed by an Ely chronicler. Such things can only be guessed at from descriptions like that of Swithun's shrine with its 300 lbs. of gold, or the picture in the *Benedictional* of an altar, redolent of the wealth of the best-endowed churches.

Although church treasures have been lost, the sumptuous effect that was aimed at can be gauged by the magnificent embroideries that are now kept at Durham because they were presented to the shrine of St Cuthbert by King Athelstan, and have been preserved with other relics that honour the saint. The embroideries were commissioned by a queen, Aethelflaed, the wife of King Edward the Elder who died in 914. A text is stitched into the embroideries to state in Latin 'Aethelflaed ordered (these) to be made' – a commissioner formula equivalent to the vernacular 'Aelfred ordered me to be made' on the Alfred jewel. The absence of the royal title on the embroideries may be because the West Saxons refused to dignify their king's consort as 'Queen', after their unfortunate experience of the wife of one of Alfred's predecessors, according to Asser.

Another text on the embroideries reads 'For the revered bishop Frithstan', who was bishop of Winchester from 909 to 931. The embroideries form a stole and maniple for him to wear during services. Against the white background of his robes, the bright colours and the gold thread that is liberally used would have made the bishop a magnificent figure glowing in the candle-light at the altar. The texts show that the embroideries were done as a gift to the bishop from the queen, and they must at least have been begun before her death in 914. Presumably when Frithstan died, they reverted to royal ownership for Athelstan to present to the Cuthbert shrine, perhaps partly as a memorial to Frithstan.

There is little doubt that the embroideries were done at Winchester. Not only were they for its bishop, and commissioned by a member of the royal family with such close associations with the town, but many of the details can be compared to Winchester manuscripts or to the Winchester wall painting. Alfred's widow founded a nunnery, the 'Nunnaminster', to the east of the Old and New Minsters (Fig. 5), so that there was a house under royal patronage where textile work would have been practised.

Textile work was the equivalent in a nunnery to manuscript painting in a monastery. Unfortunately their products are more vulnerable, so that there is nothing with which to compare the St Cuthbert stole and maniple. The other major English work is the Bayeux Tapestry, probably done at Canterbury just after the Norman Conquest to hang in Bishop Odo's cathedral in Bayeux. There are records of other such works, and seamstresses were valued members even of secular households, mentioned in several wills. They often worked in seclusion rather than in an established monastery: there was a custom that a widow would not remarry but go into semi-retirement, living quietly with a few companions to whom she was as an abbess to the sisters. Widows retained legal rights, managing their own business affairs and estates. One such lady may have been Godgythe, whose seal, inscribed in the eleventh century and describing her as dedicated to the Lord, was found at Wallingford. But she still needed a seal for her worldly transactions.

Godgythe's seal is carved onto the reverse of a seal of a thegn named Godwin, to whom she was presumably related. The seals are cut onto bone, and the handle has a superb scene on it illustrating a verse in one of the Psalms. Carving on bone and ivory was another of the monastic crafts, and some of the best work is very similar to contemporary drawings. Godwin's seal handle is comparable to similar scenes in Winchester-style manuscripts. He probably commissioned it from a monastery – Aethelstan's drinking-horn suggests that this was a common practice. Most of the work was done for use in the monasteries themselves, however, as book covers, crosses, caskets for relics or for the host, or small devotional plaques.

Carvings are much more difficult to attribute to a particular centre than are manuscripts, which may give clues in their text and in their style of hand-writing. Winchester was a major centre, but until recently only a small fragment showing two angels had been found there, just outside the town. It is a beautifully balanced design, the angels back to back as they fly upwards, the line of the arch of their backs continued in their upstretched arms as their hands reach out to heaven (Plate xiii). As in drawings of angels in manuscripts, such as the New Minster Charter picture, their robes are caught by the wind, their legs trail behind them as they fly, and their hands are exaggerated to emphasize their gestures. The drawing style is translated exquisitely into three-dimensional relief.

The recent excavations at Winchester have thrown more light on the carving practised in the town. A fragment of a carving of Christ on the cross adds to the number of known ecclesiastical works. More everyday objects have also been recovered, however, such as spoons with animal heads gripping the bowls, and combs, which were probably the work of secular craftsmen with small workshops in the town, rather than of the monasteries. Small bronzes, like strap-ends and buckles, were also probably secular products, though some of the finer ones can be compared to manuscript designs.

Some stone carvings survive also from the late Saxon period, a few both intact enough and of high enough quality to be compared to contemporary painting and drawing. The angels at Bradford-on-Avon, Wilts., or Winterbourne Steepleton, Dorset (Plate XIV), show all the traits of the angels of the Winchester style, with their kicking legs and fluttering robes. It is difficult to judge the many sculptures of which only fragments may remain, like the sadly defaced figures over the chancel arch at Bibury, Glos. Many were only outlined in stone, the finer details being worked up from plaster or gesso. Most, if not all, would have been painted. So what is visible today is not what would have been originally created. For sculptors, few of England's stones are suitable: the granites are too hard, the limestones too soft. Only a few, notably Purbeck marble and Derbyshire alabaster, neither properly exploited until the thirteenth century, can be efficiently worked in fine detail.

The sculptures that survive are not representative, therefore. A few show that there were skilled men available; others show that poor and crude work was also done. It is not known how sculptors worked. Were patterns available? Were the men trained at monasteries? Were sculptors also masons? Some carvings are an integral part of the fabric of a building, such as the leaves on the capitals of the windows at Langford. Others are panels to be set into a wall, like the two roods at Romsey, Hants., and the roods and sun-dial at Langford. Some, like the angels, can be dated at least approximately by comparisons; others are too generalized to be ascribed even to a particular century. Not enough late Saxon sculptures survive for 'schools' to be suggested. Distributions of particular types of carving cannot be made meaningful until the twelfth century: the use of 'beak-head' ornament in Romanesque churches in the twelfth century is one interesting recent study that has emphasized, for instance, the role that Reading Abbey played as a patron and an influence.

The recent Winchester finds have included fragments that illustrate the integration of the Danish and Saxon racial elements in the eleventh century. After the horrors of the Viking raids in Ethelred's reign, the Wessex dynasty was superseded by the Danish Cnut, whose acceptance of Christianity is illustrated by a drawing of his coronation in a New Minster manuscript. Political domination did not mean cultural domination, however; rather it was the Scandinavians who adapted to the English. Nevertheless, during the eleventh century and even in the tenth a few Scandinavian art forms came to be used, even in Wessex, though primarily as ornamental embellishments. That culture contacts went deeper than had been realized was shown by the discovery at Winchester of a fragment from a frieze illustrating the saga of the Scandinavian hero Sigmund. This does not mean that there was a relapse into paganism, an overwhelming of Christian civilization by the victors, but that the saga was seen as a straightforward tale of a heroic warrior. Its Scandinavian, pagan source did not preclude it. It was acceptable in Winchester just as an embroidery of the real-life story of the heroic Byrtnoth is known to have been hung in Ely Abbey, and as the epic doom of Harold was later to hang at Bayeux.

The Archaeology of Death

In many cultures much more is known about the way in which people were disposed of after they had died than about the way that they had lived, for it is easier to identify and excavate a cemetery than an occupation site. In pagan Saxon archaeology, the imbalance is at last being partly made good by work on the settlements at Sutton Courtenay, Eynsham, Chalton and elsewhere, but many more Saxon burial sites have been found and recorded nevertheless.

The balance changes with the advent of Christianity, and the gradual abandonment of most pagan burial sites and customs during the seventh century. There is evidence from a few sites that they were still used for burial in the eighth century: Cannington, Somerset, is the best known, but there is the possibility that cemeteries outside Portsmouth and at Lewknor, Oxon., were others. The practice of burying objects with the dead may have been in the process of abandonment even without Christian prohibition. There are very many seventh-century burials which are furnished with a small iron knife, perhaps a buckle, and little or nothing else. The sites of these seem to be well away from occupation areas, and it was clearly still the practice to keep the spirits of the dead away from the living. The Christian belief in the resurrection meant that the dead were not an evil force to be kept apart, but even in death were part of the community. Consequently Christian cemeteries were in the centre of the village. It is just possible that a few seventh-century pagan cemeteries became Christian sites, for there are hints of this at, for instance, Ducklington, Oxon. Such cases would not be altogether surprising, since it was the policy of the Christian church to integrate its practices with those of paganism if there was no absolute antithesis.

It is very difficult to recognize continuity of this kind, because Christian cemeteries have been in constant use for many centuries. The result is that there are very few in which earlier graves have not been disturbed and all hope of recognizing which bones come from which period is lost. Occasionally a grave may get sealed beneath an extension to a church, or the burial site may change, but these cases are rare. Even the excavation of a graveyard at a deserted village site will only give very wide date ranges to the skeletons: the church in a village abandoned in the fourteenth-century might have stayed in use for burials. There is the further problem of getting the skeletons inspected by an expert pathologist once they have been raised, for not many people undertake this very specialized research.

Human bones are studied for evidence about diet, disease, life-expectation and racial type. The last is particularly difficult. It is known for instance that there is a change in skull type from a narrow-headed (dolicocephalic) Saxon profile to a broad-headed (brachycephalic) medieval one, reverting to the dolicocephalic in the post-medieval period. These changes were explained in terms of different racial stocks when first recognized in various small groups in the Oxford area. The changes are too widespread to be seen as restricted to certain classes or districts, however, so cannot result from population influxes. Danish settlement might be an explanation if the pattern was only found in the Danish areas, but it does not appear to be regionally confined. Similarly the numbers of Normans arriving after 1066 were far too small to account for it, and it is not a trait restricted to the aristocracy. It remains unexplained.

Unfortunately most of the medieval skeletons that have been studied come from the upper strata of society, and cannot be accepted as typical. It would be wrong to judge the physical condition of Englishmen in the fourteenth century from the skeleton at Walsingham Priory, Norfolk, thought to be that of Sir Bartholomew Burghersh, who had a distinguished career as a knight before dying in 1369 aged between fifty and sixty; 1.77 m (5 ft 10 in.) tall, with broad shoulders, he had had many falls and similar soldierly injuries, but he had not suffered from rheumatism as would a labouring man. His teeth were very worn, suggesting at times a rough diet, but he had clearly had food of a quality to sustain an active and healthy life. His pathology is no guide to the medieval norm: his horses probably ate better than his peasants. He is, however, the only recent example of a member of the laity whose skeleton has been located and analysed. More typical are the burials at Wharram Percy, Yorks., which show that rheumatism and osteo-arthritis were common, as were caries in teeth. Detailed figures on ages at death or ratios of men:women:children are not yet available, nor yet from any group of skeletons from a southern site. One thing which Wharram Percy does show is that the men were not undersized, the average height being 1.68 m (5 ft 6 in.), so despite small suits of armour (usually the survivals were made for juveniles) and low doorways (usually the result of inserted floors), the population was not significantly shorter than nowadays, at least until the later Middle Ages. There may have been a height change then, but as with the skull form it may not be a change that results from diet.

Occasionally groups of medieval graves can be recognized which can be utilized in studies of particular groups. The cemetery of a leper's hospital in Norfolk provided a gruesome study, though not one that threw much light on what was already known about these unfortunates. A small group of twenty graves at Brightwell-cum-Sotwell, Berks., was probably the cemetery of the Mackney family, who held the estate and presumably had a private chapel. Congenital abnormalities in the teeth and skull occurred in several skeletons, suggesting family membership. Their heights ranged from 1.63 m (5 ft 4½ in.) to 1.70 m (5 ft 7 in.) in the adult males, and from 1.60 m (5 ft 3 in.) to 1.66 m (5 ft 5½ in.) in the adult females.

It will be interesting to discover if the teeth of the skeletons being analysed at Wharram Percy and elsewhere prove to be very worn down. It has been suggested that the average Roman Briton's teeth became ground down more quickly than the average pagan Saxon's, reflecting the difference between a grain-based and a meat-based diet. Grain has to be ground, and a coarsely ground flour needs masticating. Furthermore, particles of the mill-stones and querns that did the grinding are apt to end up in the flour. An agricultural community may have worse teeth, therefore, than a pastoral one, for meat may need a lot of chewing but it is much less rough. (The only Saxon male whom I have excavated was about my age, and had far better teeth than I have. But he nevertheless had the disadvantage of being dead: his life expectancy was much lower than mine.) Certainly the Wharram Percy people had more caries in their teeth than the Saxons, but not more than the Romans. This suggests a similarly rough fare, and consequently sore gums. If eating was painful, foods would be pounded and boiled into a soft mush, with a resulting loss of vitamin. The less well-to-do medieval peasant may have suffered not only lack of food, but may not have made the best nutritive use of what food he had. Stone mortars such as those from Purbeck for pounding foodstuffs, and cooking-pots for boiling and stewing, are a common find on excavations, and their use may have led to diet deficiencies. Aggravated by bad harvests and famine, a medieval peasant's resistance to disease was lowered, and perhaps his mental powers were also affected.

Did the peasant's normally passive acceptance of subjection partly result from his diet? The 'peasant revolts' of the thirteenth and early fourteenth centuries were on the whole confined to the south-east and East Anglia, where conditions of tenure, and probably of life, were better than in the south, with its greater emphasis on open fields, plough-lands and labour services. The predominance of ecclesiastical estates, with their managerial efficiency, meant that the southern peasantry were the most subject, and perhaps therefore also the most abject. It was only after the Black Death, and its consequent improvements for the survivors, that peasant revolts gained support in the south. It is those who have a little who have the energy to demand more.

From carious teeth to peasant uprisings is a long step, and diet was only one of many factors that divided the classes of men. In death they might be just as divided, the rich lying in graves inside a church, the monks in the 'Paradise' outside their church, and the rest in the churchyard. There were also the outcasts: the small group of skeletons on Stockbridge Down, Hants., were probably executed criminals. Occasionally isolated graves are found, which may be of suicides denied burial in consecrated ground. Sometimes there are more sinister finds, like the little child's skeleton found hidden in the wall of one of the houses at Upton, Glos. It is possible that there was a plague pit at Old Sarum, but these pits are far fewer than popular imagination believes.

Most burials were in churchyards, of course, with little apparent difference in the ritual or furniture used for burials. There have been several recent finds of late Saxon and later 'charcoal burials', in which the corpse, not itself burnt, was laid on a thick bed of charcoal. Two such graves at St Frideswide's, Oxford contained a young male and a middle-aged adult of indeterminate sex, both of whom apparently enjoyed good health, apart from rheumatism in the latter. There is no way of knowing why they were selected for such special burial. Radiocarbon dates put them in the second quarter of the ninth century. There are similar recent discoveries at Romsey, Winchester and several other sites, so there is no reason now to think that it was a Danish practice as used to be believed. Nor are they all pre-Conquest, since the practice has been revealed at Oxford's Blackfriars. Presumably it was reserved for people of status.

Another grave at Winchester, inside the Old Minster, clearly contained someone of high rank. The body had been buried swathed or clothed, for silver ninth-century garter hooks were found beside its knees, and gold braid, presumably the hem of a veil, lay round the head and neck. Finds in Christian graves are rare, though sceattas, the eighth-century coins, are not uncommon in Kent, perhaps a tradition lingering on from pagan practice. Shroud pins are found. Otherwise coffin fittings are all that can be expected, usually nails, more rarely finely made iron clasps. Winchester has produced several of the latter, fixed over the edges with tinned iron nails. The only social class which is at all set apart is the priesthood, whose members were buried with a small lead chalice and paten set, and sometimes with finger-rings, especially if they were senior clerics. At Winchester, they were laid with their parishioners, but some might be buried inside their church, as was a priest found recently at Harwell, Berks.

The recently excavated cemetery at the New Minster was in use from the late twelfth until the early sixteenth century, and its closure may be reflected in the use of St Mary's for burials at the end of the Middle Ages. The burials in it were either in wooden coffins or in chalk 'cists', in which the bodies were placed between upright slabs. It is not possible to see if any particular reason – either period, social rank, or family – dictated the choice of burial type. So far, it can only be said that some priests were buried in coffins, some in cists. An earlier group of 215 graves, dug between the seventh century and the building of the New Minster at the start of the tenth, contained 204 identifiable skeletons, comprising 49 adults (16 men, 24 women and 9 indeterminate) and 164 children up to 18–20, 100 of whom died at under 2 years of age. The death rate among infants was very high. When the full results are available, it will be interesting to see if it can be shown how many women died in childbirth, and whether life expectancy generally increased during the Middle Ages.

A contrast to the Winchester data is provided by a cemetery at the Saxon port of Hamwic, in which only half a dozen of some seventy burials were of children. The very high proportion of adults hints that it was the graveyard of a particular social group, possibly of merchants who died in Hamwic on trading expeditions. The proportion of men to women has not yet been analysed. Dark stains in the soil beside one of the Hamwic skeletons showed that it had been buried in a wooden plank coffin. Since they were mostly laid in rows, the graves must have been marked in some way on the surface, but the later graves did not respect those below. The foundations of a timber building alongside the cemetery at Hamwic have been interpreted as those of the chapel which served it. This building was burnt down, and its site was subsequently used as an extension of the cemetery. Five small cemeteries have been found in Hamwic so far, suggesting that the principle that all burials should be at the minster church had not been established in the eighth century at least, as it was later to be at, for instance, Winchester for the New Minster.

In any graveyard, a small wooden cross was probably most people's brief memorial, but a few had stone markers or slabs above them. The five British memorial stones at Wareham, with a Latin inscription containing the phrase *Hic iacet* . . . with a name and a 'son of . . .' formula, are unique in England, parallelled only in the Celtic regions – Devon and Cornwall, Wales and Scotland. Equally rare is the late fifth-century memorial stone inscribed in ogham, an Irish adaptation of Latin, found at Silchester. Saxon crosses or slabs that marked burial places are rarely inscribed: a ninth- or tenth-century copy of a Roman design, with a bust of the dead person in an arch, is at Whitchurch, Hants., commemorating Frithburg, a female name. Nothing is known of her status in life, but it was presumably high. She was probably a lady of rank and independence, like the Godgythe whose seal was found at Wallingford. It is interesting that it was not thought necessary to add her husband's or father's name, as would probably have happened later. Her stone was intended to be free-standing, for it is also carved on the back.

The Winchester excavations have revealed another inscribed Saxon gravestone, commemorating a name which may be Gunni. Gunni had an elaborate grave superstructure, with a full-length coped slab and vertically set footstone carved with a hand holding a cross. It may also once have had a headstone. Gunne is a recorded Anglo-Saxon name, but the -i ending may be a Danish usage.

An eleventh-century stone memorial slab found at St Paul's churchyard in London bears a runic inscription to Toki, certainly a Danish name, and a superbly carved animal design, also Danish in idiom; although done by and for people who were so Scandinavian in outlook, the slab was in a Christian context since the Danes, like Cnut himself, did not long remain pagan. There are surprisingly few graves recognized as of pagan Vikings, partly it is thought because many were buried by their comrades in church-yards, since these were holy places, and the precise god involved did not concern the polytheist Scandinavians. One warrior was recently found near the Thames at Sonning, Berks., who had been buried with his sword and other weapons, and an Irish type of pin. These goods showed him to have been a pagan. Sonning is close to Reading, a site used as a camp by the Vikings in 871, and where another Viking burial, with a horse and a sword, has been recorded. These are the only ones in the south of England which have been established.

Scandinavian types of memorial stone are naturally much less common in the south than in the north, where there is the series of distinctive hog-back tombstones. Indeed it is not until the mid twelfth century that a new form of memorial appears in the south, with the first of the great figural series. Initially these were not true portraits, but representations incised into Tournai marble slabs. Some of the earliest, at Wells Cathedral, were not only of recently deceased clerics, but were also provided to commem-orate the bishopric's Saxon incumbents. From incised lines to relief sculptures is a short step, and to such magnificent portrait carvings as that of William of Wykeham in Winchester. The demand for such monu-ments contributed to the growth of quarries like those at Purbeck.

Only royalty, aristocracy and leading ecclesiastics could afford such tombs. For many more, a stone slab with a long-shafted cross carved in relief was grand enough. Such slabs were more likely to be locally made than the great tombs, many of which were done at the quarries, or by London-trained or foreign masons. The simpler monuments may be grouped into 'schools' and the distribution range of particular quarries might be established, but this has not been done in the south. It is interesting, for instance, that Caen stone slabs can be found in churches which are in the 'catchment area' of the Taynton quarries.

Incised slabs continued in use alongside relief sculpture, since incised work is quicker and cheaper. Closely associated with it is the development of the monumental brass, a popular memorial for lesser gentry, clerics and merchants from the late thirteenth century. Brasses have a bad name among archaeologists because of the dilettantism of most of those who rub them. They are a valuable social record, however, and serious students have made interesting surveys of different schools, and the role of London vis-à-vis provincial makers. Where brasses have been lost, their indents in stone slabs may survive; they are at last being recorded before they all disappear, so that the history of brasses – some of which were still being made in the seventeenth century – can be more complete.

Cloistered Calm

Like churches, monasteries have long been a major part of medieval archaeology. One of the more time-wasting speculations is to consider how much could be reconstructed about the physical appearance of monasteries if only documentary sources survived. The answer is probably that enough could be worked out about a few to justify inferences about the rest, since chronicles and building accounts give great detail about some monastic houses. At Bicester Priory, Oxon., for example, a small establishment's expenditure on its church and buildings can be followed in the intermittent account rolls of its bursar, its sacristan, its hospitaller and other officials. A small payment in 1425 for a doorway into the 'locutory' next to the prior's hall would place both those buildings in their usual place on the west side of the cloister, where visiting members of the public would cause least disturbance to the inmates of the house. Such accounts show when new buildings were being constructed: £20 to a mason 'for making the new choir' in 1398, with many lesser payments for materials for it, show that the east end of the church was being rebuilt. Repairs might be major or minor. John the Carpenter was paid 53s. 4d. 'for a new roof over the vestry which was lately made anew in the time of Geoffrey the last Prior, because three great beams were broken'. So much for the myth that medieval craftsmen worked to high standards for love of their job and their God! The progress of new work depended on the money available: in a small house, a single benefaction might cause work to start in the hope that more might follow. The Bicester new choir was still being completed in 1412, when cloth had to be bought to make new cloaks 'for Brothers Geoffrey Stratton and John Wayneting, on account of their spoiling of their rochets about the work of the new roof over the High Altar'. This is a unique record of the brothers actually doing such work themselves. It is interesting that the same year saw 'tabul estrigg' – deal imported from the Baltic – being bought in Oxford, an early example of this being used away from the east coast ports.

It is bitter to have to record that the site of Bicester Priory lay under orchards and gardens until the 1960s, and that it was then developed with the loss of most of the archaeological information that could have substantiated and filled out the documentary record. Only a few measurements of the church were made, and the opportunity to study an entire complex throughout its occupation was totally lost. A small trial excavation had shown how much could have been done but civic vandalism ensured that even the east end of the church was ruthlessly cut through without any warning, in 1973. The documents would have allowed a precision in the dating of features found that would have been of great value for comparison with other sites. The trial work produced, outside the north transept of the church, the thick mortar floor of a masons' working 'lodge', almost certainly to be associated with work recorded as taking place in the late thirteenth and early fourteenth centuries. The pottery in it was therefore dated within very narrow limits, with consequences for the dating of similar types found on other sites.

It is particularly unfortunate that Bicester was treated so badly, for it was one of the few monastic sites in the south still available for archaeological investigation. Most have either been built over or have been dug by antiquarians interested in getting a ground plan of the walls, but not in unravelling the whole history of the complex, with the result that floor layers, post-holes, beam-slots and so on have been removed unrecognized. Many sites are interesting to visit but inevitably appear to be much more static than they really were. The mason's axe and the carpenter's adze were usually to be heard somewhere within the monastic compound. Interest is now in the whole of the compound, its mills, barns, stables, forges, fish-ponds and out-buildings, since the monastery was an important economic and social unit, an employer and an owner. Investigation of the great mill on a stream of the Thames within the precinct of the abbey at Reading showed that as much care went into such equipment as into the church. Stone-built on timber piles in the river bed, it had first one wheel, and later a second, presumably as the abbey's estates became more productive.

Bicester's payment of £20 in a single year was a heavy expenditure for a house which in 1535 had a total annual revenue of only £176, out of which it had to feed and clothe the brethren, pay the servants, keep all the buildings in repair and pay the travelling expenses of the prior in his many legal and business dealings, which a hard-pressed bursar wearily described in his 1440 accounts as 'divers and arduous'. The head of a house often lived a very worldly life and this was reflected in his lodgings, which tended to become increasingly comfortable, with chambers, a chapel, a hall for guests, stone fireplaces, stables, cellar, kitchen; a payment for 1000 bricks for the Bicester prior's chimney in the later fifteenth century is one of the earliest direct records of the use of bricks in the south. The heads often lived like lords: it was often their lodgings which survived as the residences of those who bought the monastic sites at the Dissolution, as at Thame, Oxon. Very exceptional is Titchfield, Hants., where the nave of the church was converted into living accommodation.

Close to the church at Titchfield there survives a very fine medieval barn, in which the produce of the abbey's three demesne farms was stored. Such barns (Fig. 30 and Plates XXIII, XXIV) are a major testimony to the carpenters' skills, to set against the Bicester vestry, and they represent a substantial investment. Investment in mills – water-mills for grinding, fulling-mills for cloth, windmills and pound-mills – was also favoured, as were town properties. The care with which estates were managed is recorded in surviving manorial accounts. The scale of the ecclesiastical holdings is shown by Hampshire, for example, in which a quarter of the land was church-owned.

The income from church estates was also capable of investment in other, intellectual forms of development. Finds of pottery and glass at Selborne Priory, Hants., included fragments of 'alembics', used in distilling. This might be for alcohol, to make liqueurs, or for nitric acid, used in assaying gold and silver, or for use in alchemy. The first two are among the rare technological innovations of the Middle Ages, the last was one of the few processes of experimentation regularly and systematically attempted. All are associated with monastic houses.

Monasteries may have had a very small role as research institutions, but their role in education was more important, for they had schools attached to them, primarily to train choristers and to ensure recruitment to the house. The development of the university at Oxford was closely associated with the small college of canons within the castle, which developed a reputation for learning during the twelfth century. The university enjoyed the support of the king and laymen as well as of ecclesiastics, but the intention was to produce an educated clergy, many of whom became monks or priests.

Archaeologically, the early university has left little trace of itself. The scholars lived in 'halls', private residences no different in appearance from other houses. Lectures were given in the main rooms of the halls. The university used St Mary's church for its meeting-place, not acquiring its own buildings until the fifteenth century. Colleges were a relatively late development, in the second half of the thirteenth century. The quadrangular

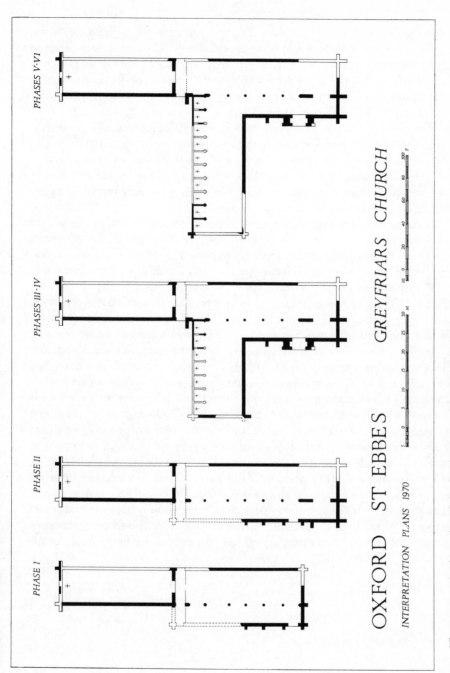

OXFORD ST EBBES GREYFRIARS CHURCH

PHASE I   PHASE II   PHASES III·IV   PHASES V·VI

INTERPRETATION PLANS 1970

22 The excavator's phase plan of the development of the Greyfriars church at Oxford, revealed by recent excavations.

plan appeared almost by accident during the fourteenth, when an existing L-shaped range at Merton had another added to it. The first college planned and built as a quadrangle, with some sense of a monastic cloister about it, was William of Wykeham's New College of the 1380s, and a similar design was used for his school at Winchester, as it was in the following century for Henry VI's foundation at Eton.

The presence of the university caused some existing monastic establishments to become famous, and brought others into being. Later, colleges like Gloucester were established so that clerks from houses of a particular Order could be together. One of the Gloucester College ranges survives in Worcester College, a terrace of tenements each separately built and maintained by a particular Benedictine abbey.

Some of the most famous medieval scholars were attached to the houses of the friars, the mendicant Orders who came to England in the thirteenth century. In Oxford, recent redevelopment has led to archaeological investigation of both the Greyfriars and the Blackfriars. The latter was built outside the town's boundaries, in water-meadows by the river (*j* on Fig. 6). To make use of such a marshy site, the foundations of the walls were dug through the flood-soils and clays, down to the natural gravel below, and stability was achieved by their enormous width, some 2 m (6 ft 6 in.). The clay was piled back up against the walls, as a barrier against floods. The Greyfriars (*i* on Fig. 6) also involved engineering works, but of a different kind, for it seems that the church stood against an artificially steepened terrace, and people on the street north of it were on a level with its roofs. The increasing fame of the church led to its expansion (Fig. 22). Originally it had a chancel, nave and north aisle. Large congregations caused a lengthening of the nave, and then a very rare feature, an extension on the north side at right angles to the east-west axis of the church, to give a T-shaped plan. The explanation of this must be that a preacher at the angle of the chancel could be seen and heard in both the 'west' and 'north' naves. The discovery of this plan was particularly interesting because it allowed sense to be made of a description of the church by the fifteenth-century writer William of Worcester, which had not previously been understood.

Chapter 5

The Rural Background

The medieval English economy was based on agriculture but the documentary evidence about the rural peasantry, which was the industry's work-force, is very mixed both in quality and quantity. A major stimulus to medieval archaeology has been the study of the material evidence surviving about the history of the countryside, and about those who lived and worked in it. In particular, much has been learnt about villages from those abandoned in the fourteenth and fifteenth centuries because of population loss, new economic demands and changes of climate.

An Early Excavation

The first recorded excavation of an abandoned medieval village site was a 'search for a church, churchyard, and village, supposed to have formerly existed' at Woodperry in Oxfordshire. It was conducted in the 1840s by the Rev. J. Wilson, an Oxford historian, whose attention had been brought to the site by a reference in the early eighteenth-century writings of Thomas Hearne, who had recorded that 'Many Foundations of Buildings appear continually, and in a plain below the Farm House, many Human Bones have been dug up at various times . . . this was the Church Yard, and therefore the Church stood there'. This implies that Hearne realized that it was a medieval site. The passage from Hearne that Wilson himself cited refers to Roman finds at Woodperry, and it is not clear if Wilson realized that Hearne had anticipated his interest in the medieval significance of the site.

Certainly Woodperry produced both Roman and medieval pottery, as have many sites that have been investigated more recently. Wilson had not only anticipated much subsequent research by his recovery of physical information, but he had also happened upon a site that had many of what are now known to be the characteristics of such abandoned medieval settlements. Woodperry was larger than most: it is recorded in the eleventh century in Domesday Book as a small *vill* with a minimum of eleven working inhabitants; by the thirteenth century, it was a parish with a church, and in the early fourteenth century between ten and fifteen householders were recorded. There is no direct record of the site's abandonment, but Woodperry was no longer a separate parish by the middle of the fifteenth century, having been incorporated into its next-door neighbour. Presumably, therefore, its population had dwindled so that it was no longer a viable individual unit, but it seems to have survived as a hamlet since a few inhabitants are recorded in the mid sixteenth century. By Hearne's time even they had passed on, except for the occupants of one farmhouse – and a stately mansion.

The presence of a mansion is not as surprising as it might seem. Although Woodperry ceased to be a parish, and ceased to be a working village, it was still an estate and a legal unit, the manor of Woodperry, as it had been in Domesday Book. Its land was not abandoned, even though the method of farming its fields changed. It was still the property of a landowner, and a manor-house was maintained, eventually becoming an elegant Georgian country house.

An outline picture of medieval Woodperry can therefore be built up from the documentary sources. Hearne's field observations revealed its precise site, though there is anyway a strong hint of its location in a recorded field name, Town Close, 'town' here having its original meaning of 'settlement' from the Saxon word *tun*. Such field names are a valuable guide to the whereabouts of sites. What did Wilson's excavations reveal that added to this outline?

The physical information recorded by Wilson was about the church and the objects rather than about the settlement. Below the altar of the church he found a very large pottery bowl deliberately buried unbroken, apparently without any contents. It may have been buried in a foundation ceremony, for the use of pots by masons as good luck tokens is certainly known. No similarly placed vessel has been recorded at any other church.

Otherwise, the main interest of Wilson's excavation is his discovery of Roman occupation on the site, and the lack of any evidence that it had been used in the Saxon period. The medieval pottery that he found dates between the twelfth and the fourteenth centuries, so that it does not indicate that the village was in existence earlier than is known from Domesday, nor that it was abandoned at a date other than that indicated by the later documents. The excavation could not tell Wilson 'by what means or at what period it became united to its neighbour', and it remains a truism that although archaeology can usually give a very broad indication of the date of the abandonment of a site, it can never directly explain why that abandonment took place. The questions that are raised by documentary history are rarely answerable by excavation. It may be possible to recognize what crops were grown, but not what were the yields of those crops. Bone evidence will indicate that animals that were reared, the different ages at which they died or were killed, even the method by which some were cooked, but it cannot reveal who cooked a particular joint, or how many people ate it. Was the pig whose slaughter is attested by a single leg-bone the property of a cottager with six dependents and no other meat source throughout the winter, or was it a free peasant's fourth meat meal in the week? How many people, in fact, benefited from its protein?

These are the sorts of questions which historians have been disappointed to find that excavators cannot answer. The evidence that is in the ground is usually either topographical – dealing with street lay-outs, house plans, manorial buildings and the other physical characteristics of a settlement – or it is evidence of the range of equipment and supplies of the settlement – the occupants' knives, keys, hones, pottery and other artifacts, and their agricultural produce. To go beyond this to questions of social status, prosperity, diet, disease, population mobility and methods of land tenure may be more than the physical evidence can stand.

More Recent Excavations and Field-work

Excavations that have been carried out since the Rev. Wilson's time have shown that the physical appearance and arrangement of medieval villages varied as much as the legal and social conditions are known to have varied from documentary sources, according to such factors as land-ownership, geography and racial customs. In East Anglia and Kent, for instance, it is being shown that partible inheritance was practised, and the sub-division of holdings might be expected to have a direct effect on the physical character of a village. It has been suggested that this different inheritance custom was based on racial differences, the customs of 'Frisian' settlers in East Anglia and 'Jutes' in Kent surviving despite the imposition of feudal tenure. For Kent, it has been argued that partible heritance and the divided holdings which result are responsible for the pattern of settlement that can still be recognized, of many scattered, 'dispersed' farms rather than 'nucleated' villages.

If race was the factor which caused different customs, then in the south of England partible inheritance should be expected in the 'Jutish' Isle of Wight, and in Hampshire's Meon Valley. There seems, however, to be no evidence that these areas did not conform to the customs of the rest of Wessex. It would be interesting to know if any specific differences could be recognized from an excavation, but no relevant sites have been attempted.

The types of settlement are not obviously different from those in the rest of the south.

Most, though by no means all, medieval southern villages were nucleated rather than dispersed, being clusters of houses and farms centred on a church. Outlying settlements may have resulted from an originally dispersed settlement pattern, from clearance of outlying areas for agriculture in the Saxon or in the medieval period, or from post-medieval enclosure. Such outliers may be single farms or hamlets, or they may be bigger than the mother village. The evidence of Saxon charters, of Domesday Book and later records, and of the landscape as revealed by maps and place-names, allows a historian to construct hypothetical settlement patterns without leaving a reference library. Sometimes such hypotheses can hardly be taken further, if the area has been submerged by a vast modern urban complex. Usually, however, it is possible for the hypothesis to be tested against the field evidence. For instance, the boundary between two Saxon estates may be marked by a surviving hedge, and the age of that hedge may be judged from the number of different plants that it contains. Botanical work recently has shown that as a very rough rule of thumb a hundred-yard length of hedge on good agricultural land will usually acquire one new species per century of its life. A six hundred year old hedge may have between four and eight species, a thousand year old one eight to twelve. Crude though it may seem, the method works; it has been shown that the Saxon park boundary of the bishop of Winchester at Bishops Waltham, Hants., can be followed for most of its length by a multi-species hedge, on a substantial bank. Such banks are a common but not an invariable feature of ancient boundaries. Furthermore, internal sub-divisions of the park can be traced from the hedges within it, and a plausible chronology for its parcelling-up suggested by the species counts from these younger hedges. Hedge boundaries may suggest sub-division of big estates in the late Saxon period, the boundary of the original estates surviving as the parish boundary around the whole complex. This can be very clearly seen in parts of Dorset.

The field-worker will look also, of course, for bumps in the ground, patches of nettles, spreads of stone in ploughed fields and so forth, which may reveal where there were once buildings. Many such sites may be better seen from air photographs, but the field-walker can hope to take his recognition a stage further, by picking up scatters of pottery which enable an approximate date to be given to the site. Long-term and systematic field-walking can produce enough evidence for a village chronology to be established, without recourse to excavation. In Norfolk, such a programme has shown that the earliest recognizable part of a village is usually round the church, and in the fields around it seventh-/eleventh-century pottery can be found in quantity. There may be evidence of Roman occupation in the same area, but as at Woodperry it is well-nigh impossible to prove continuity through the fifth and sixth centuries. The quantity of Saxon pottery increases as the population expanded. This expansion caused the village to grow out from its original nucleus, so that twelfth-/thirteenth-century sherds may be some way from the church. The village green belongs to this period, for no Saxon pottery is found round it and it is well away from the church. When population contracted in the late Middle Ages, it was the most recently settled area, round the green, that was maintained, leaving the church in isolation except perhaps for the manor-house.

This pattern can be found in the south, but it is more difficult to discover here just by field-walking than in East Anglia, both because there is less recognizable Saxon pottery, and because there is more pasture and so less opportunity of recovering what little there is, as the ground is not turned over by the plough. Many villages have a church, and sometimes a manor-house, at some distance from most of the present houses, and site shift is probably the explanation. Sometimes bumps in the fields round the church will show where there were once houses. This was demonstrated recently in a village in Oxfordshire, Tetsworth, where such earthworks were to be destroyed by the M40 motorway. The documentary evidence about the village is unsatisfactory because it was part of a large estate owned by the Bishop of Lincoln in the eleventh century, and so was not mentioned in Domesday Book. The earliest pottery found in the excavations showed that there was, in fact, a settlement there by the tenth or eleventh century, on a ridge of high ground on which the church stands. The bulk of the modern village is not on the ridge near the church, but lines the London–Oxford road. The excavations found no Roman occupation, but Roman use of the land was shown by traces of field ditches and scattered sherds. As in the Norfolk pattern, the early village was around the church, the village expanded into new areas and eventually the old centre was abandoned, isolating the church and what may have been a small manor-house. The new centre even has a village green, to complete the similarity to Norfolk. In this case archaeology not only established a settlement sequence, but corrected the misleading documentary evidence that the village was a post-Conquest development. Another example is Cheddar, where ninth-/tenth-century occupation was found around the present church, showing how the settlement developed there and not around the palace (Fig. 13). Chalton, Hants., is a further instance. Excavations at the present village have shown occupation from the tenth century on the site of the manor-house, which stands beside the church. This has Norman features, but may of course have had a Saxon predecessor. There is a small village green just outside the church – in contrast to the Norfolk pattern.

Chalton's similarity to Tetsworth and other villages may prove to be illusory. It was owned by the king, and its history was affected by the abandonment of the hill-top site (Plate III) in the eighth or ninth century. There is no way of knowing if that site was abandoned gradually or in a single operation, nor whether its occupants all moved to a single site, whether pre-existing or new, or if they dispersed themselves over several settlements in the valleys around.

The Chalton hill-top site is not the only Saxon settlement which did not survive to become a medieval village. Abandoned sites vary in size from those like New Wintles, Eynsham, which spread over at least 3 hectares (7 acres), to sites like Ufton Nervet, Berks., where only a single house is known. Some desertions may result from a tendency for settlements to nucleate in the late Saxon period, perhaps because of changing systems of land exploitation due to growing population and pressures on land space, probably leading to increasing emphasis on ploughing rather than grazing, and because of the arrival of a new factor in the settlement pattern, the Christian church.

As early as the eighth century some land-owners were building churches on their estates, and this became increasingly common in the late Saxon period (Fig. 21). The presence of a church might bestow precedence on one of several small occupation sites within an estate or an area, drawing people to a particular place, at least for compulsory Sunday worship, so that the church would become a natural focal point for settlement. Even in villages where there was no church, a preaching cross and a graveyard might be provided. The old religion treated the dead as evil spirits to be kept at a distance, which explains why the known pagan cemeteries are not on the settlement sites. Christianity, with its belief in the after-life, keeps the dead within the living community. The church or cross, and the grave-yard round it, therefore provided a new focus within a settlement area. Later medieval documents frequently inveigh against misuse of the grave-yard as a recreation centre and Sunday market-place, and laws of the early tenth century attempting to ban Sunday trading imply that this was already part of everyday life.

Another new factor in the Saxon landscape was the water-mill for grind-ing grain mechanically, rather than laboriously by hand. The earliest examples known are from the seventh-/eighth-century royal sites of Tamworth and Old Windsor, but the use of the mill spread, presumably as a landlord investment, and over 5000 are recorded in Domesday Book. Probably every village which had a suitable stream had at least one mill by the end of the eleventh century, and this may have been both a sign of, and a spur to, increased cereal production, the latter particularly in the fields closest to the mill to reduce time spent in carting the grain. The site of the mill had to be low-lying, of course, so was not suitable for settlement, and its effect on the topography of the village would be indirect for cereal production is more likely to lead to nucleated villages than pastoral farming.

It must be stressed that the new factors in the Saxon village did not lead to the desertion of all outlying settlements and farms, whose existence may be recognized both from documents and from field-work. Place-name evidence, for example, proves that Hardwick was a Saxon hamlet of Whit-church, on the Chilterns; pottery finds prove that there was another, on Bozedown. Such complementary studies of documentary and physical evidence can illustrate the development of the medieval parish throughout its history, with the recognition of such features as deer-parks, moated manors, ridge and furrow, 'assarted' (cleared) land and farmsteads, en-closure banks, water-mills, rabbit-warrens and fish ponds. One of the best of these studies is of Whiteparish, Wilts.

One limitation of this kind of work is that it only recognizes the existence of a feature at a particular time. A document may show that a village had a mill because someone paid rent for it in the thirteenth century, but unless the estate's documents are uncharacteristically complete, they will not reveal when that mill was built or abandoned, that is, for how long it had an impact on the life of the community that it served. Similarly an earth-work surviving in a field by a stream might indicate the presence of a structure that may be recognizable as a mill from its location, but will not show the date at which it went out of use – indeed the shape of the mound may be a misleading guide to what is underneath, as was found on a recent site at Daws Mill, Dorset. This is also true of occupation sites. The exca-vator of the deserted village of Holworth, Dorset, was surprised to find that the location of a house was not shown by the largest mound, since this had probably not been caused by debris from a collapsed building, but simply by the frequent digging out of sediment from the boundary ditch.

The Holworth excavation was one of the first modern investigations of such a site. The earthwork complex is particularly well preserved, with a single street lined on one side with a series of seven properties. Each can be seen to have had buildings near the road, and a back yard, the 'toft'; behind this is a long strip of garden, orchard or field, the 'croft', the whole complex being preserved under pasture fields. The excavator of Holworth was one of the first to realize the complexities and difficulties of interpreta-tion of what lay beneath the turf. A rectangular structure, 21 m (68 ft) long and 5½ m (17 ft) wide, was divided by stone walls into three separate units, but it was not clear if the central unit was an open space, or had been roofed over, perhaps with a lean-to roof since there was no back wall (Fig. 24, *b*). The largest unit was assumed to have been living quarters because of a hearth; an inner partition suggested a separate sleeping area. There was no evidence of animal stalling in the other two units, and there were no drains. The end unit, which had a clearly marked doorway, was taken to have been for storage, since carbonized grain was found in it.

The stone-built house complex was not the first building on the site, since burnt daub in features below it suggested a timber-framed predecessor. Subsequent excavations on such medieval sites have shown that frequent rebuildings were the norm, as though each generation made its alterations or extensions. The best examples of such patterns have not been in the south, but on sites like Wharram Percy, Yorks., Upton, Glos., and West Whelpington, Northumberland, where excavations over many years demonstrate the extreme complication of correct interpretation of vestigial evidence. Hangleton, Sussex, is probably the best known of the complex southern sites. There the problem was exacerbated because of property amalgamation: what had been four separate holdings in the thirteenth century were joined in a single farmstead by the fifteenth, a dramatic demonstration of reduced pressures on land-space in the later Middle Ages.

At Hangleton, different house types were found, both of different periods, and contemporaneous. Presumably these were in some way a reflection of the varying wealth and status of their occupants, but no specific social levels can be recognized. Was a man with a one-roomed cottage necessarily worse off than his neighbour who lived in a much larger building, one end of which was used to stall his animals (Fig. 24, *c, d*)? Only at the level of minor gentry do distinctions become apparent: at Tetsworth, part of the excavation may have been of a tenement of a sub-branch of the Talemasche family, who owned part of the village (Fig. 23). The first house on the site was distinct from peasant housing because it had solid foundations and had probably had stone gable walls, although in ground area it was no bigger than an ordinary villager's. An early fourteenth-century house with stone foundations at Seacourt, Berks., was a few square feet larger than average, and a semi-circular projection from it in the gable wall may have been a staircase base, to an upper floor (Fig. 24, *a*). These two factors suggested to the excavator that the building might have been a priest's house or even an inn.

As at Holworth, the Seacourt house raises the problem of identifying the internal planning of houses. It had a hearth in the room off which the staircase led, and so was presumably domestic. The same room also had a stone-lined drain, however, a surprising feature in a domestic interior, and one which is usually taken to indicate animal stabling, just as a hearth is taken to show living accommodation. One of the Hangleton buildings has some of the features of a long-house (Fig. 24, *c*), a term for buildings in which one end is for human accommodation, the other for animals or farm storage, under the same roof-line, and with a central cross-passage which gives access to each end, so that the two are not totally separated. Often the separation will be only a thin screen, indicated at Hangleton by a line of internal posts for a wattle and daub partition. The system had advantages: direct access without going outside, and warmth and shelter in winter. (Smell? The animals had to get used to that.)

The long-house was the standard agricultural peasant living-unit in the north and west until recent times. Excavations have shown its long history. In parts of the Midlands and the east, however, it is practically unknown, and it has not been found by excavation either. The south seems to be an overlap area. The possible long-house was only one of several house types at Hangleton. It has been found in Wiltshire, at Gomeldon and possibly Wroughton. There were none at Seacourt, Berks. These are the only sites in the south which have produced a representative range of excavated buildings, but it is enough to suggest that the long-house was never common, and probably became redundant to, and was perhaps regarded as unfashionable by, peasant society. This is at least suggested by the Gomeldon and Hangleton evidence, where long-houses were quite clearly abandoned in favour of separate house units during the thirteenth century. The use of the long-house in the seventeenth–nineteenth centuries was once seen as a geographical distinction between the 'Celtic' and 'English' settlement areas. The excavations of sites like Gomeldon show that an interpretation based solely on a racial explanation is inadequate, since the long-house was a feature in some 'English' areas. Its use is probably related to settlements in which it is necessary to keep stock sheltered in the winter, which in the south means only on the higher land. This distinction would explain its absence in low-lying Seacourt.

Another unexpected discovery about housing has been the change from timber foundations to stone which the Holworth site seemed to suggest. Seacourt and other subsequent excavations have shown that this was a general trend in the thirteenth century. Instead of a timber sill beam being placed on the ground, or vertical posts being dug into it, a low rubble wall was built. Occasionally, the amount of stone rubble indicates that the whole house was of stone. The one- and two-roomed cots at Hangleton were like this, another indication that their inhabitants were not necessarily at the bottom of village society. Usually, however, the stones of the walls only rose to just above ground level, and a timber superstructure was built on them. This process had the merit of protecting the timberwork from damp, and it has been taken as being a response to worsening climate conditions. If this is correct, it was a very sensitive response, for the documentary evidence of deteriorating weather is not unequivocal until the very end of the thirteenth century – there were droughts in the 1280s!

Even in a good weather period, no timber in direct contact with the soil

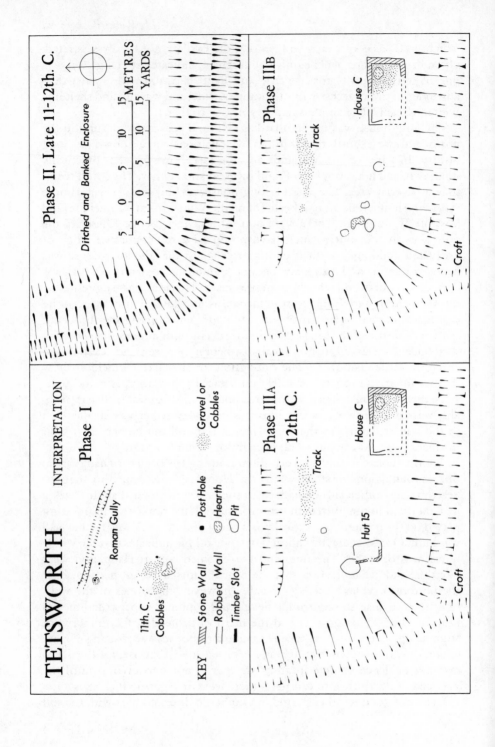

TETSWORTH INTERPRETATION

Phase I

Roman Gully

11th. C.
Cobbles

KEY IIIII Stone Wall
— Robbed Wall
— Timber Slot

• Post Hole
▨ Hearth
◯ Pit

Gravel or
Cobbles

Phase II, Late 11-12th. C.

Ditched and Banked Enclosure

METRES
YARDS
5 0 5 10 15

Phase IIIA 12th. C.

Hut 15
Track
House C
Croft

Phase IIIB

Track
House C
Croft

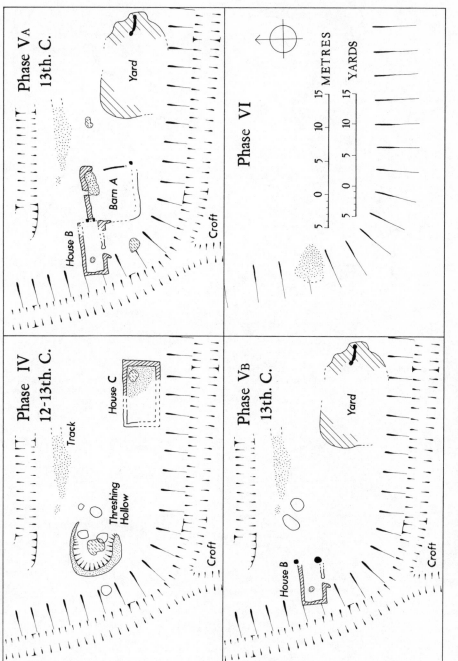

23 The excavator's interpretation of the different phases on the site at Tetsworth, one of the fourteen sites excavated before their destruction by the M40 motorway.

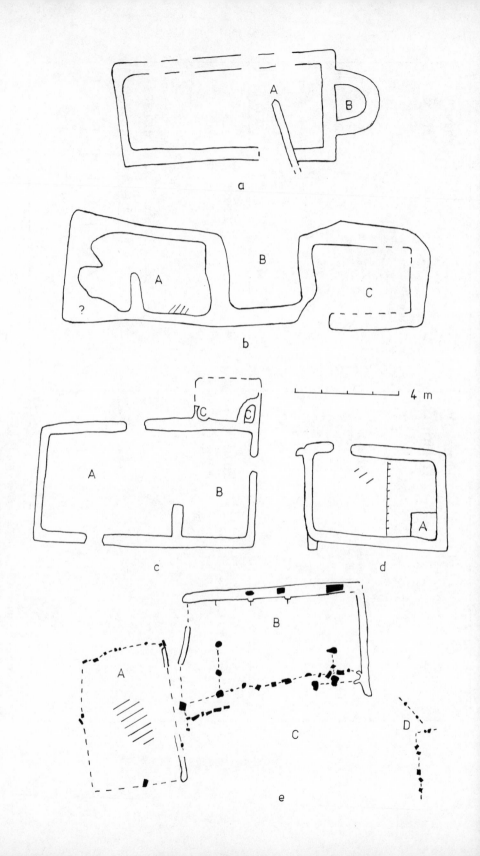

a

b

c

d

e

4 m

will survive for long. The frequent rebuilding of peasant properties on the same site was necessary because of the need to replace rotten timbers. It was probably as easy to rebuild as to repair, for the timberwork was not the properly constructed, 'framed' carpentry seen in surviving timber buildings (e.g. Fig. 32 and Plates xxv, xxvi), but was normally much more haphazard, as the irregular lines of post-holes do not indicate paired 'trusses'. The frequent rebuilding of peasant holdings was dictated by necessity, not by the whim of fashion. Presumably it was a running drain on limited reserves of capital and resources, one of the factors militating against self-improvement by expenditure on more food or land.

It is of course much more difficult to make a coherent interpretation of a series of intermittent post-holes and shadowy timber-slots than of stone-footed buildings – provided that the stones have not been removed for reuse in some later structure. The thirteenth-century farm complex postulated on one part of the Seacourt site from very limited evidence suggested a small house, with a large hearth and no trace of internal partitions, placed at right angles to a barn or byre (Fig. 24, *e*). This may have had one side open, so that animals could enter directly from the yard. The yard may have been completed by a fence and an out-house on its third side, its fourth opening onto the back croft. This reconstruction has been justified by discoveries of similar farm units, at Gomeldon in the late thirteenth century for instance.

In one corner of the Seacourt yard was a spread of dark soil and sherds which suggested a midden. It is an important record of the care taken over keeping the stable manure, and probably also night-soil from the house. It has been shown from all the excavations of peasant houses that the floor levels inside were not allowed to build up, as they did in many Roman buildings. Convenience, possibly cleanliness, but perhaps most important of all, concern for their value as manure, meant that the straw and rushes spread on the floor were frequently swept out and replaced. In towns, pits were dug for latrines: these were much more infrequent in the countryside, because the countryman could make good use of what would have gone into them. Did the midden get spread onto the fields, or onto the 'croft' behind the house? Unlike Roman pottery, not much medieval is found

---

24 Buildings excavated at various medieval village sites. (a) The stone-built priest's house at Seacourt: *A* – stone-lined drain; *B* – possible staircase foundation (after Biddle). (b) Holworth, Dorset: *A* – living accommodation in two rooms; *B* – open yard; *C* – barn; shaded area = probable hearth (after Rahtz). (c) Hangleton, Sussex ?long-house: *A* – barn/animal shed; *B* – living accommodation; *C* – ovens. (d) Hangleton, stone-built two-roomed cottage: *A* – oven; shaded area = hearth (c, d, after Holden, Hurst). (e) Seacourt, thirteenth-century farm unit: *A* – house; *B* – barn/animal shed with open side to yard; *C*, *D* – fence and possible further building; shaded area = hearth (after Biddle).

spread over the fields, suggesting that manure from the 'toft' was not carted away. The possibility is that the soil fertility of the 'croft' was higher than that of the fields, so that a peasant's garden may have had higher yields than his strips in the open fields. The value of his vegetable diet may have been underestimated.

If the 'crofts' had a higher fertility, they would presumably have been more valuable than other plots of land, and the peasant would have vigorously resisted attempts to move him away from it. This highlights another unexpected feature of village life that excavations have shown, that properties were by no means as stable as had been thought. Not only is this visible in 'shifting' villages like Tetsworth, expanding away from and eventually abandoning their old centres, but it has been found that tenements were replanned, sub-divided and amalgamated – the amalgamation of the four holdings at Hangleton is a good example. In some areas, and certainly on the continent, this was clearly done at the behest of a landowner powerful enough to over-ride the interests of his peasantry. A site at Milton, Hants., appears to have been a case in which two or three separate holdings were built over by a new manorial site in the fourteenth century, the owner presumably forcing out his tenants for his own convenience.

Most agricultural activities are hard to recognize. Part of the site at Tetsworth may have been used as a threshing hollow, with areas where the chaff was burnt – if it was burnt, not used for animal bedding. In Wallingford Castle there was apparently a corn-drier, but drying was probably not always done in a special structure. Indeed, it was probably not practised if it could be avoided, although it seems certainly to have been necessary at Holworth, judging from the amount of carbonized grain found, and further west driers were actually built into houses. Peas, beans and vetch – a crop as well as a weed – might also have to be dried. References to ovens in manorial accounts were probably to ovens mainly used for malting.

The value of medieval environmental data is reduced because of the existence of such accounts. There is no point in finding out from careful analysis of soil samples what crops were being grown, or from bone studies what animals were kept, if a document tells you. Ratios of relative quantities produced are very difficult to prove, though it is revealing that at both Seacourt and Tetsworth there was very little barley; this corroborates contemporary accounts in which, however, it might be disguised as 'dredge', a mixed oats: barley crop.

The accounts of Merton College, Oxford, give a very complete picture of a manorial farm complex at Cuxham, at the foot of the Chilterns in Oxfordshire, with its house for the bailiff, barn, fish-pond, malting oven, bakehouse, dovecote, garden, and stone gateway with an oak gate, all enclosed by a wall. Some of the buildings were particular to the manor: peasants could not keep pigeons so could not have dovecotes, a source of both food and manure, and often had to use their lord's ovens as well as his mill. Excavations have yet to take place on a total complex of this sort: useful starts have been made at Manor Farm, Chalton, and at Netherton, Hants., but it may never be possible to reconstruct all the ancillary buildings as well as the main house, because their foundations are likely to be much flimsier and even more vulnerable to destruction by later activity. Such slight buildings as cart-sheds would leave little trace, but the physical differences between such a site and the peasants' crofts might be very revealing.

Assarts and Abandonment

One discovery at Manor Farm, Chalton, has been a very large ditch – its full length not yet known – with tenth-/eleventh-century pottery in it. At present, the relationship of this ditch to the church is not clear. It may have been a boundary ditch for the manor-house, not for the whole of the village.

Such late Saxon deep ditches may not be exceptional. Another was found around part of the 'manorial' complex at Tetsworth, Oxon. (Fig. 23). Again its full length is unknown, but it did not seem to surround the complete village in the eleventh century, as it was not found in a very small excavation in another part of Tetsworth. It may only have enclosed the 'manorial' area. At Huish in Wiltshire, a similarly substantial ditch enclosed the church as well as the manor: again its full length is unknown. There are examples of complete villages being surrounded by a ditch and bank system in the Midlands, but they are not always of great size. Such ditches are too big to be just for storm water drainage, which was the function of slighter ditches known on many sites.

These discoveries show that moats around manorial complexes may not be solely a feature of the thirteenth century and later. Moated manor-houses are sites like that at Milton, Hants., where the upcast soil from the moat was used to raise an artificial island on which manor-house and outbuildings could be constructed, although that particular site did not reveal any trace of such structures. The moat was both drain and pond – fish stocks were as important a part of the manorial economy as the dovecote. Such moated sites have an uneven distribution, mainly being found in low-lying areas, naturally enough. Field-work identifying further examples is in progress in many areas, and many are still being found. Too few dates are available from them yet to see if there were fluctuations in their rate of construction, either generally or in particular areas. It seems likely that most moated manor-houses date from after about the mid thirteenth century. Various reasons may be offered. They were an alternative to the private castles which were outlawed after the end of King John's reign; the moat provided some defence, not against a proper army, but against local riots and thieves, endemic medieval problems – although most manor-houses were undefended. It became fashionable for a land-owner to live away from the peasantry, and so new sites for their houses were chosen – or, as at Milton, the peasantry may have been the ones who moved. Some probably represent new farms being set up in previously under-utilized, low-lying, damp land. Another possibility is that the climate was changing for the worse, and wetter conditions meant that the moats and islands kept the occupants dry-shod. It is difficult to see much sign of this happening before the end of the thirteenth century, however, so it was not responsible for the early growth of the fashion.

The effects of wetter weather can be seen in fourteenth-century villages also, with the digging of deeper boundary ditches for drainage and a consequent, deliberate, build-up of the toft. Holworth provided a clear example of this process. Stone house footings and cobbled yards may also illustrate weather conditions, though use of the former was occurring in the thirteenth century. In extreme cases, drainage problems that did not apply in the earlier life of the village may have been a cause of the abandonment of tenements, if not of whole sites.

The direct economic effect of changing weather is difficult to judge, as it cannot be isolated from other major late medieval factors, notably declining population and rising wage levels. Documents reveal catastrophes in some areas. There was flooding of reclaimed Sussex marshes in the late thirteenth century, but these losses were made good, permanent land losses only coming in the fifteenth. Such records are not universally applicable, however, for marine transgressions and storms may not have had any inland equivalent. Fewer references to vineyards may indicate a shorter growing season. Certainly the years after 1315 saw high prices and very high death rates, but caused by drought as well as by rain. The population may have recovered by the 1340s, to be caught disastrously by the Black Death from 1348 onwards. The erratic economy of the first half of the fourteenth century did not produce a uniform response from land-owners. The biggest southern owner, the bishopric of Winchester, tended to convert to renting from demesne farming, while the Westminster Abbey estates, some of which were in Oxfordshire, intensified demesne and ignored leasing. With such different exploitation methods depending on effectively random factors such as ownership, no uniformity is perhaps to be expected between villages and their individual systems.

The abandonment of holdings may then be as much a question of internal estate management as of external economic controls. Both the clearing of waste-land and the subsequent abandonment of the farms thus formed, which were often only marginally profitable, might depend as much on the policy of the estate owner as on the pressures on land space exerted by the rapidly growing population of the twelfth and thirteenth centuries and by the declining population of the fourteenth. An example of an 'assart' farmstead was excavated high up in Sadlers Wood on the Chilterns above Lewknor during the M40 construction. That this was marginal agricultural land is shown from its present use as rough woodland, yet in the middle of the thirteenth century it was worth building a substantial farm to exploit the high ground more effectively than could be done from the village down in the valley. The farm may have been for swine rearing rather than cereal production, because of its position. The excavator argued from the solid flint foundations, well-constructed drains with tile arches, and the use of mortar in the walls and tiles on the roofs, that this was not a peasant's cot, but represented manorial expenditure of capital. Since much of Lewknor was owned by Abingdon Abbey, it is likely that the assart was an ecclesiastical investment.

Assarts are well documented, and many clearances survive as hamlets. Names ending in -ley (-leah) or -cot (-cote) are typical clearance names. Some were farmed by peasant tenants, others were added to the demesne. Manorial sites are less well known, though Cistercian 'granges' in the north have similarities. The Sadlers Wood site does not appear in any document, nor could its presence be guessed from any field name. Only field-work could have revealed it, and only excavation could have revealed its true nature. Its discovery was an incentive to further field-work nearby which yielded two other likely sites. Yet this was in an area thought to be barren of medieval settlement.

Expense of time and resources clearly went into the Sadlers Wood farm, yet even so it was rebuilt at least once during its occupation. How long it was used, and when it was abandoned, are questions that depend entirely on the dating of the pottery found in the excavations, which seemed to make the late fourteenth century the likely desertion date, with a lifespan of anything from fifty to a hundred and fifty years. Presumably it ceased to be profitable to farm when wages began to rise, and no one could be found to rent it. Water supply must have been a constant problem, for it was high above the spring-lines. The need to conserve water was shown by the ditch that was dug all round the site, and the drains that ran into it, presumably intended to catch and hold as much rainwater as possible, although also important to prevent deer and other wild animals getting into the farmyard. Problems like water supply must have reduced its profitability. Its abandonment can be attributed to economics.

The abandonment of medieval sites cannot always be so plausibly ascribed to direct causes. Although many are on marginal land, and were therefore the most likely to go, distribution maps show that there is no absolute correlation between marginal land and desertion. In Dorset, for example, the great majority of the sites are on the prosperous chalkland in the central belt of the county. Here it seems that small villages affected by population loss ceased to be viable units and, gradually rather than at a stroke, amalgamated with neighbours. There are reasons for this in an agricultural community, particularly for peasants who are not individually rich enough

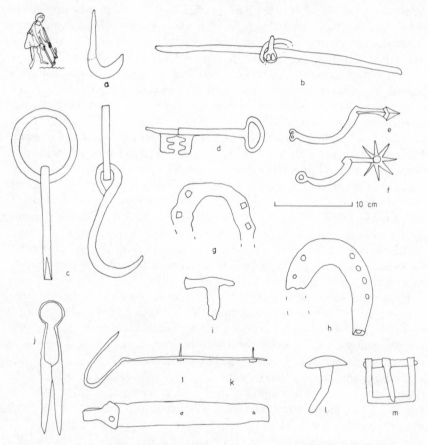

25   Iron tools and equipment from medieval sites: *a* – pruning-hook tip, with manuscript illustration of a man weeding; *b* – balance-arm; *c* – pot-hook and chain; *d* – key; *e, f* – spurs; *g, h* – horse-shoes; *i* – hammer head; *j* – shears; *k* – strap hinge from a door or large cupboard; *l* – door- or strake-nail; *m* – buckle. (a, b, e – Tetsworth; j – Seacourt; remainder – Huish.)

to own a complete plough-team. If sharing of oxen and similar co-operation was necessary, a cluster of farms was desirable. Pastoral farms do not need to be together in the same way, so that in another part of Dorset, the Blackmoor Vale, the scattered farmsteads established by medieval assarting can still be seen in the modern landscape; many sites which shrank but did not disappear probably converted to a sheep economy. This explains why sheep enclosures were later blamed for the loss of ploughlands; but the number of landlords who moved an unwilling tenantry was small. The picture is rather of landlords unable to find labourers and tenants for their demesne farming and having to convert to pasture to maintain any income at all. A worsening climate would in any case have made some former ploughlands impossible to cultivate. Different circumstances account for different individual cases of abandonment: excavation can show when an individual abandonment took place, but can no more explain it than can a document that records sadly that there is no income because there are no inhabitants.

Equipment and Furnishing

Since wood was the basic material used in medieval England, many everyday items are quite unknown from the archaeological record. Pottery is abundant from medieval sites (see Chapter Nine), but for each clay pot there may have been a wooden equivalent. Iron tools are generally few, since a broken one would have been reforged into something new, not just discarded.

The finds records of medieval iron objects is limited, therefore (Fig. 25); the only plough coulter claimed is a fragment from Huish, Wilts., not closely dated by context. The Huish collection is thought to be from a smithy, and included knives (always common); many locks, keys, padlocks, hinges and hinge-pivots, which show that houses had solid doors and contained lockable chests; buckles, which may sometimes be copies in iron of what was then fashionable in bronze, which in turn followed precious metal ornaments; a pot-hook to hang over the fire; tools like a hammer, a spike, a fork, and a butcher's cleaver; arrows; spurs, which are surprisingly common, and show that not only the aristocracy rode horses; horse-shoes and nails, also common, and also showing horse ownership; and nails, with big faceted heads to go into the rim of the wheel to give a better grip, or to strengthen wooden doors. There was also a more unusual find, a steelyard balance and its weight, for use in marketing transactions.

Two balances, simple bars with centre swivels, were also found at Tetsworth, and presumably indicate simple trading. Otherwise the range was similar to that at Huish, though it included one common object not seen there, a small pruning knife, a right-angled blade used, often in conjunction with a forked stick, on a long pole for cutting withies, brambles and the bigger ground weeds.

At Seacourt, the ironwork included shears, used for sheep and thatching, but also for all tasks for which scissors would now be used, and so not symptomatic of any specialization. Like many objects, shears have a typology that can be traced, largely through representations on memorial brasses, tomb figures and manuscript pictures. One typology partly confirmed by Seacourt was the suggestion that the principal type of knife changed in the late thirteenth century from having a pointed tang fitted into a solid handle to one with a flat tang which was riveted to handle-plates on each side. Such classifications can rarely be given more than very general dates. Changes in types of horse-shoe nails, with the abandonment of the 'fiddle key' types in the thirteenth century, first suggested from evidence at a site at Ascott Doilly, Oxon., were confirmed by stratified deposits at Tetsworth.

Unlike Roman sites, coins are very rarely found: Tetsworth was far from untypical in producing none whatever. Seacourt only had two late medieval jettons, used as reckoning counters. The value of the penny was too great for its loss by a peasant to be viewed with equanimity. A man takes care of half a day's wages. Until farthings were struck in the late thirteenth century, only illegal cutting in half or quarters of pennies gave a small denomination. Even afterwards, foreign jettons and small foreign coins were used in large numbers, at least as reckoning counters; at Huish, a Venetian *soldino*, and two French or Low Countries jettons were found, all fifteenth century in date. It may be that expedients were resorted to, such as the use of bone gaming counters, and even perhaps of curiosities, like the six ground-down Roman pot bases found in undoubted medieval levels at Tetsworth. How did a villager buy a chicken or a cooking-pot or a drink of ale? Presumably most such rural exchanges had to be by barter. There are a few more coins found in towns, because more transactions involving currency took place in them, but they are never more than lucky finds on any medieval excavation.

There are occasional exotica found on rural sites. A piece of Mediterranean glass at Seacourt could have arrived as a traveller's souvenir. Imported pieces that were obviously traded because there are so many of them are small hones, for sharpening blades, some of which came from the west, others from Brittany or Norway, like the two at Huish. A fragment of coal at Seacourt had probably come from fifty miles north near Coventry, but one piece is too slight evidence to suggest that it was a regular trade, and none has been recorded in Oxford, where it is perhaps more to be expected. Coal has been found at other village sites, however, including

Hangleton and Gomeldon. Purbeck marble mortar fragments are quite common, as are quern-stones, although their use was illegal, since grain had to be ground at the manorial mill.

The most frequent finds are, of course, of discarded pottery and bones, and more will be said about both later. Because of the quantities involved, reports on them take a long time to produce, and there are many difficulties, especially with bones. The occasional finds are more easily interpreted than the frequent: a merlin's bone at Tetsworth was one of the clues to the site's probable 'manorial' status, and partridge bones show one of the merlin's targets. Such finds stand out, for there are surprisingly few bones of wild animals or birds such as deer and pheasant. Poaching was probably too dangerous an occupation to be worth the pursuit. Rabbits, probably introduced in the twelfth century, were also a manorial perquisite, bred in 'coney-garths', long mounds which can look deceptively prehistoric.

I have a friend who now works as a Refuse Disposal Consultant. When asked her qualifications for the job, she replied that she had spent five years of her life as an archaeologist, studying nothing but what other people had thrown away. Evaluating rubbish is what archaeology is all about.

Chapter 6

Castles, Weapons and Fortifications

An anthropologist claimed recently that despite appearances there is nothing in man's nature which impels him to fight. It would have been difficult to explain this to a medieval man to whom fighting was a natural activity, being the *raison d'être* of one of the three categories of society, those who fought, frequently assisted by the category of those who worked. Not all those who prayed excluded themselves from it, either.

An archaeologist usually studies the defensive works of those being attacked, for the man on the offensive leaves little trace of his path. The Saxon defensive *burhs* can be traced, but not the horses and rarely the ships on which the Viking raiders travelled. A sword dredged from a river bed (Fig. 16) is a record perhaps of a chance loss, perhaps of a skirmish at a bridge-head, perhaps of a full-scale battle. It cannot often be ascribed specifically to attacker or defender, however, for even when different races or nations were involved, there was little difference between the weapons that they carried. An eleventh-century sword rarely has ornament distinctive of Saxon or Dane. An excavation on the battlefield of Hastings would show that the technology of the weapons used by the two sides was the same, even though the way that they made use of those weapons varied slightly.

The Saxon *burhs* like Wareham were communal defences, maintained by each locality for its own shelter and protection. Some residences were within fortified enclosures, like the unidentified eighth-century royal *Meretun*, and the excavated sites at Cheddar (Fig. 13) and perhaps Old Windsor. Although it was a *burh* in the *Burghal Hidage* list, Portchester probably functioned as a private fortification, with its timber halls (Fig. 19), its stone tower-chapel and its lack of town life. There may have been something similar at Corfe, Dorset, where King Edward was slain in 978. An eleventh-century document describes the type of residence suitable for a thegn, indicating a gated enclosure – which might imply a ditch and bank with a timber palisade – containing a chapel. Sulgrave, Northants., is an excavated example.

The Feudal Castles

One of the two common Norman fortifications is the 'motte', a steep earth mound surmounted by a wooden or stone tower, with an enclosure or yard, the bailey, at its foot. That mottes are not Saxon was established many years ago, but recently the argument has gone a stage further, with the suggestion that the motte was not introduced at the Conquest, but appeared some years later. It has been shown at Castle Neroche in Somerset that the earliest fortification was a 'ring-work' or 'enclosure castle' and that the motte was added to it later.

One reason for assuming that the Normans built mottes in 1066 is the picture in the Bayeux Tapestry which shows press-ganged Saxons throwing one up at Hastings, under the baleful eye of Duke William (Fig. 26). It has to be assumed that the Tapestry, which was probably embroidered in the 1070s, was being anachronistic, showing a castle of the type that had by then become normal, but was not actually the type that would have been

26 Scene from the Bayeux Tapestry showing press-ganged Saxons throwing up an earth 'motte' round the base of a timber castle. The man on the right is using a one-sided, iron-tipped spade; the other tools are shovels and a mattock.

built at Hastings in 1066. An attempt to solve this problem by excavation proved abortive, because of later reconstruction on the site. The Tapestry is quite correct, however, in the method of labour that it shows. The motte could be very quickly constructed by a small number of men, whether soldiers or press-ganged local labour. So, of course, could a ring-work, so that neither type had the advantage in terms of efficiency. The point of both was that a small team could build the strong-point, and a small garrison could defend it. The Norman castles were effective because they were ideal for a few military overlords holding down a much larger number of hostile natives. As a contemporary stated, the Normans won because they had castles – and because the English failed to co-ordinate efforts to oust them.

William needed castles, for himself or for his baronial supporters, to dominate key towns and to control key routes, like the one through the south-western peninsula controlled by Neroche. Precise dating of castles is always difficult: some are referred to in documents at an early date, but others may not be mentioned until many years after they were first constructed, for building expense accounts are not preserved until well into the twelfth century, and earlier dates rely on entries in chronicles, with references to sieges and such-like events which might have taken place years after the castle was first built. Even when there is a chronicle entry at an early date there is rarely certainty about which bit of a castle was then standing. It used to be assumed that the first part of the castle at Oxford was the surviving motte, and that it was to this that a chronicler referred when saying that Robert d'Oilli, the first Norman governor of Oxford, had built the castle by 1071 (*e* on Fig. 6). Reconsideration has shown that this cannot be proved. It is just as likely that the line of the bailey was the earliest feature, dug as a ring-work with a ditch and bank, surmounted by a timber palisade or a stone wall. Two stone buildings in the castle are either contemporary with or immediately subsequent to the ditch – a subterranean crypt, whose columns have early Norman carving on their capitals, and a tower (Plate xv). The crypt has been dismantled and re-erected on a new site at least once in its history, and the chapel that stood above it has been demolished, but the gaunt, four-storey high tower of St George remains.

Documentary references are even more difficult to use at Winchester, since they may refer either to William's extension to the existing royal palace west of the Minster, or to a site by the West Gate (Fig. 5). That the latter was not begun until the 1140s was only disproved by the recent excavations, which showed that the later Saxon activity in the area was brought to an abrupt end by the construction of the castle's earthworks. This involved a bank and ditch to isolate the castle from the town, and a motte, probably with a timber tower, beside and dominating the West Gate. A stone chapel was provided – a normal feature of castles, whether separate buildings as at Winchester and Oxford, or incorporated in the keep, as in twelfth-century examples like Portchester.

The other town which certainly had a castle inserted to dominate it soon after the Conquest was another of the *burhs* which had successfully developed into an urban centre, Wallingford (Fig. 10). Here too Robert d'Oilli was the builder, and its date is known because the abbot of Abingdon had the misfortune to be imprisoned in it, an event recorded in his abbey's chronicle. Castles were not only for active defence, they also provided a strong-point as a centre of administration, and a gaol for those who fell foul of that administration. Historical continuity means that Winchester Castle is now the site of the assize courts; Oxford Castle is a prison, although for a time it passed out of royal ownership.

Archaeologically, castle sites provide the best evidence of the late Saxon period, for their earthworks cover and seal such features as the early streets at Winchester and Oxford (Plate IX), where the castle was located to control the east-west road at its crossing of the Thames, and was actually built across the existing street, causing the road to swing round it (Fig. 6). At Winchester, the castle commands the West Gate, but not the river: it was sited to use the highest ground in the town and did not dislocate the main north-south street. In Wallingford's case (Fig. 10), the castle was by the river, but slightly north of the crossing point. It perhaps overlay Saxon streets – this has not been proved – but it did not cause this northern entry to the town to shift westwards until the castle was extended in the thirteenth century. The earlier gate site and road were found in excavations to be about 30 m (100 ft) east of the present entry point.

Another urban centre which may have merited a castle was Wareham (Fig. 4). Here the documents are particularly unhelpful, for Domesday Book confuses 'castellum Warham' with nearby Corfe. Certainly Wareham had a motte, but its date of construction was not established in excavations in 1910. The castle commanded both the west gate, the only easy land access to the town, and the river. The street plan suggests that the castle was inserted as disruptively as at Oxford, but this is partly misleading. It used to be thought that Pound Lane, the curving street in the south-west quarter of the town, had originally been straight, but had been forced to alter course in order to circumnavigate the motte, following the line of the outside of the bailey ditch found in 1910. A small excavation in 1975 (*n* on Fig. 4) revealed, however, that there had been a second, outer ditch round an outer bailey, causing the slight curve in West Street. Later encroachment over the outer bailey must eventually have led to the con-struction of Pound Lane, which results therefore only indirectly from the construction of the castle. The hope of finding sealed Saxon levels within the outer bailey was frustrated. This may have been because of a medieval levelling-off operation, rather than because the Saxons were never there, but I suspect that in our small hole we had a back garden or field where luckier excavators would have found streets and buildings!

The other hint that the Wareham castle may be an early one is the Domesday record of the town's population. Like very many towns the prosperity of Wareham was considerably less in 1086 than it had been before the Conquest. Frequently such devastation resulted from the forcible seizure of house properties for castle sites, a process that is directly recorded in a few places, and inferred at others. Much of Oxford's waste property may have resulted from the annexation of what the excavations have shown to have been a thriving Saxon zone. At Wallingford, on the other hand, only eight properties are recorded as having been destroyed for the Norman castle.

The effect that the urban castles had on their immediate surroundings is seen clearly enough topographically, though their long-term impact is more difficult to assess. As an administrative centre, the castle brought people to its courts, and thereby presumably increased the market potential of the town in which it was located. The garrison had to be supplied with food, goods and services, and these had to be purchased. Trade would receive a particular boost when the king or a major baron was visiting. On the other hand, a castle provided a focus of less welcome attention in civil wars and rebellions, when a besieging army would pay scant regard to the rights and property of the local people. Even then there could be compensations: Wallingford received a very beneficial charter as a reward from Henry II for its loyalty to the Angevin cause. In some cases, a castle has been blamed or commended for something for which it was not responsible. Domesday Book records the presence of a large number of French burgesses at Southampton, presumably boosting its trade. It was thought that they came because of the protection to their interests given by the castle overshadowing the hostile Saxons. Excavations have not shown anything to suggest that the castle was not a later development, however, so that the French, although sponsored by the Conqueror, did not shelter under its walls.

The effect that the early Norman rural castles had on their immediate localities is even more difficult to estimate. In a few places, Windsor for example, the castle led to a town developing at its feet, but this process might produce only such small markets as Corfe (Plate XVI). Architecturally there was probably not much difference between the construction of urban and rural castles. The latter might be less constrained in terms of space, since it was an expensive business to buy town properties for the sake of the castle – even by the end of William's reign such sites were being paid for, not merely commandeered. Some extensions were made: the precise location of a barbican constructed as an outwork to Oxford Castle by Fawkes de Bréauté in the early thirteenth century was established by a recent excavation. Its construction had involved the demolition of a church, and possibly of other properties. On the other hand, neither in town nor in country would a castle grow unless its owner could be sure of defending it, and an extension involved the use of a larger garrison to cover the extra length of wall. Large outworks were put up, as at Corfe (Plate xvi), to reduce the effect of improved siege techniques and machines, but such measures were a desperate expedient. Wallingford also had its surrounding earthwork defences enlarged in the thirteenth century. Recent excavations revealed remarkably well-preserved cob-built structures, their walls standing to roof height, below a bank added to the bailey. Presumably it had been as easy to pile the bank round them as to bother to demolish them.

Excavations at castle sites recently have thrown an interesting new light on the construction of the mottes. Not only may they be post-Conquest additions to ring-works in some cases, but they were not generally built as mounds on which stone or timber towers were erected – newly thrown-up earth would take years to settle sufficiently to take the weight of a tower safely. At Ascott Doilly, Oxon., it was shown that the stone tower was constructed at the same time as the motte. The earth layers of the mound contained the chippings from the stones worked by the masons building the tower. As it went up course by course, so the earth round it was piled a stage higher. A similar process is implied by the Bayeux Tapestry which shows a completed tower, probably of timber, projecting higher than the motte which is still being finished by the digging labourers (Fig. 26). The motte is shown as a series of layers, and it even seems to have an outer 'skin', equivalent to the layer of clay found to have coated the outside of the Oxford motte to prevent the inner layers from slipping. At Ascott Doilly, the motte only went up for a few feet, and then the rest of the tower was built free-standing. Sometimes previously completely free-standing towers were encased in a motte, a precaution against having the foundations mined or battered. A good example of this process is at Christchurch, where a door in the wall of the tower below the present top of the motte shows that the motte had been added later, blocking the door (Plate xvii). An extreme case of this is Middleton Stoney, a small motte and bailey in Oxfordshire. Excavation has shown that the motte was the final, not the first phase, for it not only enclosed a well-built free-standing tower, formerly entered at first-floor level by a flight of stone steps still sealed in the motte, but the motte was partly made out of the demolished upper storeys of the tower.

The Middleton Stoney excavation is intended to produce information about a common type of medieval earthwork fortification, for it is not clear from documents how such sites functioned. Were they only occupied in times of war? How long were they utilized? What resources in terms of money and man-power were needed to build and maintain them? How did they affect the district round them? The only direct references to Middleton Stoney Castle are in 1215 and 1216, the latter an order for its demolition.

The site has a complex series of earthworks (Fig. 27A). There is a fairly normal looking bailey on the west side of the motte, surrounded by a ditch, mostly still visible as a slight depression in the ground. There is a similar enclosure on the east side, but beyond this is an outer ditch and bank, covering an area roughly 130 m (440 ft) × 120 m (400 ft). To understand such a site fully would really involve excavating not only all the banks, but the whole area inside them, and then the fields beyond. As it is, samples have to be taken. It was more than a little surprising that one of the samples, a large area inside the inner eastern enclosure, produced the rubble foundations of a Roman farm building almost at the foot of the motte. So unlikely was it that a Roman wall base could survive despite what must have been fairly intensive medieval activity on the site that at least one sceptic insisted on digging part of it himself to see if the director was missing something – the director was right, of course, and I was wrong. So a site which should have produced evidence of the stables or other such outbuildings of a typical twelfth-/thirteenth-century bailey has instead produced a second-/third-century barn. The fact that it could remain there is an indication that it was probably the west bailey that was used for the castle's buildings. The ground on the east side was carefully kept as open space in the Middle Ages to ensure visibility. The presence of the barn shows that it cannot be assumed that the castle was built in an empty landscape. Roman field boundaries at least may have survived, affecting the layout of the later work. There was also late Saxon use of the site.

Like many other castles, Middleton Stoney's military use probably ended in the thirteenth century, when the ditches were filled in. The pottery evidence is slight, but is consistent with the 1216 order for destruction of the castle. An important aspect of the excavation was the opportunity taken to extract information, not only from the objects found but also from environmental data, in this case soils and snails. Snails are sensitive creatures: a woodland snail cannot survive in an open field, for instance, so the different types of snail whose shells are found in a particular archaeological layer will reveal the vegetation of the land-cover from which the soil in that layer came. There are some snails which cheat the archaeologist by burrowing, and others that were removed from their natural habitat by an archaeologically insensitive thrush; but on the whole they can provide some useful data. At Middleton Stoney, the soil evidence showed that before the castle was put up, the land round it was pasture, or possibly woodland, but was not ploughed; the site was perhaps chosen, therefore, because it was in fairly open territory, and since it was not intensively used local opposition to its construction probably did not have to be quelled. The lack of snails in the lower part of the ditch seemed to show that it was filled fairly rapidly, confirming the effect of the 1216 order. The upper part filled only slowly, the snails and the soil types in the various layers showing that at various times the area was grazed, at others left fallow. Although not much can be made of this historically, it is interesting to see that there was no proof of the speed of the filling of the ditch from the rest of the archaeological record, since no pottery from later periods had penetrated into it; but for the environmental data, it might have been claimed that it was completely filled early in the thirteenth century.

By the end of the thirteenth century, the great age of the medieval castle had almost passed. The most dramatic buildings and the largest expenditures that resulted from castle building were over, except for Edward I's Welsh castles. Castles continued to be built and altered, won and lost, fortified and demolished, but their heyday as invincible private strongholds had gone. Changes in society, and in social demands, meant physical changes that made defence a subordinate consideration. Castles were still important, and their very existence threatened the crown with the spectre of un-controllable subjects. Many did not see action until the seventeenth century, when places like Corfe proved themselves still to be militarily effective, despite gunpowder and other sophistications. Their absolute predominance did not outlast the early Middle Ages, however.

'Pro bono publico'

The Normans were interested in defending themselves from the native inhabitants, not in defending the inhabitants from outsiders. As a result there is very little in late eleventh- and twelfth-century records about the communal defences of the *burhs* and their maintenance, although there are hints of work due at Wallingford and half a dozen other places. Nor does archaeology add much to the picture. Some towns seem to have allowed part of their first ditches to be filled in at an early date: Southampton's has tenth-century pottery in it, Oxford's had a Saxon street over it. Basic lines were probably kept up, however. A series of 'waste' strips owned by the king immediately behind Oxford's stone walls in the thirteenth century represented the land formerly covered by the town's earth bank, which had therefore survived intact whatever might have happened to the ditch.

The mid twelfth-century civil war might well have caused a frantic campaign of repairs to town defences, but evidence of this is hardly

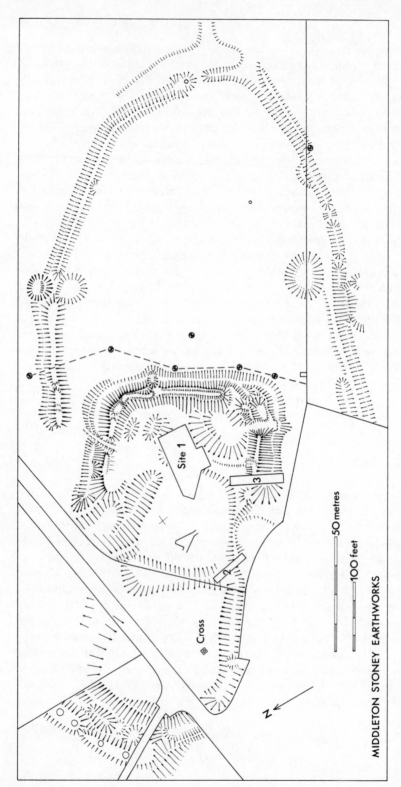

MIDDLETON STONEY EARTHWORKS

50 metres

100 feet

Site 1

Cross

27A The excavator's survey of the earthworks of the motte and bailey castle at Middleton Stoney, Oxon. They have survived so intact because the village which originally stood round the cross by the church was moved to a new site by an eighteenth-century land-owner, who turned the whole area into a park.

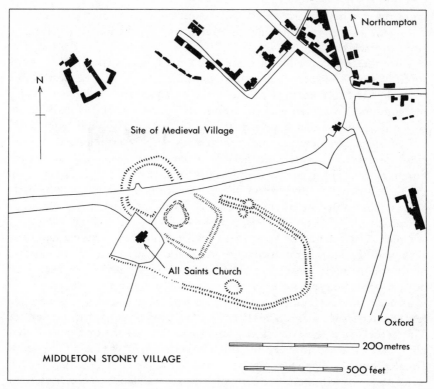

Northampton

N

Site of Medieval Village

All Saints Church

Oxford

200 metres

500 feet

MIDDLETON STONEY VILLAGE

27B   Middleton Stoney village.

forthcoming. At Wareham, excavation showed that the town's ditch was recut (Fig. 9). Recent work at Cricklade hints at the same thing. But there is no evidence of such work at Oxford or Southampton – even Winchester fails for once to add to the story.

Southampton is the first town to show renewed interest in urban defences, in the early thirteenth century. Its receipt of a sum of money from King John 'to [en] close the town' probably went towards the earth bank and ditch found in excavations in 1956–8. Construction of a stone gate (Plate XVIII) over the road leading north out of the town – its only approach by land (*G* on Fig. 2) – had started some years before, for the mouldings on the central archway indicate a late twelfth-century date. Gates were of course well known from earlier days, either of timber, as indicated by the South Cadbury excavations, or of stone as presumably in the reused Roman towns. There may be eleventh-century work in the core of Winchester's standing West Gate. Southampton's Bargate and John's

137

grant mark a new phase, however, resulting not from fears of civil war but from the spectre of French invasion caused by the loss of the English lands in France.

Since the invasion when it came was a disciplined expedition to assist some of the English barons against the king, it was not the destructive force that had been anticipated. Nevertheless a panic had led to emergency measures which set up a chain reaction. Towns demanded walls, even though the worst dangers were temporarily past. As often happens in human affairs, the need was met after it was over. Nevertheless, there were fresh demands for walls, and new ones were subsequently built at each public alarm. The records of murage grants, made from tolls taken on goods entering the town, allow the process to be followed into the early fourteenth century, after which it became more likely that a levy would be taken directly from the citizens themselves for use on wall building.

Unless some grant survives, it is usually difficult to ascribe a date to a town wall. In Southampton changes in the social make-up of various parts of the town might provide a clue; in an Oxford excavation, sherds of pottery indicated a date after the late twelfth century. Otherwise the evidence would have to be that of the structures themselves, and there are few characteristics that can be described as typical of any particular period. The actual walls give no hints, and even the projecting bastions that punctuate them are not very helpful. The earliest of these seem to be semicircular, but this shape was retained when square, stilted apsidal, and even horse-shoe shaped ones appeared, which gave a defender a better view of the base of the wall below him. The circuit which survives for much of its length around Southampton has three different types, but they cannot be dated typologically.

Southampton not only has a fairly complete circuit, it also has several gates. These range from small posterns to substantial structures like the frequently enlarged Bargate which has a prison, a Gildhall, and other rooms on the first and second floors (Plate XVIII). A chapel or church was often incorporated in the structure of a gate; these survive at Langport in Somerset and in Winchester's Kingsgate. Gates were frequently lavishly decorated, especially on the exterior to impress strangers arriving at the town.

The Southampton circuit proceeded slowly. The earth bank was strengthened by stone walls in the second half of the thirteenth century, but the line was not complete, certainly along the shore, by 1338 when the French finally did raid the town, as had been feared over a century before. Even this disaster did not spur the citizens to complete the walls, for to do so was to block their wharves from the town. Their reluctance is shown in the quality of the work done, for excavations have revealed that the walls were built on carelessly laid, unmortared foundations. When the government finally insisted on the west wall, in the process incorporating existing stone houses whose windows can still be seen (Plate xix), it prevented goods from being unloaded straight into warehouses. Instead they had to be hauled round through one of the gates. No wonder the citizens at Portsmouth petitioned against the levy of a murage grant. The wall there was not finished until the fifteenth century. Other southern towns to have walls include Chichester, Poole and Melcombe. Not surprisingly there is a coastal bias; Salisbury was one of many inland towns which never finished its circuit, and anyway never had stone walls, only an earth bank and a ditch. Many inland towns treated their circuits as legal rather than protective barriers. At Oxford (Fig. 6), the Grey Friars were allowed to breach through the wall with their church, provided that there was no access through it for the general public.

The walls at Southampton that belong to the later fourteenth century contain provision for a new weapon, the gun. A series of gun-ports sited to rake the western shore is one of the first instances in which accommodation was made for these fearsome if not yet very lethal weapons. They may have been built into the sea gate at Quarr Abbey on the Isle of Wight at a slightly earlier date, in the 1360s. Thereafter gunports became a standard feature in gates and walls. Often existing arrow-slits had a circle added below them to allow for guns. It is significant that care went into siting the gun-ports to give maximum fire-power. This was a lesson that had been learnt very slowly with archery. The earliest stone defences did not even provide arrow-slits. St George's tower in Oxford Castle presents blank walls to the outer world (Plate xv). Introduced in the late twelfth century, it was not for some years that proper thought was given to the siting of arrow-slits to cover the widest possible area, and especially the base of a castle's walls.

Arrow-slits and gun-ports provide a point of direct comparison between castles and town walls. In general, however, it does not seem that the two were closely inter-related. Walls were likely to be the work of local builders, not specialists. Lessons in gate construction might be learnt, but there was not a great deal of exchange of even the limited ideas available. Southampton's twelfth-century Bargate was apparently quite small, though later enlarged and heightened, but it was not as solidly built with such thick masonry as a castle gate. Forward-pointing drum towers were added to it in the early fourteenth century, but the defensive value of these was reduced when the space between them was filled in the fifteenth century, so that they no longer commanded the entrance approach (Plate xviii). Many town gates, like Winchester's West Gate, presented only a flat facade to an attacker, and were a screen for traffic and riot control rather than an active point of defence. The intentions were not always the same as those that dictated the building of castle gates.

Castles of Comfort

It is appropriate to return to private and royal castles after a comparison of their gates with those of towns. An increasing emphasis on the strength of the gate developed from the building of strong defensive curtain walls around castles, with a relative reduction in the role of the internal keep. This process, resulting from the need to prevent sappers and siege engines getting too close, is not well illustrated in southern castles, except at Corfe (Plate XVI).

As with churches, the history of a castle cannot be fully understood from a study of the surviving fabric alone. Ludgershall Castle, Wilts., for instance, has only a very small stump of masonry surviving above ground within its double-enclosure earthworks, yet excavation on the site has revealed that it was replanned and altered time after time. The earliest documentary record is in 1138, at the start of the Civil War, but there were buildings, not necessarily within a defensive circuit, before that date. Indeed, one of the problems at Ludgershall is to decide where the 1138 date comes in the chronological phasing of the site: it may be that it was already a castle by that time. Certainly there was a great deal of activity on the site in the twelfth century, including the digging out of a subterranean chamber, probably for storage purposes rather than for some dramatic last-ditch defensive stand.

The late twelfth century saw the start of changes to the whole character of Ludgershall. Its defensive structures such as the small keep were taken down, many more timber buildings appeared, mural towers were placed around the rampart circuit, and a sequence of chambers with fireplaces appeared. These thirteenth-century developments were because the castle was not required for defence, but as a royal palace from which the king could go hunting in the nearby forest. Lodgings for himself, his followers, his horses and his dogs meant that the inconveniences of a barrack were replaced by the comforts of a mansion. Ludgershall's new role did not long outlast the thirteenth century. It declined into an ordinary manor-house, with farm buildings encroaching into the baileys, and by the sixteenth century all that remained was 'a pretty lodge made by the ruins of it', and even that has now gone.

Ludgershall demonstrates how the changing function of a castle is reflected in its buildings. Social demands were for comfort rather than security. Fireplaces, *garderobes* (lavatories) and small private rooms were required, and these were put in at the expense of defensive needs.

Private castles developed on broadly similar lines, the earlier gaunt tower giving way to less martial buildings. Many were fortified houses rather than castles. Bishop Henry de Blois was deeply implicated in the twelfth-century civil war, but his residences at Wolvesey, Winchester and Bishop's Waltham, Hants., were not impregnable strongholds. The latter has a strong stone tower largely surviving, but big windows in it show that it was not built solely for defence. The Bishop's hall was built for administration and convenience.

Taste and demand for private castles revived in the late fourteenth century, as soldiers who had made money in the French wars returned to newly bought estates where they wanted residences to suit their characters. Central government had little to fear from them, and licences for castles were easy to obtain. They would not withstand a proper siege, though they served as useful strongholds in the lawless fifteenth century.

There are several of these late castles in the south. In Somerset, Nunney was licensed by a returning soldier in 1373; it was small, but modelled on both Edward I's and on French examples (Plate xx). Four drum towers protected the corners of a rectangular four-storey building, approached by drawbridge over a moat. One tower served as a stairwell, another for garderobes and there was just enough accommodation for kitchens, a hall, a chapel and smaller chambers. It was essentially a family dwelling unit, however, rather than a real stronghold. The bases of its walls were not thickened out into massive plinths to prevent undermining, but relied on a moat for protection; it was sited in a valley bottom, overlooked by a ridge of high ground from which a cannon or a mangonel could have played havoc among its tower tops.

More substantial were Donnington, Berks., and Farleigh Hungerford, Somerset, both of which had gate-houses, the former still very impressive, its projecting drum towers pierced only by arrowslits. The window above the gate arch shows that the wall is thin, however, and would not withstand an intensive battering. Wardour, Wilts., and Farleigh Hungerford have buildings round a courtyard, not contained within a central keep-like block. In this they were following Bodiam, Sussex, one of the few castles which was built for an explicit purpose, 'the defence of the local neighbourhood' against the French, who did not however put it to the test. It has been suggested that the gate at Bodiam was made its strongest point, and that this could be effectively cut off from the rest of the castle. This may have been so that the owner could if necessary barricade himself and his family against a rebellion by his own men, an important consideration at a time when loyalty was expensive to buy and keep. More probably it was realized that the castle, once penetrated by an external enemy, could not all be held but that a last stand might be possible in the gate tower.

The castle tradition lingered on, especially visible in gate-houses such as that at Wolfeton House, Dorset, put up *c.* 1490; it has two tough-looking drum towers forward of the entrance arch, which it covers with gun loops. But the towers are not serious: the top of one was used as a dovecote! Few fifteenth- and sixteenth-century houses even made a gesture towards fortification. The Lovells at Minster Lovell were deeply, profitably and in the end disastrously involved in the Wars of the Roses, but even they did not bother to provide themselves with anything more than a small stone tower in one corner of their great courtyard.

Although it was a private castle, Bodiam was built with a public purpose in mind, and was intended for use if necessary. Some of the king's castles also received attention in the fourteenth and fifteenth centuries because of the threat of the French. At Southampton, the castle had not had any money spent on it for a hundred years when in 1378 work on a new tower-keep began, an expensive and impressive structure on top of the old motte Two of the most famous English builders of the period, Henry Yevele and William Wynford, were employed on it and the surviving accounts show how much effort was put into bringing together men and materials so that it was largely completed within four years, wholly within ten. Nothing of this now survives.

Southampton received this special treatment because of its coastal position. Carisbrooke on the Isle of Wight was actually put to the test, successfully withstanding a French siege in 1377. Fortunately much money had been spent on it during the previous century, and it was in good repair. Further work was done in the 1380s but it was then left to decay for two hundred years. Other royal castles affected by the French wars because of their coastal situation included Portchester, which had been ignored in the thirteenth century because of the development of the better harbour at nearby Portsmouth. It was refurbished, with new works on the gates. Most was spent on chambers and the hall, however, for the castle's use was as a supply base. Its constable looked to its fortifications in the 1380s; but after 1396, and peace with France, money was again being spent on the royal apartments, not the defences. It was totally neglected in the fifteenth century. At Windsor, a favourite royal residence, expenditure was frequent and considerable, but the defences were not strengthened significantly. Winchester on the other hand was near enough to the coast to occasion alarm, and the defences were repaired though even here the only actual new building was a royal hall.

Winchester was a castle which had an extra reason for being maintained, for it was the administrative and judicial centre of the area. At Oxford, however, the stone tower on the motte was actually taken down in 1240, and other towers are recorded as having collapsed. The castle's condition grew steadily worse. Wallingford was probably kept better, and served as the royal strongpoint in the Upper Thames, although often held by wives or siblings rather than by the king himself.

The excavation which showed that Wallingford Castle had been extended over the original north gate of the town provided one of the very few cases of a castle which was enlarged in the thirteenth century (Fig. 10). In towns particularly the economic value of the internal space was a strong counter to any such ideas. It is interesting to see how quickly castles were built over if the opportunity arose. At Wareham, the king's castle passed to the Earl of Essex in 1216 and in baronial occupation was probably not kept up at all. The pottery found in the outer ditch suggests that it was filled in the thirteenth century (though five glazed sherds should not have to bear too much weight!), and probably the outer circuit was built over by houses lining the road out of the town. The inner road may have developed at this period, along the inner bailey ditch. By 1461, the castle site was being rented out to an ordinary citizen. In most towns, this sort of encroachment did not occur until the sixteenth century. At Dorchester, Dorset, the castle was sold by the king to a local citizen in 1290, but it had never been a very large or substantial one. Wareham may also be a special case because it was not retained by the king throughout the Middle Ages. It may be possible to 'test' it against Banbury, another small town with a non-royal castle, where excavations are revealing more about its history.

The medieval castle served a variety of roles and has an important place in any understanding of the functioning of medieval society. Many castles saw action for the first and last time in the seventeenth century, and many even then withstood the battering of cannon for many weeks. A strongpoint never quite loses its strategic value. The castles were essentially garrison defences, and thus different from the chain of forts that Henry VIII built round the south coast, which were the first of a new series of entrenchments designed to protect gun installations from bombardment. The direct purpose differed, but a romantic view can still see the horizontal machine-gun slits in a 1939–45 pill-box as the lineal descendant of the arrow-slit in a medieval castle tower.

Chapter 7

Town and Country Buildings

If archaeology is the 'study of the past from its material remains', an archaeologist interested in the Middle Ages must be concerned with standing buildings as well as with excavations. Internal and external changes of plan, removal and insertion of doors, windows, chimneys and even of whole floors, change of use, alterations to walling materials and surface finish, and replacement of rotten timbers or even of complete roofs, all make the 'archaeology of standing buildings' a very complex exercise, usually hampered because – quite properly – the building has to remain standing and the investigator cannot chip away at the plaster to see if there is a timber beam hidden behind it.

A building's chances of survival depend on many factors. A well-built stone structure is more likely to last than even the best of timber frames. If the latter are totally protected from damp, be it rising or falling, they still have to contend with beetle infestation and, of course, with the much worse risk of fire. The financial value of a plot of land in a prosperous town demands maximum economic use of its surface space, and buildings cannot grow sideways without encroaching on neighbouring property. Town buildings are therefore more often under pressure for total demolition and replacement than are rural ones. Furthermore, the nature of town life has changed, since fewer people now live in the actual centres of towns than they did in the Middle Ages. Very few town buildings that began life as houses have not been converted to offices and shops, if they survive at all. Demands for purpose-built and supposedly more efficient accommodation have at all periods led to the destruction of old buildings. Consequently it is very difficult to use the numbers of surviving buildings as an indication of the relative prosperity of a particular period or a particular place, for the record is not complete, nor have losses occurred at a uniform rate.

Economic and practical requirements are not the only ones that lead to changes in buildings. Fashion also plays a major part, especially of course in housing, for a man's status is judged by his contemporaries as much by his home as by his clothes, his accent or his horse. Castles like Ludgershall and Nunney (Plate xx) have already shown the aristocracy demanding smaller and more private rooms, with such comforts as fireplaces and inside lavatories. These refinements were seen and admired by visitors who wanted them in their own homes thereafter. The external appearance of a house has a particular importance, for it is a public statement to every passer-by about the self-esteem of its owner. From this came the elaborate display of timber-framing that can still be admired on buildings in both town and country. Although stone was more durable and more expensive, it was not necessarily the material chosen by the rich, for it does not lend itself to the decorative self-assertion of timber-framing.

Timber-framing is often picturesque, and timber-framed buildings have been a favourite subject for sketches and drawings since the later eighteenth century; many buildings that have been demolished can be studied from their pictures. It may not be possible to rely on these for absolute accuracy, however. J. C. Buckler was perhaps the most reliable and industrious recorder in the last century, but minor details of even his drawings are not always accurate.

Town Buildings

Although status required that the houses of the upper ranks of society should be the aspiration of those below, different functional requirements as well as financial limitations would obviously prevent mere copying on a smaller scale. Just as pressures on space meant differences between town and country building, so also the needs of a merchant differed from those of a landed gentleman, who would not need a shop to display his goods or a strong-room in which to store them, but who would need a large hall in which to handle his tenants' affairs and to hold the manor court.

Excavations are as yet too incomplete a record to allow clear distinctions to be made between urban and rural building types, although surviving buildings show that certain types would appear only in one context or the other. This is particularly true of cellars, which are desirable for storage space in towns, but are not worth the expense of digging and stabilizing in the open countryside.

Cellars were already appearing in later Saxon towns, as the Oxford Castle site has recently shown (Fig. 19). There is nothing to suggest that the house there was large, or for a particularly wealthy citizen. There is a hint from the sites in Oxford's 1954–5 Cornmarket excavation (*f* on Fig. 6) that subterranean provision either for latrines or for storage was quite common by the twelfth century, but this perhaps varied from town to town. The Southampton evidence is of timber buildings mostly without cellars, and there is only one feature at Winchester's Lower Brook Street which might have been a cellar – at least it was the right sort of size, but it was not quite rectangular, and did not seem to have had posts for a house super-structure above it.

The sides of the cellar pits would soon have caved in if they had not been revetted in some way, so presumably most were wattle- or plank-lined. One at Oxford had a smear of clay round its edge, which may mean that it was lined with puddled clay, perhaps in addition to planking. From timber to stone cellars is an obvious transition. At Oxford, part of the 1954–5 Cornmarket site also had a twelfth-century stone cellar, from which a vault-rib survived; its footings were found in the excavation. It was probably built by Oseney Abbey, a monastery on the edge of the town, which acquired the property between 1140 and 1166. The cellar was some 11 m (35 ft) long by 6 m (20 ft) wide and, with its stone walls and ribs, repre-sented a substantial investment by the owners in a property in the best commercial street in the town.

Stone cellars are fire-proof and thief-proof. Similar considerations meant that a 'house-over-warehouse' type of stone building was favoured by merchants in the late twelfth century. Southampton had at least four, of which three partly remain. Living quarters were on the first floor, in which was an open hall with fire-place and windows: on the ground floor below was storage space, and no fire-place. In three of the Southampton examples one wall faced the quay and was built with wide arches in it so that goods could be brought straight into the warehouse from the ships. The ceiling of the ground floor was of timber beams and joists, supported by pillars in the centre if the span was more than about $4\frac{1}{2}$ m (15 ft). The evidence is uncertain, but in towns there was possibly internal access between ground and first floors. This type of house is not effectively any different from similar buildings in different contexts, such as the 'Constable's house' in Christchurch Castle (Plate XXI), small manor-houses in the countryside, or the misnamed 'King John's Box' at Romsey, Hants., built by the abbey. These 'first-floor halls' had external staircases, and the ground floors may often have been for kitchens and servants' use rather than storage.

That stone-built houses were not an entirely new phenomenon in twelfth-century towns has been shown by the excavations in Winchester and Oxford, where secular stone buildings were the core of certain churches (Fig. 20), and also by the excavation of the castle site at Winchester, where the corner of a late Saxon stone building with ashlar quoins was found sealed by the castle earthworks. These were rare, however, and were generally to remain so. Leases in Southampton show that the rich merch-ants provided themselves with stone accommodation in the late twelfth century almost as a matter of course, and excavations have shown that this involved building over the sites of earlier timber-framed structures. These might seem exceptional because they were in the wealthiest quarter of the town, but an artisan site, Lower Brook Street, in Winchester, has also recently produced the foundations of a twelfth-century stone building interpreted as having a first-floor hall. It almost certainly had an internal staircase, for there was no sign of external stairs up to the first floor. The flint walls were substantial, with dressed stone door jambs. A fine stone ground-floor fire-place was inserted into a side wall soon after the house was built, and it was extended, also in stone, up to the street frontage. A wall within the extension showed that the front area was partitioned off, probably for a booth in which an artisan worked.

Although few twelfth-century stone buildings have survived, it is clear both from excavations and documentary evidence that once built they were used by many subsequent generations. Changing ownerships and functions might lead to physical changes, but within the existing stone wall framework – a good example is the insertion of the ground-floor fire-place into the Winchester house. Whatever happened to the upper floor's function, it is clear that the ground floor thereafter was to have at least equal status. Indeed, first-floor halls in towns may have gone out of fashion for private use by the early thirteenth century, if lack of survivals is a true guide. Unfortunately, thirteenth-century Southampton leases which specify stone houses and cellars do not clarify whether the cellars were subterranean vaults or ground-floor warehouses below first-floor halls. Nor have any thirteenth-century houses survived at Southampton. Indeed it is remarkable that town houses are lacking throughout the country in the thirteenth century, despite documentary evidence that they were being built. The implication is perhaps that despite fire risks, the great majority were timber-framed.

Excavations have not yet filled this gap in the structural record. At Winchester's Lower Brook Street site, apart from the twelfth-century stone house, the buildings were not of high social status. The cloth-workers and tanners had small houses which probably only gave them ground-floor accommodation, comprising a living-area, and a small partitioned-off bedroom. Up to the middle of the thirteenth century these houses were entirely timber, either with posts dug into the ground, or with timber sills laid directly on it. After that date, low walls were used as foundations, sometimes mortared, sometimes not. There was not enough rubble on the site to suggest that stone was used for more than just a foot or two, and clearly a timber superstructure was then built on the walls. Exactly the same was happening in contemporary peasant houses in the countryside. Similarly, houses were built, altered, reconstructed, demolished and rebuilt as often as in the countryside, but with much less tendency to change alignment.

At one stage in the fourteenth century, a row of four cottages was put up in Lower Brook Street, probably as an investment development by the owner, a small monastery. Documentary sources reveal many such speculations by ecclesiastical owners: Oseney's cellar in Oxford was an early example there of a process that played a major part in the town's history. Leases show that, from the late twelfth century, a favourite development was a building with a line of shops along the street, the shops being little booths often no more than 2 m (6 ft) square. A narrow passage gave access to the rear of the property; behind the shops, often along the length of a whole row, might be a single room, the hall, and chambers over the shops. The rest of the area, often round a small courtyard, would be for kitchens, stables and other minor buildings, latrine pits, wells and gardens. Such properties were let out quite separately from the shops, which might not even have the use of the chambers above them, in which case the shop-keeper and his family had to live elsewhere in the town, or in one of its suburbs.

From the twelfth century onwards, shops might also be in a cellar like the one built by Oseney Abbey in Oxford. The floors of these stone under-crofts would be a few feet below the level of the street, from which they were entered down a flight of steps, partly or wholly external. Iron-barred windows would look out onto a narrow light-well, though most of the lighting would have had to be artificial. Southampton had at least thirty thirteenth-, fourteenth- and fifteenth-century vaults, some used as shops, often combined with workshops, so that a tailor's customers, for instance, might order their cloth at the front of the building, while his assistants made up the clothes in the background. Others were inns and beer-cellars, and some would have stored the 'sacks' of wool, the bales of hides and, in-creasingly in the fifteenth century, the bales of cloth, ready for export, as well as the imported wines, silks, spices, dyes and luxuries which were the port's chief interest. The finest undercroft has an early fourteenth-century ribbed vault and fire-place, with corbels and bosses as finely carved as in any contemporary ecclesiastical work. Others have built-in seats, well chambers and privies.

Cellars were secure, and were therefore especially suitable for the port of Southampton. Although not unique to it, the only comparable quantity is in another port, Winchelsea, and there seem to be many fewer in other towns. There is a twelfth-century one in Winchester, and Oxford has two late thirteenth-/early fourteenth-century examples, as well as the earlier one in Cornmarket. Even quite small towns might have a merchant who needed such premises: there is a very big fourteenth-century cellar with a central pillar in Burford, Oxon. There may be many others, unrecognized because a few small alterations would remove all dating evidence, particu-

XIII Ivory panel carved with two 'Winchester School' angels; late tenth or early eleventh century. Height 7.5 cm. Found at St Cross, Winchester and now displayed in the City Museum.

XIV A carved limestone panel at Winterbourne Steepleton church, Dorset, showing a 'Winchester School' angel. Length about 50 cm.

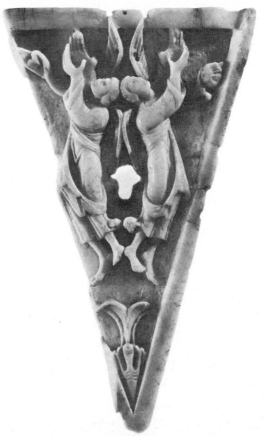

xv St George's tower, Oxford. The top storey with its arrow-slits is an addition to the Norman structure, which avoids weak points by having only a single opening. In the foreground are the remains of the mill demolished in the 1930s, on a site where there had been a mill since the Conquest.

xvi Despite the importance of its castle, Corfe never became more than a small market town. The first reference to Corfe is the murder there of the king in 978. The structures visible from the town are the square Norman keep, and the outer defences added later as a counter to siege machines. Destruction was by Oliver Cromwell, since the castle had proved a very effective defence even in the Civil War.

XVII   The castle at Christchurch, Dorset, where the stone tower can be seen to be earlier than the earth motte piled up round it, blocking what had been a window. The houses in the background must stand over the castle ditch; the bowling-green is in the castle bailey.

XVIII   Southampton's Bargate began life in the late twelfth century, though the earliest work survives in the core of the present structure, for it was enlarged by half-round towers in the early fourteenth century. The space between these was filled in the fifteenth century by the forward-projecting facade, on which the row of shields presents a show of civic pride.

XIX Southampton's fourteenth-century west wall. The modern road was the sea shore in the Middle Ages. The spaces in the wall arcades are the windows of houses which existed before the wall was built and which were retained as part of its structure. The block of flats is on the site of the castle motte.

XX Nunney, Sir John de la Mare's late fourteenth-century private castle in Somerset. The decorated windows are those of the hall and chapel.

XXI   The 'Constable's house' in the bailey of Christchurch castle is a good example of a late twelfth-century 'first-floor hall', with service and storage on the ground floor, living accommodation above. The fine round chimney is original, serving the fire-place in the hall.

XXII   The late fifteenth-century three-storey shop in Cornmarket Street, Oxford. The ground floor has been extended forward on both street fronts, to increase the space inside.

XXIII   The spacious interior of Shaftesbury Abbey's barn at Bradford-on-Avon. It provided both storage and working space. The stones in the foreground were used as a threshing floor, set in the entrance way so that the dust and chaff would blow out through the open doors.

XXIV The barn built on their estate at Great Coxwell, Berks., in the first half of the thirteenth century for the monks of Beaulieu Abbey. The gable entrance is fairly modern. There is a second cart porch on the opposite side, over which was a small room to accommodate the bailiff. For the interior roof construction see Fig. 30. The roof is of stone slates and weighs several tons.

XXV A cruck building at Ibsley, Hants. The paired cruck blades show clearly in the gable wall. Later alterations to the building can be seen to include a slight raising of the roof, and a heightening of the front wall to give more first-floor space inside, attested by the dormer windows.

xxvi   A 'Wealden' farmhouse reassembled at the museum at Singleton, Sussex. The door gives access to a screens passage, with two small service rooms on the right and a single chamber above. On the left is the open hall, lit by the tall window. Beyond the hall is another ground-floor room, with first-floor chamber above. There is no chimney because the fire was in an open hearth in the centre of the hall.

xxvii   Thirteenth-century tile pavement from Muchelney Abbey, Somerset, now in the church. The tilers had probably come from Clarendon Palace.

XXVIII Pottery chimney from a site in Oxford. This medieval jester may be a scholar in his cap poking fun at authority.

XXIX Part of the hoard of rings and coins found at Thame, Oxon. The hoard was probably lost in the 1460s or 1470s, the date of the latest of the coins in it, and probably also the date of the largest ring.

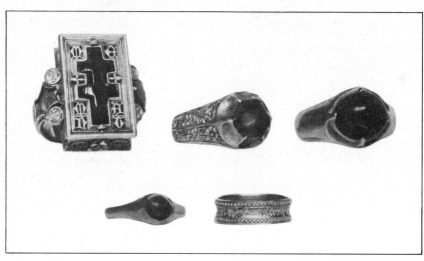

larly if the roof was not of vaulted stone, but of timber, as must usually have been the case.

The undercrofts were often without any internal staircase to the buildings above, which had separate entrances from the street, and could be rented off separately. The superstructures were usually timber-framed, and have not survived. One exception is at 58 French Street, Southampton, and is stone-walled, but with a timber-framed front (Fig. 28). Here, as in many examples, the roof of the vault is slightly higher than the level of the street, so that the ground floor was reached by a short flight of steps. Along the front of the building was probably a small covered gallery, below the over-sailing jetty of the first-floor chamber. From the gallery, a door led into a shop. In this way, both ground floor and cellar could be used for commercial purposes, taking full advantage of the street frontage.

58 French Street is a rectangular building, now 18.9 m (62 ft) by 4.8 m (15 ft) internally. The ground-floor shop may have had access at the back into the rooms behind, or have been rented off separately. The centre part of the building was the hall, open to the roof, and probably with a central hearth. It was entered by a door from the outside, which was screened off by a wooden partition to make an entrance corridor. At the rear of the building, the moulded ceiling beams and joists and the finely carved stone corbels on which the main beam rests (the early fourteenth-century style of the leaf carved on one of the corbels is one piece of dating evidence for the

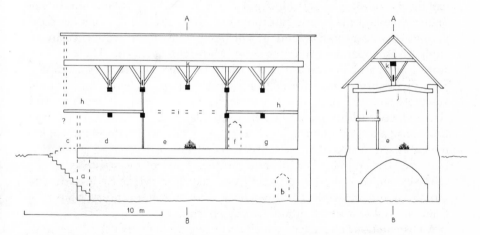

28 58 French Street, Southampton. Cut-out sections through the early fourteenth-century merchant's house. Some details hypothetical, for example, details of crown-post roof structure (collar-beams omitted in longitudinal section). *a* – entry to cellar; *b* – side entry; *c* – access to shop (details lost); *d* – shop; *e* – open hall with central hearth; *f* – door; *g* – 'counting-house'; *h* – first-floor chambers; *i* – gallery; *j* – tie-beam; *k* – collar-plate or -purlin; *l* – collar-beam.

building), shows that the room was a very special one, perhaps the merchant's counting-house. On the first floor there was a chamber over the shop and another at the back. As the open hall lay between them, a gallery was provided above the ground floor corridor, to link them. Even at 'the earliest complete town house in England' (P. A. Faulkner), there are discoveries to be made. A Southampton University team has just (1977) revealed that a blocked side door in the cellar led to a flight of steps that gave a second entrance to the undercroft. It also confirmed the early fourteenth-century date of the building, by the pottery that pre-dated its construction.

Slightly later, and a storey higher, than 58 French Street is the Red Lion, in Southampton's High Street. It has had its street block completely rebuilt, but the open hall with its gallery, and the rear block, survive substantially intact, though with a chimney-stack added in the early sixteenth century. Unlike 58 French Street, it was entered by an enclosed passage from the street on one side of the shop, there being no separate side door into the hall. This meant that the whole width of the plot of land was used for the building. Similar land values presumably account for its extra storey. Because of the buildings on both sides, there could be no windows in the walls of the hall, which was lit by a sky-light in the roof. This would also have served as a louvre for the open hearth which the chimney-stack replaced.

A type of shop known in the fifteenth century but perhaps earlier also, had the use of the rooms behind and above it. The shop itself might be no bigger than a single booth, but the door into it also led to a side passage giving access to a room behind, in which might be a fire-place and a stair or ladder to an upper floor over the shop. Above this again could be a second storey, or an attic known as the cock-loft. Late fifteenth-century examples of this type survive at Oxford (Plate xxII; *k* on Fig. 6), Henley-on-Thames and elsewhere at Exeter and Tewkesbury, where there is a superb line of twenty-three such shops. They were a speculation by Tewkesbury Abbey. Exeter had a row of nineteen butchers' shops which were a development by the city itself. Some of the wealthiest merchants had very big properties built round a courtyard, with more profligate use of the street frontage. Large examples of these survive in places like Norwich and King's Lynn, but the south has only the small, and late, fifteenth-century Scaplen's Court at Poole, although others are known from documents.

An ostentatious house type which is very common in towns, villages and farms in the south-east, but is only known in towns in the south and the Midlands, has a central open hall and two-storey chamber blocks at both ends, the upper storeys of which are jettied (Plate xxvI). Since these 'Wealden' or 'recessed front' houses lost their point if they were not fully visible, they were never built at right angles to an urban street, only parallel to it, so they are only found in the fringes of towns, away from the most valuable frontage space. An example in an Oxford suburb, owned by Oseney Abbey, seems from the abbey's Rental to have been built in the 1450s. The most westerly of the known Wealdens, at Yeovil, Somerset, had stone side walls. These served as a useful fire-break between properties which had a timber-framed front along the street. In the west country, stone gables were used in late medieval rural houses as well, because of lack of suitable lengths of timber and because of easily accessible stone, as much as a precaution against fire.

Some town buildings had to serve a communal not a private role. In many cases, the upper floors of the wall gates provided rooms for guilds. Southampton's guild met above the Bargate (Plate xviii). Most towns had separate guild halls, however, although none survive in the south. A vast warehouse at Southampton by the main quay was built in the early fifteenth century, either by Beaulieu Abbey, or by a wealthy merchant, but later became communal. It survives as the 'Wool House'. A hall to which all non-burgesses had to take cloth so that customs could be charged was being repaired in the fifteenth century, and Southampton's 'Tudor Merchant's Store' is in fact the Cloth Hall in its upper storey. Below, unenclosed, was the Fish Market. This building was taken down in the 1630s, moved to its present site, and reassembled, without the open ground floor. This is not a difficult process with a timber building, which can be literally unpegged. The 'Tudor Merchant's Store' is the first known structure to have been moved in this way, though there are documentary references to it happening earlier.

A favourite ecclesiastical investment was accommodation for travellers, both in towns and in the countryside. The word 'inn' was used for any private house, and inns in the modern sense did not become physically distinctive from ordinary houses until late in the Middle Ages. There were plenty of places where travellers and pilgrims could stay, often probably sleeping communally in a hall. Merchants, travelling with money and valuable goods, were among the first to require private, secure rooms, and eventually special buildings were provided for them, with small rooms each with direct access to a gallery or corridor. Many are known from documents, others still survive. Changes in economic systems led to increasing demand for 'hotel' space. The end of demesne farming meant that most religious houses lost their direct interest in trade as suppliers of wool from their own flocks. Often they had also acted as collecting agents for their tenantry. They were likely to negotiate the entire sale to a single merchant – who would be warmly received in the monastic guest-house. A few monasteries continued this system, but most abandoned it. The increasing numbers of English merchants dealing in smaller quantities, whose business was not with the monasteries' own officials, were not so welcome to disturb the calm of the cloisters. The construction of an inn to provide for them, and for pilgrims, increased revenue for decreased inconvenience. It may not be coincidence that Bicester Priory's last recorded payment on repairs to its guest-house occurs in the same decade as does the first reference to The Bell, an inn which it owned in the town's main street.

In towns, these buildings had an entry from the street, but the frontage space was likely still to be used for shops. There was less restriction in the countryside, and an inn like The George at Norton St Philip stretches proudly along the road. It was built by a Carthusian monastery. Glastonbury Abbey's George and Pilgrim has an impressive, gate-like frontage on the main street of the town, but most of the accommodation is behind. The Golden Cross in Cornmarket Street, Oxford, has a wide entry arch but the accommodation was in a range down one side of a long yard at right angles to the street, its ground-floor frontage having a different landlord as well as different occupiers. The Golden Cross was purpose-built in the 1490s by New College, but the site had been a hostelry long before that.

Neither documentary evidence, nor any surviving or excavated building, suggest that any inns were specially built in Southampton. This may reflect differences between the port and other towns like Oxford. Firstly, most of the property was privately owned, so that long-term investment motives were reduced. Secondly the port had a system of 'hosting' by which foreign merchants lodged with Southampton burgesses who took an active role in their trading activities. Presumably English merchants could find lodgings, but there is no direct evidence of purpose-built inns. It is interesting to see how different factors – of ownership, of commercial systems, and of spatial pressures – could produce different kinds of building in different places.

Rural Buildings

It was a phenomenon of later English medieval society that successful merchants sought to set themselves up as country gentry not as burgess-oligarchs – just as is implied by the eleventh-century statement that a merchant who crossed the sea three times in his own ship was 'thegn-worthy'. Although there were still substantial town houses, they were not enlarged, even in Southampton where the burgesses enjoyed greater independence than in most towns and might have preferred to remain in their own environment. Instead, they bought themselves country estates, one of them in the New Forest, where he could entertain visitors and easily remain in contact with Southampton. The sons of such men might with-draw from trade completely. This factor, and the frequent failure of male lines to last beyond a second generation, prevented the development in England of great merchant dynasties like those of Italy. It also took capital out of the towns and into the countryside.

Others who bought rural estates as an investment were lawyers; crown servants might hope to receive them for faithful service; and successful soldiers retired to estates bought from the profits of ransom. There were large numbers of new men entering the countryside, with enough capital to build for themselves houses suitable to their rank. The soldiers might build miniature castles, like Nunney (Plate xx), but most men had no aspirations beyond a comfortable and commodious manor-house. Some of these might be existing ones adapted; most, perhaps, were newly-built, for many villages had not previously had a resident lord of the manor and so had no manor-house.

The possibility of associating a surviving house with a particular person whose career is known adds greatly to the historical significance of the building. It is a study that has produced interesting recent results in north Berkshire, which has a large number of surviving houses. Unfortunately it is a study that can only go to a certain level down the social hierarchy. Smaller farmhouses cannot be tied to a particular name until the sixteenth century, and peasants' houses do not even survive until the seventeenth. Nor is it always possible to ascribe a particular manorial building to a particular owner, even when the ownership record is complete. The interesting complex of thirteenth-century and later house, barn and chapel at Rockbourne, Hants., descended through members of local families, none of whom seems more likely than another to have paid for any one of the new buildings. Since at present these cannot be dated more closely than to within a century, their builders remain individually unknown.

The actual accommodation provided in a manor-house was not signifi-cantly different from that of the larger town houses. The focal point was the open hall. First-floor halls, with service rooms below, were one twelfth-century type (Plate xxi), but ground-floor halls were more common, with detached kitchens, chambers and service rooms. After the twelfth century, these were increasingly linked to the hall by covered walks, or directly, as crosswings (Fig. 29). Smaller houses would have only one end block. Unlike urban merchants' houses, there were no first-floor galleries through the hall to connect the two end blocks. A standard feature from the four-teenth century was the screens passage across the 'lower' end of the hall: this contained the front door, and led through to the back yard or garden. On one side was the entrance to the hall, on the other a pair of doors, one into the pantry, the other into the buttery where the wines and ales were kept. Larger houses might have a passage between these service rooms for access to chambers beyond.

Except in castles or very big houses, chamber blocks were only two storeys high, there being less pressure for three storeys than in towns. In the country, it was easier to extend sideways. Although attached to them, the hall and its roof construction were structurally separate from the cross-wings in most larger houses, and so one or other element might be added, pulled down or extended without affecting the rest. So houses were easily adapted to new demands.

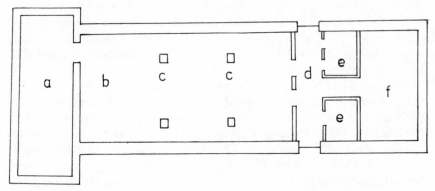

29 Ground-plan of a hypothetical manor-house of the later thirteenth century with an aisled hall and two end-blocks: *a* – solar block (lord's private chambers, two-storeyed); *b* – open hall (perhaps with raised dais); *c* – aisle-posts; *d* – screens passage; *e* – buttery and pantry; *f* – service room (this block two-storeyed).

The owners' family's rooms would be in the chambers behind the 'upper' end of the hall, and increasingly these had the comforts of fire-places, windows with cushioned seats and, very rarely, garde-robes. The social phenomenon of 'the withdrawal from the hall' meant that the private rooms became a more and more important part of the house. The hall was still necessary as a court room and for formal entertaining, but its role declined. In particular, its great open fire came to lack appeal, and it was this feature which dictated the hall's height, for the smoke had to find its way up, perhaps through a hood, to a louvre in the roof. Removal of the open fire meant that an open hall was not necessary. Although many grand houses retained it, to give a display of elaborate timber-work in the roof, many had stone or brick chimney stacks built into them.

The first reference to a hall with a chamber over it occurs in the 1380s. Thereafter single-storey halls might be built, or existing open halls might have a ceiling inserted so that the first-floor space could be used for chambers.

The twelfth-century first-floor halls in the urban house-over-warehouse and its rural equivalents had of course had side fire-places not open hearths, and first-floor halls continued to be built, at least in the countryside, throughout the Middle Ages. Their disadvantage was that their width was restricted. A ground-floor hall could be made much wider by using vertical posts inside the room, but such aisle-posts encumber the interior space. This mattered in a house for reasons of prestige, and aisled halls were not built in the south after the end of the fourteenth century.

Another major type of rural building is the barn, an impressive record of the medieval economy. It was one of the few capital expenditures of a landlord, apart from the initial purchase of the estate, or 'assarting'. Most barns that survive are therefore on estates of ecclesiastical institutions, the only landlords with the money for building, and with estates whose produce needed to be collected and stored, eventually to go to the monastery for consumption or to go to market (Plate XXIII). The other major corporate land-owner was the Crown, yet no medieval barns survive on what were royal estates. Their lack is probably a reflection of the inefficiency of the system by which the royal estates were run. The largest barns, like Great Coxwell, Berks., built in the first half of the thirteenth century, involved huge quantities of timber, stone and roof tile (Plate XXIV). The biggest are mostly thirteenth- and fourteenth-century in date, the period of demesne farming. Leased farms required only smaller barns, though the monastery's home farm might still require a fairly large barn, such as the fifteenth-century one beside Titchfield Abbey, Hants., and others were still built on other farms, such as Winchcombe's at Church Enstone, Oxon., uniquely dated by an inscribed stone to AD 1381, a much smaller barn than Great Coxwell. Since the inscription says that it was built at the request of the bailiff, presumably the estate was still being directly farmed by the monastery, not leased out.

It is often a misnomer to call monastic barns 'tithe barns', for the biggest were on estates owned by institutions and used to store the whole of the produce, not just a tenth. 'Tithe barns' were required only where the monastery had the advowson of a parish, that is, the right to appoint its priest, but did not necessarily own the estate. In such cases the priest was paid a salary as vicar but did not receive the tithe, which went to the holder of the advowson. There are a few barns which are true tithe barns, either built by an advowson-holder, or by a rector. There is an interesting group of three in north Oxfordshire, near the Church Enstone barn and probably built at much the same time; Adderbury, Swalcliffe and Upper Heyford were all Winchester estates, the rectories of which William of Wykeham gave to New College in the 1380s, and barns were provided on them for the college. Adderbury has a documentary record of building work done on its barn in the 1420s, but this may refer to alterations, not to a new barn: this is typical of the problems of associating buildings with particular events and records, for some authorities have ascribed the Adderbury barn to the early fifteenth century. Its construction is so like its neighbours', however, that a late fourteenth-century date seems more likely. The New College barns are not typical, and few parishes had such large produce returns that they justified large-scale expenditure on barns by their rectors.

Advowson – holders had to provide a priest's house – a rector had to pay for his own, of course, but had his tithe to do it from. A few priests' houses survive, differing little from lay houses, but often at an interesting intermediate point between a small manor-house and a farm. All had their open hall, a first-floor one in the case of Congresbury, Somerset, where Bishop Beckington's coat-of-arms over the door suggests a date between 1443 and 1464.

Apart from the manor-house, if the lord was resident on the estate, the priest's house was perhaps the only one in a village which might be significantly different from those of the villagers. Excavations occasionally recognize buildings that have some small difference of ground plan or use of material to suggest an interpretation as a small manor, as at Tetsworth, or a priest's house, as at Seacourt (Fig. 24, *a*), but these are few. Villagers' houses begin to survive from the thirteenth century, but cannot be attributed to precise social grades any more than can those found in excavations.

The increasing number of smaller late medieval houses to survive, at least in part, is partly explained by the time factor. It is also, however, attributable to the phenomenon that both rural and urban excavations have revealed, that after the mid thirteenth century new houses were likely to be built on dwarf stone walls which provided a solid, damp-free footing for timber superstructures. These foundations were enough to give timber buildings the potential to survive, and the corollary to that is that it became a sensible investment to build a more durable type of house. Certainly for the poorer peasantry the change meant little, since extra expense was beyond its resources. But for the better-off villeins, and particularly for the tenant farmers who prospered in the land-abundant century after the Black Death's visitations, a well-built house was a possibility. It is not surprising, therefore, that recent evidence is suggesting dates in the second half of the thirteenth century for a few quite small surviving houses, nor is it a mere accident of survival that increasing research is producing more and more examples of fifteenth-century buildings. These were the houses of the first English yeomen.

These smaller houses copied the greater ones in having an open hall with a central hearth. Plans were rectangular, and extra size could be obtained by extending at either end of the hall – both the Radley house (Fig. 32) and the Wealden house at Singleton (Plate XXVI) were probably enlarged in this way. The end blocks might have been two storied, the upper a loft entered by a ladder. Just as excavations have suggested that the long-house (Fig. 24) was obsolete in the south by the end of the thirteenth century, so also do the surviving buildings show no trace of having had animals stabled under the same roof as the farmer, and although no doubt there was minor storage in the end blocks, no barns with loading facilities were attached.

Although tenants prospered, there were still many labourers for whom conditions did not improve sufficiently for their higher wages to be reflected in surviving buildings, One- and two-room insubstantial cots must still have been frequent. Unfortunately, we know little of them, for the sites available for excavation are those that were abandoned in the late Middle Ages. No site has yet produced an unequivocally fifteenth-century labourer's house.

The surviving medieval buildings in a village are likely to be the church, much altered by each generation; perhaps the manor-house, with some medieval features in it, and very occasionally one or two of the buildings of its *curia* – a dovecote, a chapel or traces of a gate-house; a barn may have medieval work in it; the exterior of houses will sometimes show medieval timbers; and the diligent researcher can find more hidden in roofs and attics. But a village is a constantly evolving unit, and despite fond beliefs, the mellow stone walls and the thatched roofs, the dovecote, the mill and the inn, cannot be accepted as medieval unless there is firm archaeological evidence of the antiquity that is often spuriously claimed for them.

Timber-framing

Most medieval buildings had walls with timber frames. Even stone-walled buildings need timber to support the roof, which will weigh many tons if it is slate or tile. Thatch is lighter but has to be supported by a framework that will not give way when there is a heavy layer of winter snow on it. It is snow rather than rain which dictates the need for a steep pitch to a roof, so that the snow will slide off quicker, but an even more important consideration is that the steeper the pitch, the less is the outward thrust exerted on the side walls. The steeper it is, however, the greater is the wind pressure on it. A flatter roof must be sealed with lead, which is heavy and also expensive, thus quickly becoming a status symbol. Its increasing use in the later Middle Ages explains why so many churches had their roofs altered, and often the line of the earlier, steeper gable can be seen against a tower or outlined in a wall.

Church and cathedral roofs have recently been recognized as one of the keys to an understanding of the development of timber roofs generally, for techniques developed in a church might be used elsewhere. The problems were not always the same, however, for a major church's timber roof is often not visible from below, because it is hidden by a stone vault – which is not of course load-bearing. The timbers in a medieval hall would all be exposed, and therefore had to be decorative as well as functional.

The earliest secular timber roofs that survive reasonably complete are in barns. Great Coxwell (Plate xxiv), for example, probably dates to the first half of the thirteenth century: scientific tests and stylistic details agree. It has

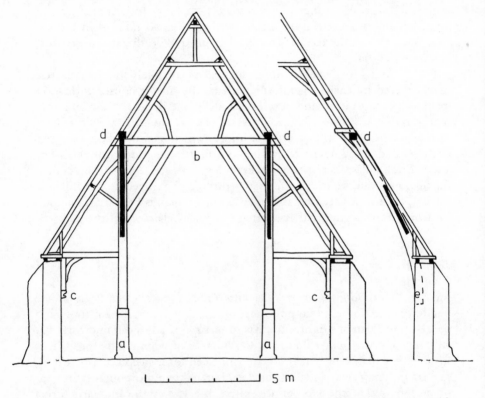

30   The roof construction of the barn at Great Coxwell uses aisle-posts, alternating with base crucks (right) down its length: *a* – aisle-posts; *b* – tie-beam (note that this is not needed in the base-cruck trusses); *c* – stone corbels in the side walls; *d* – collar-plates or -purlins; *e* – curved base-cruck slotting into the stone wall (after Horn and Born).

a church-like plan of nave and side aisles, with a double line of aisle-posts standing on low stone columns (Fig. 30). A tie-beam joins each pair of posts at their tops, about half-way up the roof, and the rest of the roof superstructure is built up from the tie-beams. Already it was being found that the aisle-posts were an inconvenience to carts entering barns, and a second system of timber-framing was also being used at Great Coxwell. Alternating with each pair of aisle-posts were pairs of long, curved timbers called base-crucks; each base-cruck had its foot built into the wall of the barn, its curve formed the angle between wall and roof, and it went up to the same height as the aisle-posts. A length-wise timber, the collar-plate (or collar-purlin – terminologies are various), joined post to cruck. The alternating system gave a wider uncluttered bay inside the barn.

Great Coxwell is an elaborate building, using a sophisticated and carefully thought-out system of roofing. If the earliest surviving roofs are of such calibre, have they evolved from a long tradition of skilled carpentry, or do they indicate a rapid improvement in carpentry techniques, showing that earlier buildings could not have survived because they were not cleverly enough built? Certainly Great Coxwell has features which show uncertainties of construction principles: for instance, the tie-beams are linked to the aisle-posts by two braces where one would have served just as well.

Excavations like that at Portchester have shown that aisled buildings were used from the tenth century onwards (Fig. 19). They were certainly large; but they did not have very long lives. This suggests that they were not very well built, and this is borne out by their ground plans, which show that the bay widths between the pairs of posts are not always identical, as they are in a carefully carpentered 'trussed' building like Great Coxwell or Bradford (Plate XXIII). This raises another question: how skilful were early medieval carpenters in cutting joints?

The study of carpentry joints has been one of the most revealing in recent medieval archaeology. A master carpenter is one who devises a joint which will hold two pieces of timber together so that the joint will resist any strain that is put on it both while the building is in use and while it is being put up. It may have to be complicated because some thrusts will be pulling it apart, others forcing it sideways. The master carpenter will work out precisely what it will have to do and will cut it accordingly: but to save himself time and effort, he will not make it any more complicated that it has to be. A study of joints, based on the ways that they change, may enable fairly close dates to be assigned to the introduction of particular types.

Most of the Great Coxwell joints are mortice-and-tenons. The joints had to be cut into the timbers while they were on the ground and then each in turn had to be lifted into place, slotted into its partner, and the joints secured by wooden pegs. The alternative jointing method is to cut notches or trenches into the beams, so that they will overlap each other (Fig. 31). Overlapping is the only way to add timbers to a standing structure, and may be used also in the initial construction of a building. Its major disadvantages are that it offers little resistance to sideways pressure, and that it needs thick timbers, into which deep trenches and notches can be cut without making them so thin that they are unsafe. Thin timbers are more economical, and allow less cumbersome-looking beams to be used. One of

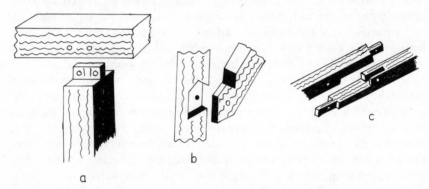

31   Various types of timber joints: *a* – mortice and tenon; *b* – notched lap; *c* – a scarf for joining separate lengths of timber (after Hewett, Currie).

the developments of the thirteenth century appears to be the use of 'uniform scantling' timbers, that is, narrow beams cut lengthwise from a branch or tree to produce perfect pairs. This pairing is an aid to skilled carpentry. Another thirteenth-century development may be the use of purlins to give longitudinal strength. The evidence of twelfth-century church roofs is that they were not used, and this would explain why the post-holes in excavated buildings are so close together, to prevent twisting, which is the purlin's main function.

Surviving timbers from water-logged deposits are not representative of what early medieval carpenters could do. The joints that we know of are from submerged features like well bottoms, which did not need any great skill; ship-building was clearly advanced enough. The Graveney boat and others like it had to have keels made from more than one length of timber, and these had to be joined together by a 'scarf-joint'. Churches like Breamore had timber spires, which are complicated and difficult to put up.

The negative side is, as we have seen, that the pairing of timbers in early building plans does not suggest the mathematical exactitude of trussed framing. Although a carpenter can do much with an adze, an axe, a chisel and a drill, he needs a saw for the fine detailed work of an elaborate mortice-

and-tenon. Although fine saws would have been much in use for cutting bone and wood combs, only two Saxon saw blades have been found, and the carpenters in the Bayeux Tapestry are not shown using them. Their use may have been very limited, as also may that of chisels. Certainly stonework shows that masons generally used finer chisels in the twelfth century than before, and this may have implications for carpentry. Better saws and chisels perhaps became available because better iron was available. It is argued that this accounts for a change observed in iron sword blades: tenth-century and earlier blades were usually 'pattern-welded', made by a technique in which flexibility is achieved by welding strips of iron together. The abandonment of this process, and the use of solid bars instead, without loss of quality, indicates that better iron was available. This technological improvement may have come to affect the quality of carpenters' and masons' tools.

Stonework is also a clue to carpentry techniques in the Saxon period, because stone churches were not very wide. This suggests a distinct limit on timber roofing potential. Timber spires may have been achieved by the use of very thick timbers. The 'receding pyramid' designs suggested for Breamore (Plate XII) and the New Minster could be because timber lengths had to be short, to maintain their strength. It is often said that the decoration on such towers as Earls Barton, Northants., reproduces in stone what was common in timber-work: if this is right, then the stone corbels represent projecting beam ends, and these in turn indicate joists that overlapped wall plates and were not morticed into them.

The cumulative evidence is, therefore, that although Saxon timber buildings were large, they were not particularly well built. The story of St Dunstan who was miraculously saved when the building in which he was sitting collapsed and his colleagues fell to their deaths, is usually taken to show that by the 970s there were first-floor halls in England. It might also be a reflection on the standard of the carpentry involved!

It may well be, therefore, that the thirteenth century was indeed a formative one in carpentry techniques. Lap- and halved-joints were used, but were increasingly replaced by the mortice-and-tenon, with its greater potential for fitting timbers securely together. The great series of late medieval roofs, epitomized in the magnificent engineering involved in the hammer-beam of which the Pilgrims Hall, Winchester, is a fine early example from the first half of the fourteenth century, seems to have resulted from revolutionary changes in carpentry methods.

The quantity of surviving later medieval timber-framing has enabled 'regional schools' of carpentry to be identified: certain forms of construction were only used in certain areas. Differences may be in fairly minor details, such as the style of 'studding' in walls, or it may be fundamental, such as the type of roof truss used. It used to be assumed that these 'schools' reflected age-old geographical distinctions, but it has recently been pointed out that they are probably better seen as a result of increasing provincialism in the later Middle Ages. More money being spent in small quantities by the growing yeoman class meant that carpenters were kept busy building modest houses, and did not travel or come into contact so often with outside ideas. Carpenters employed on barns like Great Coxwell by Beaulieu Abbey might have come from far afield; a farmer building his own barn used his local contact.

The dating of the Great Coxwell barn to the first half of the thirteenth century has been confirmed by recent radio-carbon tests on it. Radio-carbon dating of timbers involves measuring how intensely the carbon-14 in a specimen glows when placed under a nuclear reactor. Since a growing plant takes in carbon-14 until it dies, and thereafter the carbon-14 content fades away at a steady rate, the less it glows, the older it is. A variety of complications makes the method unable to give absolute dates, and even if it could say that a tree was felled on 23 April 1472, it could not say for how long the wood was left to season before it was cut up into beams for a building, nor can it say if the beams have been reused. Fifteenth-century beams often get a second life in a seventeenth-century building. Neverthe-less, some recent radio-carbon dates have coincided closely with dates that were expected on stylistic grounds, or because of documentary evidence, as at Great Coxwell, and the method is giving a very useful objective criterion for dating timber buildings.

The other scientific method, dendrochronology, is still in a very formative stage: it involves counting the number of growth-rings in a piece of timber. In theory, a tree planted in 1875 and felled in 1975 will have 100 growth-rings. A dry season will produce a narrow growth-ring, and an exceptional run of three dry (or wet) summers will therefore show clearly in the timber. Unfortunately, there may have been three successive dry years in East Anglia, but they might not have been dry in Kent. Furthermore, a tree grown in a hedge with a ditch would have received more moisture than one grown in a hillside wood. Sometimes a tree will produce two growth-rings in a single season. So it is very difficult to make comparisons between timbers. The technique has major implications for the study of climate, as well as of buildings.

Radio-carbon tests on two small houses in Berkshire have recently given thirteenth-century dates. Both houses were cruck-built. Whereas a base-cruck, as used at Great Coxwell (Fig. 30) or Bradford (Plate XXIII), reaches only about half-way up the roof, a 'true' cruck goes from the wall right up to the apex (Plate XXV; Fig. 32). It is a type of construction used throughout the Midlands, the north and Wales, and a variant form, the 'jointed-cruck', in which the cruck blade is actually separate timber lengths scarfed together, is common in the west where longer timber was scarce and where stone, not timber-framed gables, were used. It is unknown in eastern England and the dividing line between the cruck and the non-cruck zones is roughly the line between the Hampshire and Sussex Downs. It is similar to the known distribution of long-houses, except for its use in the south and the south Midlands in the fourteenth and fifteenth centuries. As with long-houses, explanations that attempt to use racial distinctions between Celts, Saxons and Scandinavians are inadequate.

Cruck buildings are constructed by assembling the blades, tie-beam and collar-beam on the ground, and then 'rearing' the whole unit into place by heaving it up with ropes rather than assembling it piece by piece. Although in the south mortice-and-tenons were used, elsewhere the principal timbers were halved over each other, and the method does not demand the same care in construction as assembly. Technically, therefore, it could have been used earlier than the thirteenth century. The two north Berkshire thirteenth-century examples both have details which suggest an evolutionary stage of a construction principle, having for instance, two collar-beams where one would have been enough – like the double braces at Great Coxwell. They may have been evolutionary, however, not in the use of crucks but in the application to crucks of the mortice-and-tenon. The use of long, curved principles may have been of great age, although they may not have been properly trussed. Excavation evidence, unfortunately, is unlikely to produce clear-cut answers: the only early building for which crucks have been claimed is a late Roman barn at Latimer, Bucks., but their use there is unlikely, and there is some doubt about whether the post-holes there indicate a building at all! The origin of the cruck construction remains a problem.

The social range of crucks is interesting. They were standard for farm-houses, outbuildings and barns – even in quite grand barns such as the 1381 Church Enstone one and its neighbours, in which they are 'raised' from the ground and built into the wall. Apparently there were never used as far up the social scale as the manor-house, even though base-crucks were used in manorial halls. Nor were they much used in larger towns. They could be found in market-towns – Burford, Thame, Wimborne Minster – and Buckler drew two on the fringes of Oxford. They may not have been used in town centres, partly because they may have been thought crude, partly because of the difficulties of transporting the heavy timbers through a town, and putting them up on a site which was narrow and left little room for manoeuvre. More important, the width and height of a cruck building are both limited by the size of the tree. Crucks cannot be used to construct buildings that have two full storeys, such as were a prerequisite on valuable urban sites. The same restriction did not apply to the Wealden houses (Plate xxvi), although even they were not used in the central areas of towns.

The Wealden house allows more opportunity for display than the cruck; its higher walls and its jettying showed off decorative timber-work. The use of jettying, in which the first-floor joists project beyond the wall of the ground floor giving a larger upper room, was primarily for prestige. Had it been to gain floor space, or to achieve safer joints by relieving strain on the posts, or for weather protection, it would have been used at the backs of buildings, not just at the fronts and the sides; in a few farmhouses, and never elsewhere, it is found at the back, but only where the fronts and sides are also jettied. Jettying demands skilled carpentry and uses a lot of wood, and these factors made Wealden houses relatively more expensive than crucks. Their use in the south-east appears to show the wider spread of wealth in that area, and the greater spending power of its yeomen farmers.

Both cruck houses and Wealdens allowed provision for an open hall, with central hearth (Fig. 32). The hall would be two bays long, and the central truss would therefore have no partition built into it. In cruck halls, a tie-beam at the curve of the blades would have been dangerously low and close to the open fire, and so in the open truss the tie-beam was omitted, and the collar-beam was strengthened by an arch-brace, as in grander buildings. The Wealden had its tie-beam set higher, so the problem did not arise. Either in arch-braced collar, or in crown-post set on tie-beam, the carpenter had to display his talents where they were most visible, as did carpenters working in grander houses. The lesser houses also had their 'screens-passage' at one end of the hall.

Increasing use of chimneys led to the decline of the open hall, and so of the construction types which best provided it. In the south it is unlikely that cruck or Wealden houses were built after the middle of the sixteenth century. Those that survive have invariably had chimneys added to them and a ceiling built across the hall at first-floor level to give upstairs chambers. An interim form of this process occurred in the Yeovil Wealden, in which an upper storey was jettied over the screens passage into the open space of the hall. In many houses only one bay was left open to take the smoke from the hearth, and this 'smoke-bay' tended to become narrower, until it was virtually a central chimney.

The remains of an arch-brace, or a crown-post, the lack of mortices for the studs of a partition, and smoke-blackening (not invariable) are the clues to the previous existence of an open hall in an old house, which are more frequently to be found than is generally realized. Our knowledge of medieval life would be greatly extended if more detailed surveys of standing buildings were undertaken.

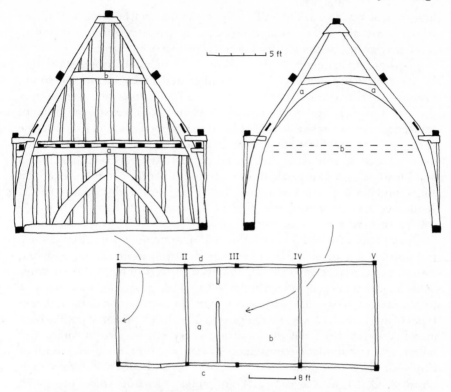

32 Drawings of the cruck trusses and ground plan of a four-bay house at Lower Radley, Berks.: top left – gable truss, I on plan (*a* = tie-beam, *b* = collar-beam); right – open truss over hall, III on plan (*a* = arch-braces below collar-beam; *b* = ceiling inserted in sixteenth century); bottom – plan (*a* = screens passage; *b* = open hall; *c* = front door; *d* = back door).

Building Materials

Both excavations and standing buildings produce information on construction techniques, and on the materials used in the construction. The main building material was, of course, wood, and it is oak beams that survive in buildings today. Chestnut, elm, beech, ash, poplar and sycamore may all have been used: all present problems of warping or beetle-infestation and their use would perhaps have restricted the time and cost worth investing in a building. Unpaired post-holes do not necessarily show that in other, contemporary buildings properly trussed roofs were not used, since untrussed roofs probably continued in less durable woods. Waterlogged deposits at such sites as Portchester with a well bottom, or Hamwic where some pits retain enough moisture to preserve seeds and pollen, show that woods were available but not how they were used.

Occasional documents, such as those from Bicester Priory, show that by the fourteenth century there was imported pinewood in the south, presumably for use in rafters and wall-studs. Most woods were home-grown, however, and there is little evidence to suggest long-distance transportation of timber. It is possible that pedunculate rather than sessile oaks were grown where conditions gave a choice; the former throw off a lot of branches, producing the natural curves required for crucks, braces and for ships' ribs. It is partly this that accounts for the common belief that ships' timbers were used in houses, but there is no truth in the romance. It may be true, however, that timber was used in houses which would otherwise have gone to the shipyards.

Documents such as Bicester's also tell of stone quarrying: local rubble for walls, good quality free-stone brought from more distant quarries, rare stones carted from far away, and even 'hewed stones' from the walls of an abandoned castle fifteen miles away. That quarrying was already a major Saxon industry has been shown from the distribution of the different types of stone in churches and sculptures. The development of the Purbeck marble quarries from the late twelfth century can be seen in tombs and pillars, and in humbler circumstances as mortars, throughout the south of England. The limestone industries of Portland (after the thirteenth century), Quarr, on the Isle of Wight, and of the Cotswolds, prospered despite competition from imported Caen, which could be carved to a finer finish. Granite reached Southampton from the Channel Islands for it has been found in excavations, but there is nothing to show that it went inland. Chalk was quarried where the harder seams of 'clunch' were found, but it was not worth taking very far.

A major Devonshire industry from the twelfth century was the pro-duction of the thin blue slates which are found all along the south coast. They were used on roofs, but also in some cases as damp-coursing in foundations. In towns slate was required as a fire-proof roofing material and was much used in late twelfth-century Southampton, as well as on grander buildings like Portchester Castle. Thin slabs of limestone served the same purpose in Oxford: the famous frost-split stone tiles were not produced until the sixteenth century, but there are quarry-beds from which tiles can be manually produced. It is strange that tiles were required for fire-proofing urban buildings, yet there is no direct evidence of increased use of solid stone walls in the thirteenth century.

The man-made substitute for stone is baked clay, but the availability of stone in the south of England meant that brick made little impression before the late sixteenth century. It was used in a few great houses like Stonor, in the Chilterns, or by the prior at Bicester for his chimney, but was never important, and had not spread any distance down the social scale before it was boosted by the immigrant Huguenots at the end of the sixteenth century. The art of brick- and tile-making was known to the Saxons, and charters not infrequently refer to clay-pits. It may be that some of the 'Roman brick' seen in Saxon church walls is not in fact always a reused material. Odd fragments like those found below Oxford Castle could come from such workings. Since the Saxon word is 'wall-tile', the products were presumably not for use on roofs. Clay roof-tiles were certainly in use by the end of the twelfth century, however.

A major Winchester find has been of Saxon glazed tiles for the decoration of the Old Minster. Although found in a rubble layer, their context suggests that they may have come from the east end of the church, and have decorated the steps of the altar. Glazed tiles of this period have been found in a church at York and there are fragments also from St Albans. The Winchester ones are either plain or have simple geometrical patterns in relief (that is, the pattern stands proud of the surface), and slip was used to give different colours to the background fields.

The Winchester tiles are exceptional, and no further glazed tiles are known until the art was reintroduced from France in the 1220s, under Henry III's patronage. Clarendon Palace, Wilts., had some of the very first tiled floors, in the king's and queen's apartments and in the chapel. Some were glazed and plain, but most had pictures showing the Royal Arms, Richard and Saladin, texts, and floral or geometric designs. These were made by cutting the patterns into a wooden block, stamping the block into a square of red clay, and filling the hollows with white clay. The whole surface was then glazed and the tile fired. One of the Clarendon pavements that has been excavated is circular, 4 m (13 ft) in diameter, made up of ten bands alternately plain and patterned, each band composed of separate short tiles cut to fit the circle.

The difficulty of making a circular pavement is in ensuring that each tile shrinks by a uniform amount in the kiln. Similarly with the patterned tiles there was the risk that the red and the white clays would not shrink by the same amount, so that the white inlay would be unstable. On the whole the French tilers had enough skill in their choice of clays and their firing techniques to avoid these problems.

The tile industry provides a rare opportunity for study of both documentary and archaeological evidence. The pavement in the apartments at Clarendon for Henry's new French queen was paid for in 1252, and has been excavated. It is less elaborate than the circular one, having relatively simple but pleasing designs of lions, griffins, birds and various cross patterns. These designs were copied by English tilers as the fashion for pavements spread. Most were in churches, monasteries and colleges.

The designs in the queen's pavement at Clarendon occur at many west country sites. Clearly the tilers dispersed after the Palace contract was complete, taking their skills and patterns to new markets. Salisbury Cathedral was one of their first. Some of the tilers who had made the circular pavement in the king's chapel must have made the similar circles at Muchelney Abbey, Somerset (Plate XXVII). The patronage of Henry's brother Richard took tilers to his monastic foundation or to the houses that he patronized, like Cleeve in Somerset. In tribute to him, the two-headed eagle from his coat-of-arms, and a shield with chevrons on it (the coat of the de Clare family, of which his first wife was a member) entered the tilers' repertoire, and were to appear in places with which he had no connection – the chevrons of the de Clare coat were easy to cut, which probably explains why they stayed a favourite pattern! The castle of Eleanor of Castile was another that is frequently found. The Richard and Saladin motif became steadily debased into an ordinary mounted knight.

By the late thirteenth century, it is probable that the 'first-generation' French tilers had died and their craft had passed entirely into native hands. These men were less skilful, and did not attempt circles or involved designs. In the south, two 'Wessex' schools have been recognized: the Dorset–Somerset–Wiltshire–Oxfordshire belt being mostly served by designs developed from the more straightforward of the Clarendon tiles, east Hampshire and Sussex looking rather to the work that had been done at Westminster and at Chertsey, Surrey. It is surprising how quickly localization of patterns happened: at Middleton Stoney, a tile fragment was found which I completely failed to recognize, although a more skilled eye at once knew it as part of Queen Eleanor's castle, a common enough design but one that had not previously occurred in Oxfordshire.

Middleton Stoney also produced a few fragments of tile decorated in a way slightly different to the 'inlaid' technique. A very narrow line was impressed into the clay, and not filled with white clay. This 'line-impressed' technique was used in the east and north-west of England and in Northamptonshire, but not south of the Thames. Similarly 'relief' tiles are not found, except at the very end of the period, after the Saxon ones at Winchester, although they were used in East Anglia and the north. 'Mosaic' tile – plain tiles cut to form geometrical patterns – is known in the south at Beaulieu Abbey.

The 'inlaid' products were challenged in the early fourteenth century by a new process which simply involved 'printing' the design onto the red clay tile in a way which is not yet understood. The advantage of the printed tiles was that they were much quicker and therefore cheaper to make; the disadvantage was that they could not be used for finely detailed designs. It is not known where 'printing' was invented, but it was first put into large-scale practice at Penn, in the Chilterns. Vast quantities of tiles, smaller at about 10.5 cm (4½ in.) square than most inlaid ones, were made and distributed along the Thames Valley and down to London, and there can have been few churches without tiled floors. Again, documents help the study of the industry. In 1350, 10,000 tiles for Windsor varied between 4s. and 8s. per 1000 according to quality, carriage added another 10s. or so, and laying probably cost 2s. per 1000 – this was the rate elsewhere.

The Penn industry probably exhausted its market well before the end of the fourteenth century, and many of the tilers dispersed to find commissions on a random basis. Certainly localization is then recognizable in the 'printed' tiles, as it had become in the 'inlaid' tiles, with some groups in the Midlands, some centred in Oxford and some in London. It is doubtful if the Black Death of 1349 and its subsequent outbreaks had much effect in causing this dispersal, since there was generally little more than temporary interruption to building programmes: the tilers' markets were hardly affected, but there is no way of knowing if many of the tilers themselves died. 'Printing' was labour-saving, but it was not introduced because of rising wage costs, since these did not begin until 1350. It is not a process that can be interpreted as a response to demographic forces.

Tiles were also imported. In 1396, Winchester College bought 45,800 tiles from Flanders for £15 5s. 4d., plus 4s. 10d. for unloading costs, and £3 0s. 6d. for carriage from Southampton. These were plain, so took less skill in laying. It is far from clear why the college could not have bought them from William Tyelere, of Otterbourne (a village about five miles south of Winchester), from whom they bought 8000 tiles for £4 in 1396. His tiles were decorated, since white clay had to be dug at Farnham, Surrey, and carted to Otterbourne by Richard Porteur for 18s. 6d. One wonders why William Tyelere lost his market; he was also supplying the cathedral, but was apparently not too proud to make roof-tiles, so he could have made plain floor-tiles. Southampton had a well-established import trade from at least the end of the thirteenth century, supplying such religious houses as Romsey and Salisbury. Low-cost imported tiles, although they were plain not decorated, may have prevented the growth of a low-cost 'printed' industry south of the Thames.

The 'inlaid' tiles had a short-lived renaissance in the Severn valley in the mid fifteenth century, but none of that school's products reached the south. A few tiles were being made for private houses with the family's coats-of-arms, in Wiltshire and Somerset. Well-to-do citizens might have tiled floors in their houses, as chance finds have demonstrated; the remains of a floor with fourteenth-century tiles was found in a private house in Oxford recently. Despite this potential market the trade was effectively operating only on a very small local scale for patching and repairing when it was finally brought to an end by the Reformation.

The floor-tile industry is a classic case-study of a product, introduced as a luxury by foreign and very skilful workers, being taken over by native craftsmen serving a broader market with less expensive and less carefully made goods. A technological change led to factory-style mass-production, but this could not be maintained because of the saturation of a limited market. There was no diversification, so there was no alternative to dispersal and localized production for geographically limited distribution. Medieval economies were not sophisticated enough to allow for capital accumulation to lead to the 'take-off' stage necessary for development beyond a simple primary level. Unfortunately the documents do not reveal enough of the Penn organization to see if the tilers were mainly small independent craftsmen, or labourers paid wages by a capitalist distributor.

At Otterbourne, clay roof-tiles were being made as well as floor-tiles, and there were many such kilns, like the recently excavated one at Naish Hill, Wilts., which produced pottery as well. Roof-tiles had to compete with slates in towns where fire-proofing was required; in the countryside, only the most substantial buildings were not thatched. Wooden shingles were also used. Clay tiles were probably available by the end of the twelfth century, but the evidence is not very specific. Ridge-tiles, however, exhibit a definite typology: the earliest ones are from thirteenth-century levels, and their crests were pinched up by hand, giving an undulating effect. From the end of the thirteenth century, the crests were cut by knives, giving a row of sharp triangular 'teeth'. Ridge-tiles were usually glazed, though this was often so sparse that it had little weather-proofing value and was mainly decorative. Clay roof-tiles were in competition with slates, and so are generally found in areas away from the Cotswolds distribution area, or the coastally distributed Devon (and later Cornish) slates. Ridge-tiles were ubiquitous, because natural slates cannot be used so effectively for crests.

Other clay roof-products were finials: horses' heads, a crowned king or a monk might stare down into the street from a gable end. Similar decoration might serve as louvres: smoke from the open hearth below would pour out of the eyes, ears and mouth of an Oxford head whose tongue poked out at authority (Plate xxvIII). So far, these gew-gaws are only known from town sites; thatched roofs probably did not always have a louvre. An opening for smoke might be left in the apex of the gable wall, but the smoke would find its way out through the thatch anyway. Large clay louvres attached to ridge-tiles, with many holes and finials, have been found to be a much more common urban or grand-building find than had been realized until a recent study identified many of them. Those in the south all have attached finials, unlike ones from further east.

Glass for windows – and for vessels – was an expensive luxury until the Huguenots developed it in the late sixteenth century. A very few fragments, probably imports of the eighth or ninth centuries, have been found at Hamwic: up to 7 mm ($\frac{1}{4}$ in.) thick, with very uneven surfaces and full of air-bubbles, they would have been opaque, but were of attractive colours – the largest piece is a very delicate light blue. This glass was probably made by blowing a cylinder of glass which was placed while still hot and malleable on a sanded surface, cut lengthwise with shears and flattened out. Later the crown-glass technique was used, which involves spinning the glass on the end of a rod so that centrifugal force creates a disc that can be cut to size. Saxon window-glass has yet to be found at Winchester but there is some from the Saxon palace at Old Windsor, and it was made at Glastonbury Abbey, for three furnaces were found in a pre-970 level, with fragments of both window and vessel glass. Wasters were few, however, because waste glass is remelted, 'cullet' being a necessary ingredient in many glass mixes.

Like floor-tile production, Saxon glass industries failed to develop into anything significant. Also like floor-tiles, glass became available again in the thirteenth century, because of Henry III's tastes. Royal accounts contain many references to the glazing of palace windows. 'Stained' glass became more frequent in church buildings also, but most people kept their windows small, barred and shuttered. A window was indeed the 'wind's eye'.

Chapter 8

Towns, Trade and Transport

At a time when more time and money are probably being spent on medieval urban archaeology than on any other archaeological topic, the reasons for undertaking excavations on town sites should be carefully examined. Since we already know what many sorts of later town buildings looked like, there is no point in duplicating the information, especially since excavation rarely presents an unambiguous picture. Unrelated walls, post-holes and hearths are of minimal interest, but it is these which are all that many urban sites provide. Later disturbance has often removed the shallow foundation walls and slots of what were once substantial buildings. One recent site in Oxford was known to contain a major courtyard dwelling, but hardly any trace of it could be located in the excavation.

New Towns and New Problems

The evidence that excavations can give about the development of house types is exemplified in, for instance, the change at Southampton from timber to stone buildings in the late twelfth century, or the use at Winchester of dwarf foundation walls after the mid thirteenth. Winchester has provided the first opportunity to study a large, well-preserved artisan area of poorer-quality housing, industrial buildings, drying-racks, pits, vats, drains, stream-courses and gullies, mostly associated with the dyeing industry – a smelly and unhealthy rabbit-warren of activity.

The expansion and growth of town life in the late Saxon period continued in the early Middle Ages. Increasingly these developments are recorded in documents such as rentals, tax lists, legal and legislative records, and royal, ecclesiastical and secular letters, charters, grants and donations. Physical growth is visible. Development is shown by new suburbs, such as that demonstrated in one of the earliest major urban excavations, in Broad Street, Oxford, in 1936 (*l* on Fig. 6). The pottery found on this site proved a flourishing settlement outside the city ditch from the late twelfth century.

Oxford's ditch and bank, replaced in the 1220s by a wall, had the effect of making a clearly visible distinction between what was inside and outside the town. There is a possibility that there was a market for stock just outside the North Gate, which would explain the great width of the road there. Similarly at Winchester the wall circuit makes extra-mural suburbs easily identifiable. Southampton apparently had no such Saxon boundary, and the establishment of its northern defence after the late twelfth century meant that people who lived north of this new line wanted to move into the enclosed part of the town. Extra-mural tenements were abandoned, and there was corresponding pressure on the southern areas. This can be seen in documentary evidence that more people had houses in previously fairly empty districts, and can be seen archaeologically by developments in the south-western quarter, where stone houses were built over what had formerly been open yards. At the same time, a new side street was laid out. Clearly substantial replanning was effected.

Although no new streets are known to have been constructed, twelfth-century Oxford also saw replanning, with the change in width of Corn-market Street, described in Chapter Three. Powerful interests must have been involved and Oseney Abbey, as the main landlord and builder of the stone cellar found in the 1954–5 excavations, was probably one of them. Boundaries between individual properties fixed in the twelfth century were very stable; Nos 44–6 Cornmarket Street, excavated in 1970, were three properties which had remained the same sizes since they were assessed for tax in 1279, except that No. 44 had then been sub-divided (Fig. 33; *m* on Fig. 6). However, it was shown that this stability was only a phenomenon from the twelfth century onwards, since there were earlier rubbish pits straddling what were to become the property boundaries. Similar results had been obtained in 1954–5 in the Cornmarket, for the twelfth-century stone cellar's vault did not follow the same building lines as earlier pits. In Winchester's artisan quarter, stability was not even maintained in the thirteenth century, for there is physical evidence of sub-division and amalgamation of properties, and even of realignments of lanes and passages. This could rarely be achieved in more substantial areas, for even if landlords were ready to make changes, tenants with legally binding leases would resist them. They were in a much stronger position to uphold their rights, and thus their property boundaries, than customary tenants and villeins in the countryside. Substantial stone buildings would also be a stabilizing influence, since to destroy them would be bad economics.

Despite the Civil War twelfth-century towns generally prospered as landlord investment, attractive rents, stone buildings, growing suburbs, shop development, new parishes, guilds, and burghal communes for self-government, all testify. An archaeological demonstration is the discovery in old Roman towns like Winchester and Chichester that demand for stone

OXFORD   44 · 46 CORNMARKET STREET

1279

N·W W 69   *John de Hanekinton*
N·W W 68   *Nic. Gerdun*
N·W W 67   *Hen. Owen*
N·W W 66   *John de Bedeford*

1772

17´5˝   *Mr. Fell*

8´9˝   *Mr. Thomson*

10´0˝   *Mr. Smewing*

1970

44
45   *Cadena Café*
46

33   The excavator's diagram of the changing ownership of 44–6 Cornmarket Street, Oxford, as revealed by surviving documents at different periods.

was sufficient to justify the effort of digging out the foundations of the Roman buildings, since all the surviving above-ground walls had been pulled down by the thirteenth century. Another witness is the increasing number of towns: not only did existing ones grow but new ones were founded, many by ecclesiastics. The largest and most famous is Bishop Richard Poore's Salisbury, the town founded to serve the cathedral which he moved from Old Sarum in the 1220s (Fig. 34). Old Sarum was not completely abandoned, but the excavations there have not shown how occupation altered because of the new town. The effect on nearby Wilton was very marked. That town was by-passed by traders, and its bailiffs resorted to violence to try to retain them. There was always jealousy between markets that were too closely situated, in Wilton's case with justification.

Salisbury was planned as a grid around a large central market. It was enclosed by a ditch and bank – fourteenth-century attempts to wall it were unsuccessful – and the cathedral occupied a major quarter of the enclosure, later divided off from the town by its own wall and gates to maintain peace and quiet. Salisbury was a commercial success; it had a major church establishment to serve; it was well-placed for road communications, particularly after a new bridge across the Avon was built; it had a prosperous hinterland for which it was a market and distribution centre; and it established industries which carried it through the difficult fourteenth and fifteenth centuries, when older towns like Oxford and Winchester were in decline.

Salisbury's surviving testimony of its medieval history has been sadly maltreated since 1950, with the demolition of many timber-framed buildings. A typical piece of vandalism was the loss of the hall built in his court-yard by John Balle, one of the town's wealthy late fourteenth-century merchants; it had a fine hammerbeam roof with delicate mouldings. Excavations have revealed something of Salisbury's history, which could perhaps not have been found in documentary records. Part of the eastern area of the town seems to have been an 'industrial zone' with metal-workers and potters concentrated in it. It would be interesting to know more about the procedures behind the laying-out of the plots and the first houses on them, but such information is elusive. In another, smaller 'new' medieval town, Thame, Oxon., I have both excavated and back-filled a site in the space of a single Good Friday, for all traces of early levels had been scraped off by an eighteenth-century cottage floor! This situation is likely to be typical of the new towns, certainly the small ones, for they did not have the length and intensity of occupation which causes a build-up of levels, and the consequent protection of at least parts of the earliest, which can make the archaeology of sites in Oxford, Winchester or Southampton rewarding.

Thame, like Salisbury, was an episcopal foundation, probably though

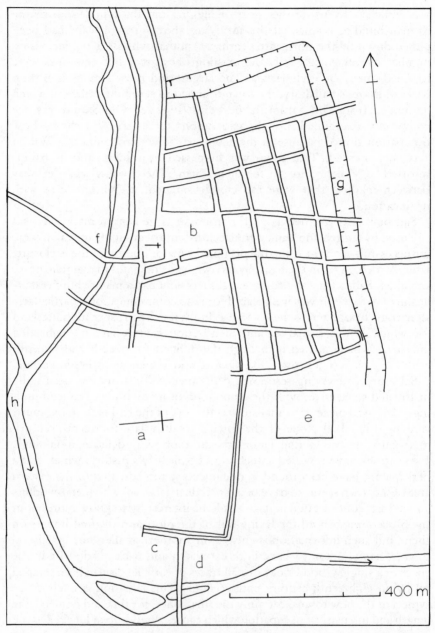

34   Ground plan of Salisbury, a new town of the early thirteenth century: *a* – cathedral and precinct; *b* – market-place; *c* – site of college; *d* – hospital; *e* – Franciscan friary; *f* – Dominican friary; *g* – town ditch; *h* – River Avon.

not certainly set up by Bishop Alexander of Lincoln in the 1120–40s. The original village of Thame, an estate owned by the bishopric, was presumably centred on the church (Fig. 35). The new town was grafted onto this existing settlement by laying out a long, wide market-place, and dividing up the ground on both sides into 'burgage plots', each with a narrow frontage onto the market and a long yard reaching to a back lane. The profit to the bishop was the rent from these plots and the tolls paid by those coming to the weekly market or the annual fair. The bishop had to buy licences from the king for these. To increase the traffic passing through the town, a later bishop diverted the main road so that it ran into the market square. Thame was a success, and in the early thirteenth century the bishop rented out the central space of the market for permanent stalls because of the high rents he was offered. All these features survive in the modern topography, and they are typical of small planted towns like those of the bishop of Winchester – Downton, Alresford, Yarmouth (Isle of Wight), Witney – and of other land-owners, not necessarily ecclesiastics. Henry II

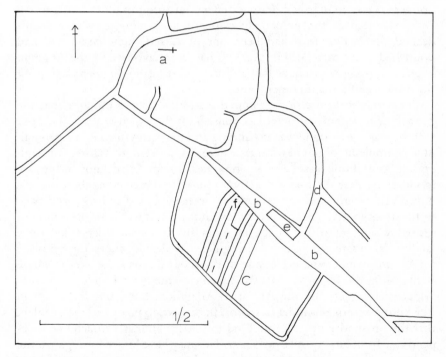

35   Thame, Oxon: *a* – the church; *b* – market-place; *c* – line of some of the surviving burgage plots; *d* – diverted road; *e* – thirteenth-century encroachment in market-place; *f* – site of 1973 excavation.

encouraged the growth of Woodstock, for instance, so that his court would have somewhere to stay when he was at the palace, and Richard I fostered Portsmouth because bigger ships could not reach Portchester harbour.

Existing settlements with markets were often replanned in the Middle Ages, and only archaeology can then reveal if the market-place visible in the modern topography is in fact the original one. Places like Great Bedwyn may well have had earlier centres than the present ones. Many existing centres had large new additions set out on mathematical lines. Wimborne, Dorset, had two, each made by a different landlord. The one on the south of the town was not successful, and is now an open field. Excavations on this very interesting site should have been able to reveal a sequence of twelfth- to fourteenth-century structures, but they failed, a demonstration of the importance of systematic, long-term excavation on such sites, as at Lower Brook Street, Winchester.

The development of markets depended on many factors, but most important was the hinterland that the market could serve and ease of access to it. The diversion of roads was a standard practice, as was the building of bridges. These could have a dramatic effect: the bridge built at Abingdon in 1416 was seen as the immediate cause of its neighbour Wallingford's decline, yet Wallingford had been one of Alfred's new *burhs*, and had flourished in the early Middle Ages; it had been favoured by the Angevin kings, and is known to have had at least one 'stone house', demonstrating the presence of a wealthy merchant.

Trade was seen in strictly competitive terms. It was thought that the growth of prosperity of one place must be at the expense of another, not that the volume of trade was expanding and that growth could be general. Many complaints about new centres were exaggerated, therefore, although not all, as Wilton's case shows. Some new towns failed, mostly the late foundations after the boom was over, but not all thrived as their owners hoped. To avoid clashes, rival markets were supposed to be six and two-thirds miles apart; in practice very few in the south were. Markets did not 'grow' where there were gaps in the system, for they depended on a landlord's initiative. It is an amusing game to decide where a good place for a town would have been; one of my own choices is Lewknor, where traffic using the Icknield Way crosses one of the main London–Oxford–Gloucester routes. But the Abbot of Abingdon, the main landowner in Lewknor, was not a founder of towns. In his own town he had the problem that the prosperity of its market led to violent attempts to achieve independence from him by the townsmen. This may have biased him against the town-founding activities of the bishops of Lincoln or Winchester. Villagers did not necessarily go to the nearest market: Abingdon was the market to which men are recorded as going from Cuxham long before 1416, although

Wallingford was closer, and many of them had to go much further afield on carting services. The nearest market was not the limit of a man's horizons.

A few of the new towns developed industries, but most depended entirely on their market role. Apart from small-scale production of articles needed locally – clothes, shoes, buckles, trinkets – little was manufactured in them. Their economic lives hinged on the activity in their market triangle or square, in which the market cross gave the blessing of the church to the transactions effected at its foot. Such crosses might be simple columns with heads carved with religious scenes, as at Ludgershall in Wiltshire, or more elaborate enclosed structures with tiered steps, like Witney's. Although the size of the population of many new towns might be no bigger than that of many villages, they were clearly differentiated, both by their appearance and by the occupations of their inhabitants. Surviving documents from such towns as Fairford, Glos., or Titchfield, Hants., show that those who held properties in them were in trade, almost none in agriculture.

Although Salisbury was set up as a town to serve the cathedral, most new towns were initiated with no such service role in mind. The presence of an early monastic house had often led to the development of a market-town, as had happened at Abingdon with its 'ten traders outside the gates' recorded in Domesday. Similarly the presence of castles had led to towns developing at Windsor and perhaps Corfe. Some castles continued to provide opportunities for urban settlements, as belatedly at Portchester or, eventually unsuccessfully, at Middleton Stoney; Woodstock served the palace; but very few church foundations of the twelfth and thirteenth centuries led to new towns. In some cases, as with the Cistercians, such a thing was specifically forbidden. A different case were the friars, who came to preach, not to retire from the world. Their houses were therefore in centres of population, not on isolated sites. The presence of a friary may be used as a test of the way in which an existing town was flourishing. In Oxford, the Black friars (*j* on Fig. 6) could not afford a large enough site within the town and had to use most unsuitable ground outside it. The Grey friars (*i* on Fig. 6) were given a special licence to build across the city wall, though their cloisters were outside the boundary. In Southampton (*F* on Fig. 2), the Franciscans were inside the town, but in the south-west corner, the least expensive land in the town. Next door to it was a hospital for the old, sick and infirm, known as God's House. The location of institutions such as these is also a clue to the size of a town at the time of their foundation. A leper hospital would, of course, be well outside the town's boundaries.

The major industry on which England's expanding towns depended was that associated with wool production. Much of the wool left in an unfinished state, increasingly during the twelfth century for Flanders and

Italy, where great industrial centres developed, and whose best products could under-sell English ones. This resulted partly from the replacement of the vertical loom by the horizontal which was much more productive but, since it involved a treadle, was a piece of industrial plant and might limit the weaving activities of part-time peasant producers. The vertical loom's steady replacement is shown by the absence from the archaeological record of the clay loom-weights and bone pin-beaters which were used with it.

Just as the weaving process changed during the twelfth and thirteenth centuries, so did 'fulling', which is the next stage in cloth production. English records from the end of the twelfth century show the introduction of water-driven fulling mills, the earliest being monastic investments. The new mills required fast streams, and so were likely to be built in the countryside. They were likely to draw weavers away from towns to the new sites, more than countering the 'industrializing' effect of the new looms, which would have favoured urban production.

It is impossible to be sure how much justification there was in complaints about this drawing away of weavers, but it certainly often happened. The effects of such developments varied from place to place: in Oxford, it seems to have caused a rapid decline. Winchester had mills of its own, but lost trade nevertheless: the Brook Street dyeing industry went by the end of the fourteenth century. Salisbury on the other hand managed to set itself up as a cloth-making centre, as did smaller places like Newbury, Witney or Romsey. Southampton never had the industry, although so many of its products passed through the port, because it lacked streams to provide water and water-power.

In many areas, rural industries flourished remarkably independently of towns. Generally, their products were coarser than the towns', and so were cheaper. They were not therefore in direct competition with the Flemish cloths, but they were not worth exporting, at least until the Flemish industries collapsed because of the fourteenth-century wars, which provided new opportunities for towns like Salisbury. The north Berkshire area was one of the most prosperous in England in the early fourteenth century, as the number of medieval houses there still shows. But its prosperity had little direct benefit for nearby Wallingford and Abingdon, nor were new towns established to act as new markets for it, as they would surely have been in the twelfth or thirteenth centuries.

The fluctuations of the medieval economy are difficult to measure, and can rarely be seen as having direct and immediate physical consequences. The decay of towns in the fifteenth century is a general reflection of poor trade conditions, especially between 1440 and 1470, but it is very difficult to assess the individual impact of the very many fourteenth-century developments: decline of wool exports, changes and increase in cloth production, wars and overseas losses, and population fall. The relative importance of these different factors in each individual town is impossible to assess.

Some towns were certainly in decay in the second half of the thirteenth century. Winchester was badly hit, and excavations in the prosperous western areas of the town have shown that they were already being abandoned. This was partly a special case, caused by the withdrawal from the town of the royal Exchequer and the Treasury in the 1180s. Fewer coins were minted there also. In Oxford, falling property values meant that founders of colleges for the university could afford to buy the sites of what had previously been houses. The earliest colleges are extra-mural or very small. Merton, however, was built in the 1270s on the site of a dozen houses, just inside the walls (*n* on Fig. 6). Oriel, in the 1320s, was on a site closer to the centre, and swallowed up seventeen house sites (*o* on Fig. 6). New College (*p*) in the 1370s used over thirty houses but was rather further out. All Souls, however, (*q*) was able to establish itself in 1438 right along a substantial part of the frontage of one of the main streets. This dramatic encroachment contrasts with what had happened to the two large friars' houses in the first half of the thirteenth century, for they had had to be built across and well beyond the walls, on very unsuitable land (*i* and *j*). Yet a century later, much of the Broad Street suburb on the north of the town (*l*) excavated in 1936 was being abandoned for want of population; the pottery sequence comes to an end in the fourteenth century.

If the hypothesis that the university grew at Oxford because the decline of the town commercially meant that students could afford to live in it, then the failure of Salisbury to become a university town may have had the same cause. A very successful college was established in 1262, and could easily have developed into a rival to Oxford (Fig. 34). Salisbury's success with its cloth production kept its rents high, however.

The declining fortunes of towns are shown by abandoned suburbs, new markets that failed to get established, empty properties, static or falling rents, parishes amalgamated for lack of population, lower taxation returns and the vociferous complaints of the townsmen. Individual cases had different causes, however. In Winchester and Oxford, the cloth trade was blamed. At Wareham, it was because Poole took over the trade of that part of Dorset.

As an agricultural market, Wareham had only a limited hinterland because of the barren heaths north and south of it (cf. Fig. 21). It was just too far from the Purbecks to take advantage of the expanding output of the quarries; instead, the stone was shipped out of various small harbours closer to the hills. It is interesting that the industry was not big enough to establish any one place as a major centre. Corfe, the market town for the area, was never more than a small settlement round a triangular market-place at the foot of the castle (Plate XVI). An attempt to set up a new town at Ower in the Purbecks failed – throughout Europe, mining industries failed to spawn towns. Similarly Dorset's agriculture was not enough to make for much trade: its sheep were numerous, but their wool was the least valuable in the south of England. The northern part of the county traded out through Salisbury, but was not enough to make more than small towns out of Shaftesbury or Blandford.

Roads and Rivers

The decline of Wareham has always been attributed to the use of bigger ships which were unable to get up the narrow river to reach it. Another possibility is that the river was changing as much as the ships, with rubbish from the town fouling the stream, fishnets impeding navigation, but perhaps most important of all, increasing numbers of water-mills upstream reducing its flow, so that the channel did not get scoured by flood-waters which were now held back in the mill-pools.

A similar hypothesis has recently been proposed to explain the decline of Oxford. The suggestion is that navigation up the River Thames became impossible, and that this choked the town's trade and cost it much more dearly than any movement out of the town by its weavers. Documents show that in the late Saxon period navigation on the Thames was sufficient to justify the Abbot of Abingdon in digging a new and better channel, and boats paid a substantial toll to use it. Perhaps the large numbers of water-mills and their attendant weirs, for which Old Windsor and Domesday Book are evidence, were aiding rather than impeding the Thames navigation, since they controlled the water flow, caused deeper channels and prevented the river running dry in summer. Archaeologically, excavations in Oxford show that the Thames flowed through many small streams, but became increasingly concentrated into bigger channels. This was partly caused by new bridges, whose cut-waters acted as dams, and would cause flooding if deep channels were not made upstream of them.

Some mills and their attendant weirs were desirable; too many were disastrous, and the thirteenth century added fulling-mills to the grain-mills. So important was the problem that even Magna Carta had a clause to deal with it, but neither that nor subsequent legislation was enough. At least by the fourteenth century, goods from Oxford are recorded as being carted either all the way to London, or carted to Henley and loaded onto barges for the second part of the journey. The extra expense of transport could have made trade prohibitive.

This argument can be sustained only if it can be proved that cost differences between carting and boating were very great, so that loss of use of the latter would be economically ruinous. The evidence is not there, however. Figures are not exact, and are mostly for dates later than those required. But boats could not carry all that much more than carts, and although they might be quicker going downstream, they were probably very slow going up, despite improvements to the water flow, in a river like the Thames with a steep fall. Boats involved more capital investment, and a sunk cargo was ruined, whereas almost everything could be salvaged from a cart that tipped over. There was also the risk of drowning. A boat might have less to fear from robbers, but nevertheless there were planty of places where it could be held up, and the thieves' reward was greater. Towns in the east, like Boston, Lynn, Norwich, Lincoln, Hull and York, depended heavily on river and canal systems, as Bristol depended on the Severn and Avon. In the south, the network was lacking. Nor were roads necessarily as bad in the Middle Ages as in the seventeenth and eighteenth centuries. Medieval travellers rarely used coaches, which were uncomfortable and regarded as unmanly, and it is coaches which are destructive of road surfaces because they require narrow wheels to give a better-sprung ride. Broad-wheeled carts do not cut deep ruts into unmetalled roads, and although there are occasional documentary references, it seems that wheels were very rarely iron-clad, and this would have reduced the damage that they caused. Excavations have not produced any identifiable iron tyres, though some nails with big, domed heads may have been strake-nails for wheels. Unfortunately it is almost impossible to separate these from large door-nails (Fig. 25).

Apart from the Thames there are no rivers in the south that are navigable for more than a few miles, and many new towns, like Salisbury, prospered although they could not be reached by boat. Southampton had two rivers leading into its hinterland, but the Test probably did not even get boats as far as Romsey, (although a recent (March 1976) find may disprove this statement), and the Itchen to Winchester is not recorded as having played any part in the town's trade. One bishop attempted to improve its navigation at the beginning of the thirteenth century, and intended his new town upstream of Winchester at Alresford to act as an entrepôt where goods for London would be unloaded, to go the rest of the way by land. There is nothing to suggest that this was effective, however, and within a century the bishop was himself petitioning against improvement of navigation on the river, because it would have involved destroying his mills. The loss of water carriage did not prevent Alresford from being one of the country's ten largest wool-collecting centres in the fourteenth century, with a thriving cloth production. It might be argued that the decay of the western part of Winchester was because people were drawn to the riverside, but there is no proof of this, and no evidence that there were wharves there, only that the river was divided into several streams to supply various different properties. There is no record of the annual St Giles fair outside Winchester being accessible to cargoes brought up the Itchen by barge.

Southampton did of course have a very extensive coastal trade: slates and stones were part of it, and grain from Sussex is known to have been important. Some ships went to London, others to more local ports. Unfortunately the documents only tell of goods leaving the town by road, but it is reckoned that this was at least 50 per cent of the trade. Carts regularly went as far as Coventry, and pack-horses even reached the Lake District.

Roads were important in the Anglo-Saxon period: charters frequently refer to them as boundaries, a network of saltways stretched out from Cheshire to royal estates like Bampton, and an eleventh-century law gave special royal protection to four roads, including the Wiltshire/Berkshire/Chilterns ridgeway, the Icknield Way. Is it coincidence that a large early eighth-century hoard of sceattas was found recently alongside the Way? Certainly the distribution map of the sceattas shows that merchants used the land (Fig. 7), and that the Southampton–Oxford route was important. Oxford's growth was because it was a good crossing-point of the Thames, superseding the old one at Dorchester because Silchester had been abandoned, making the old Roman north-south road obsolete. Late Saxon pottery shows that Oxford's links were also strong with the area to the north-east of it, and later documents record the importance to it of Stourbridge fair, outside Cambridge. There is no river-link from Oxford to the north-east. Although the documents tell of boats on the Thames, access to London was not Oxford's main early medieval *raison d'être*.

If the loss of the Thames as a highway during the thirteenth century was so disastrous, the later Middle Ages should have seen fewer contacts with the capital city. Instead, London's economic and administrative role was growing, its relative importance in the kingdom generally becoming greater. After the 1180s, the Treasury and the Exchequer were at Westminster, not Winchester. Parliamentary attendance took men there who would not previously have had to leave their own shires. The number of mints steadily declined, and the new coinage of 1279 was nearly all struck in London, with small outputs at Canterbury, Bristol and York. There were occasional additions to and deletions from this list, but only Reading in the south struck any later medieval coins, and then only for a short period in the mid fourteenth century. London merchants played an active role in provincial trade: they owned property in Salisbury, used Southampton as their out-port, gained monopolies by making loans to the king, and seem to have been more rather than less in evidence in the Upper Thames Valley, especially since by the fourteenth century the era of the great fairs was over, and there was more direct marketing. Of the four roads given royal protection in the eleventh century, two were not connected with London whereas the fourteenth-century Gough map shows London as the centre of a network of roads.

Another guide to the increasing use of roads is the building of bridges. It has been said that the Romans were content with fords because their men and their goods travelled on horses which could wade through rivers. Use of carts in the Middle Ages made bridges necessary. The effect of new bridges has already been seen at Salisbury and Abingdon, and the consequent decline of Wilton and Wallingford respectively; in 1429 the bridge at the latter was described as ruinous, and ten years later the town's eleven parishes were amalgamated into four 'because many burgesses have departed'. Local villages were also affected: Harwell, for instance, no longer had traffic through it, and retired into isolation. This is a major reason for the large number of fourteenth-century buildings that survive in it. As so often, the needs of later traffic have caused rebuilding of Wallingford's bridge, but its westernmost arch retains medieval masonry, with strong stone ribs holding up a barrel vault. Other bridges had stone piers but a timber superstructure: there were even timber towers on Wallingford in 1153. In Gloucester, a recent excavation has enabled a complete sequence of the bridge over the Severn to be established, but this has not been done for any southern bridge. Occasional bridges survive: the earliest documented record of a bridge over the Thames at Radcot occurs in 1209, and there is still a bridge there which is certainly medieval, if not the original one.

The main bridge over the Thames at Oxford was attributed to the first Norman governor, Robert d'Oilli, in later centuries, but there may have been at least a timber one there previously. The medieval stone bridge was a causeway of forty-two arches, its great length necessary to cross the many channels of the river – the bridge itself being a factor in the creation of fewer and deeper channels thereafter. Bridges were not new to the country in the eleventh century, for bridge building had been one of the estate holder's compulsory duties since at least the eighth century. Presumably the Norman reputation for bridge building was largely the result of the replacement of timber by stone. When the Viking Olaf destroyed London bridge in 1009, he did it by pulling down the piles so presumably they were wooden. Medieval records of maintenance by bridge-guilds, by groups of parishes, by 'hermits' who took the tolls, by estate owners, by local religious houses or by charitable foundations are numerous, and a testimony to the importance of safe, dry crossings.

Traders were frequent travellers, but their direct archaeological record is not great. Weights, used on steelyard balances like the ones found at Huish and Tetsworth (Fig. 39), are not infrequent, but the Huish example suggests that they may not have been exclusively used by merchants. Many seal dies are known, but very few from recorded find-spots. The lead seals used on bales of cloth, potentially so informative, have almost all decayed to illegibility and are of no help. Roads and rivers were used by everyone from the king downwards, however, not just by merchants; the royal itineraries show that enormous distances could be covered in short periods. The king's agents, his sheriffs, judges and messengers, were constantly on the move. Frequent finds of Papal bulls show how ecclesiastical messages were always being passed. Increasing numbers of pilgrims were a growing source of profit to saints' shrines: many monasteries attempted to take advantage of this devotion by encouraging new cults, of which there were many in the later twelfth century, from Glastonbury's Arthur to Bicester's St Edburg, whose superb early fourteenth-century Purbeck marble shrine survives in the church at Stanton Harcourt. Large numbers of pilgrims' pewter badges are found, a record of the visits made to various holy places – King Edward's tomb at Shaftesbury was popular in the west. One found recently in excavations at Portchester had been the property of a pilgrim who had been to the shrine of Our Lady, at Walsingham, Norfolk. The earliest road map, the fourteenth-century Gough map, was probably compiled for ecclesiastical use, showing routes between institutions. This accounts for its omission of known routes such as that from Southampton to Oxford. It includes rivers and streams, not because they were navigable but as land-marks, and also presumably to show where they could be crossed. Another of the earliest known travellers' guides is an itinerary compiled at Titchfield Abbey, for the use of Premonstratensian houses.

Other travellers included landlords' stewards visiting distant estates. Reeves had to travel long distances to purchase stock – the reeve from Cuxham in Oxfordshire went as far as Winchcombe, Glos., to buy horses. Drovers moved large flocks over long distances, occasionally to market, more often between estates. Tenants owed carting services, which took them on journeys for their lord beyond the local market: the Cuxham tenants often had to go across the Chilterns to Henley, for instance, to collect mill-stones or similar things which came that far up the Thames on boats. It was a peasant's cart that carried the corpse of William Rufus from the New Forest to Winchester – proof that eleventh-century peasants had carts, as manuscript drawings suggest.

England was relatively a very stable country, and although there were robbers, and occasional civil wars, it was probably safer for travellers than any other in Europe. It was only in the early Anglo-Saxon settlement period that men avoided roads, the *here* (= army)-*path*, because of marauding

war-bands, and built their homes well away from them – another reason
why so many of the medieval 'new towns', sited on roads, were at some
distance from their 'mother village'. Medieval roads were both more
useable and more used than is often realized. They were not, however, the
straight, paved, narrow highways of the Roman period. Only in towns
were they surfaced, and when rain and traffic turned some patches into
bogs, travellers skirted round them, making the road wider. Several
alternative tracks would go up steep hills. Nor were the roads straight.
They meandered to stay on the best-drained land, and they led from market-
town to market-town. Much more perhaps than Roman roads, they were
communications links and the travellers on them brought not only goods
but also information. Although there was much provincialism, there was
no isolation.

Bones, Butchery and Breeding

Despite roads, bigger towns were dependent on the villages round them
for some of their immediate food supplies, since journeys were too slow to
allow for long-distance transport of perishables. It is surprising to find that
butter was a commodity that was widely traded but milk, meat and fresh
fish had to come from local sources. Salt was a major coastal industry,
largely for the salting of meat and fish so that it could be stored and, in the
case of fish, transported; salt-pans can be seen round the New Forest coast,
for example, but imported salt was increasingly used. How far this had a
direct effect on any salt-producing settlements cannot be adequately
measured, but it certainly still continued in places like Titchfield.

Sea-fishing was also an industry at Titchfield, and one which is very
difficult to investigate archaeologically. A substantial by-product of
milling was the fresh-water fish and eels caught in the weirs, and documents
show that catches were in their thousands each year. Fish-ponds at most
monasteries and many other sites can still be seen, though it is often very
difficult to date them. A recent excavation on one at Thame showed that it
was probably post-medieval, not part of the medieval manorial estate as
had been thought. Most villages had streams that provided fish.

Fish therefore provided a substantial vitamin content in medieval diet –
at least for part of the population. Was it too expensive for the poor, and
eaten only by the wealthy, yet another manorial perquisite? This question
may one day be answered by archaeology, but unfortunately it is difficult
to recover fish remains on excavations. Fish-bones are usually too slight to
survive long in the soil, and although excavators are increasingly sieving
material from their sites and recovering much larger quantities of data as a
result, only the bigger fish have bones that can be expected not to have

187

decayed and disappeared. Cod-sized bones have been found at Wharram Percy in Yorkshire, but not in large quantities, and the availability of sea-fish in inland villages may have been sporadic. At Tetsworth, sieving of certain deposits only produced two fish-bones – yet the finesse of recovery was such that three frogs' bones were found. Southampton, although a sea town, has so far produced only eleven fish-bones!

It is highly unlikely that it will ever be possible to talk in terms of species, quantities and ratios about fish-bones. There is a hint of what was happening to be gleaned from the more durable shells of edible molluscs. At Tetsworth, only one fragment, of a cockle, was found. At Seacourt, there were a few oyster fragments, and others that were indeterminate. In Oxford, returns from specimen pits have produced much higher ratios of oyster-shells to animal bones than did the two rural sites – twenty-four upper shells and twenty-eight lower shells in a fourteenth-century pit that had only ninety-five bone and rib fragments, for example. It might be possible to argue from this that, except close to the coast, townsfolk were more likely to be eating marine shell-fish in quantity – and therefore by inference other sea-fish also – than villagers in the town's hinterland. It would hardly be possible to extend this argument to fresh-water fish and eels, however.

A diet that included fish was likely to be more varied and better-balanced than one which was only grain- and meat-based. It is still too soon to say much about bone evidence: many reports only show the presence or absence of species and give no clue to the potential meat contribution of the bone. The Tetsworth bones showed a selection of the best cuts of meats and were one of the clues to the relatively high status of the site's owners. An interesting rubbish pit from Romsey had a remarkably high quantity of fowl bones, suggesting a rich household or possibly a specialist producer. In Southampton, specialist butchery was being practised in the thirteenth century, but not in the twelfth. In the wealthy part of the town, later pits produced only the remains of the best joints instead of whole carcasses, as well as a wider range of small animals such as rabbit, poultry and wild fowl, and more of the young and tender meats, like veal and sucking-pig. Similar butchery, with bones cut for roasting and stewing, is suggested in the Oxford fourteenth-century pit.

Butchery and the selection of joints help to show the economy of the countryside that supplied the towns with their meat, from beasts killed while still young and therefore bred for their food value, or killed – or eaten when dead – after a long life providing wool or pulling carts and ploughs. From villages in the south, bone results are not suggestive of deliberate large-scale breeding solely for one purpose or the other, but suggest rather a mixed, non-specialist economy. In general, this is consistent with documentary evidence, but not entirely. One of Glastonbury

Abbey's estates in Dorset had no pigs, for instance, and another specialized in sheep. Such records are only of the demesne farms, however. The stock kept by the peasants on those estates may have been much more varied, so that the bones would be a more accurate record of the meat actually available there. Meat is not in any case the only product of dead animals: their hides make the tanning of leather a major industry, and every big town had its cordwainers' (shoe-makers') district. Bones were a product to be used – not just for glue but for small objects like combs, needles, pins and gaming-counters, which are common finds in the early medieval period (Fig. 3). Occasional curiosities are found: Southampton yielded a high concentration of cat bones, perhaps suggesting skinning for smart coats, a practice not unknown to-day, or an indication of the need to keep down the number of rats in the warehouses. Foxes were being bred at the royal castle at Ludgershall.

Bone evidence is some of the most difficult in archaeology. Species recognition, and bone weight:meat weight ratios are two of the problems; the date of the bones is another. It is wrong to assume that the whole contents of a fourteenth-century rubbish pit will be products of that century. Constant turning-over of urban gardens meant that pits were always partly back-filled with rubbish that had been thrown out by previous generations. The pit at Oxford with the fifty-two oyster shells must have been filled in the fourteenth century, because at its bottom were two fairly complete jugs of that date; but it also contained pottery of the twelfth and thirteenth centuries. The pots can mostly be sorted into their centuries, but not the bones. Were the oysters specifically twelfth, thirteenth, or four-teenth century, or were they spread over all three? Their dating does not affect the general argument, but the fluctuations in the supply of oysters to medieval Oxford cannot be gauged.

It is not often possible, therefore, to be precise about the dates of the contents of the rubbish pits and wells which are found on all urban, though not rural, sites, unless the pottery all belongs to a particular period, or there is particularly good stratigraphic evidence. This severely limits the value of the most frequently collected form of data, for the bottoms of pits will survive even when all the upper archaeological layers on a site have been lost. All the environmental information suffers from this disadvantage; the recognition of grains has little value if the crops grown locally are already known and there are few plants whose seeds are informative about the immediate area in which they were found. Nettles and fat-hen, for instance, might seem to be weeds showing uncultivated empty plots, but since the former were used in tanning and the latter were acceptable vegetables, they may just as well have been deliberately grown or may have been brought to the site from some distance away.

The rubbish pits and wells are a record of urban conditions which show how easily infections and diseases could spread. Analysis of parasites' eggs from a Winchester pit produced a blood-curdling array. There is some evidence of efforts to keep the pits separate from the wells on each site, but foul water must have seeped in nevertheless. In most towns, it is easy enough to dig wells deep enough for their purpose: a few towns were on solid rock or chalk, but most lay on gravel, sand and other easily worked subsoils. Wells dug into these would soon collapse if unsupported, and often a central shaft is found showing that there had been some form of timber or wattle-lining: an old barrel was probably often used. When this collapsed, or the well became too foul to clean out, it was used as a rubbish and latrine pit until it was full. Some of the sherds found in it may have been an uncomfortable predecessor of lavatory paper. Rubbish pits with unmortared stone linings are sometimes found in wealthy districts, in Southampton, for instance. The fourteenth-century pit in Oxford was one of the very few in the town that was stone-lined, and there is no clue as to why it should have been treated differently from its dozens of earlier and later neighbours. Stone-lined pits were presumably regularly cleaned out, and had a much longer life. Some may have begun their lives as cool places for storage.

One of the Southampton pits contained a seal-die that had been cast for one of the town's wealthy late thirteenth-century burgesses, Richard of Southwick. The other contents included fine imported pottery and glass, pewter, tally-sticks used in counting-houses, fine leather goods and shoes, weapons and ornaments. Someone had kept a pet African monkey, for its bones were there. Other bones showed a wide choice of diet, and seeds included figs as well as native fruits. A building collapsed over this pit, so it was not emptied out, and its contents were securely sealed. The ascription of them all to one individual's household has been criticized since rubbish can so easily get mixed, but they do indicate the standards of luxury of rich Southampton merchants with far-reaching commercial contacts.

It is unfortunate that small mammal bones are as difficult to recover as fish-bones, for it would be valuable to have more information about rats and mice in medieval England. It is said, for instance, that the black rat is a town-dweller and certainly only one of the Tetsworth deposits produced any of its bones; unfortunately the rat is a burrower, like the rabbit, so its bones can get into a pit long after the pit had been filled up. On the other hand, the storage of seed-grain in pits seems to have stopped at least by the end of the twelfth century: there are a few pits, at Wareham for instance, which may have served this purpose, but rural sites like Chalton so far lack them. Recent tests have shown that germination from such pits is greater than from grains stored in barns. Were storage pits abandoned because of increasing numbers of burrowing vermin? There seems to be an increase in the use of large pottery storage-vessels in the same general period, which may have been a response to new needs for vermin-proof storage. This problem is one that more work on bones may answer, and it is important to solve it because of the light it will throw on a major feature of medieval agriculture, low returns from high sowing rates, as well as on health hazards. Was the Black Death caused by a plague among the rat population, causing fleas to find new hosts, or was it caused by a new strain of flea or germ, or by a sudden insurge of rats? Certainly it would be useful to know if there were significantly more rats in fourteenth-century England. Medieval towns must have been ideal breeding grounds for them, with their open cess-pits and water-courses.

Timber-framed houses, even those on dwarf walls, offer little resistance to rat penetration. Stone buildings are better, but there were few enough of these. There is some evidence, though, that those who lived in them were more likely to survive. The Black Death mortality rates among most social classes are unknown, and it is not possible to tell if the wealthy merchants, for instance, suffered less than other townsfolk. But the higher clergy seem to have been at a distinct advantage, with very much lower death rates. Any visitor to a monastic site will admire the system of stone-lined drains, usually flushed by a running stream (and usually also the origin of countless legends of underground passages), which were a healthy contrast to urban cess-pits. It is interesting that there were efforts to keep town streets clean, and water-courses like those by the Itchen at Winchester running freely. The richest Southampton merchants had stone-lined drains to carry away their refuse. The legislation reveals the general squalor of the situation, however.

Removing rubbish was one problem, providing clean water another. Increasing populations meant greater demands, and some towns probably had so many wells dug in them that the water table was lowered. This has been suggested as the reason that so many friaries in the thirteenth century had to have supplies from extra-mural well-heads brought to them down lead pipes – some have been excavated in Exeter. Clay water-pipes for Salisbury and for the palace at Clarendon were made by the potters at Laverstock. A better water supply was a major reason for moving the cathedral from Old Sarum. At Southampton, the city bought out the friary's supply in 1420, but this is a rare example of civic action. Some citizens could afford a private supply, but very few. Of their charity, some ecclesiastical houses provided taps in public places, as Oseney Abbey did in Oxford.

Such corporate facilities are not known in the archaeological record. There are other things which may one day come to light. It would, for instance, be interesting to see one of the communal ovens which are recorded, but excavations have only found the ubiquitous private ones, small hearths with stone linings and clay domes, sometimes within houses, often in small separate bake-houses to try to reduce fire risks.

The physical conditions of medieval towns are being slowly elucidated by excavations, although for every new discovery there seems to be the recognition of some other problem which archaeology may never answer. That conditions of life in the big towns were bad for all but a very few is obvious enough. Towns offered material compensations, however, and better diet possibilities may have been one of them, marginally reducing the risk of infection. Insanitation may have been a major cause of the infertility which stopped even the best-housed merchants from begetting many male heirs. If the urban wealthy were infertile, so were the urban poor, and towns must have grown on a constant influx of the more ambitious of the countryside's surplus, men like the descendant of one of Cuxham's successful villeins, who set himself up at Henley. The surnames of townsmen in fifteenth-century Titchfield show that they had come from the local area, none originating from beyond the Wiltshire/Hampshire Downs, a contrast to the Londoners' names, which show a much wider distribution. When, after 1350, the countryside had no surplus to supply, and had opportunities to offer which it had not had previously, the townward migration was checked. The decay of many late medieval towns may have resulted in part from biological conditions.

Chapter 9

Possessions – from the Precious to the Prosaic

An archaeologist spends much of his time studying his predecessors' possessions, some large, like houses, some small, like brooches, some surviving, like many buildings and small finds from excavations, some only shadows, like a line of post-holes. There are also documentary records describing possessions, which may vary from the poetical to the practical, from verses rhapsodizing over Beowulf's treasure, to a property inventory of a merchant's stock-in-trade.

Gold and Silver

'Treasure fascinated the Anglo Saxons' (H. Mayr-Harting), for a man's social status was measured partly by his ornaments. A lord bought his men's loyalty with precious finger-rings, finely decorated swords, brooches and bracelets (Figs 8, 16). Some of these objects have survived, like the gold rings given to their followers by King Aethelwulf and Queen Aethelswyth, in the ninth century. The Alfred Jewel (Fig. 15) can be seen as a gift made in the same tradition as the rings, the bestowal of a costly object as a mark of the king's favour, though to a churchman not to a warrior.

There is some evidence that the ring-giving tradition, and the emphasis on treasure, died away in the tenth century. No swords with gold mounts on the hilt are known, and many fewer even have silver: the workmanship is less elaborate. His sword was of course still a warrior's most prestigious weapon, and its importance to him is shown by the practice of stamping a maker's name onto many blades. The difference in the decoration suggests a change in attitude to personal ornament, however, which is borne out by the jewellery: there are no successors to the inscribed finger-rings, or to the enormous silver disc-brooches like the ninth-century Fuller brooch.

Craftsmanship in precious metals was increasingly restricted to church plate rather than to personal adornment. The king was no longer a 'ring-giver to men', for the social system which tied a man to his lord by the giving and accepting of precious objects had become obsolete. Society was stabilizing, and it was land which gave prestige, status and power.

Such finger-rings as there were after the eleventh century, were usually not very elaborate, being plain hoops with uncut stones in their bezels, usually a single one, sometimes two or three in a cluster. There were *Lapidaries* which listed the various properties attributed to semi-precious stones: the sapphire in a ring found recently at the Blackfriars site, Oxford, would have helped its owner to think on the Heavenly Kingdom, to have relief from the sweating sickness, and even to escape from prison! A more elaborate gold ring with chip-carved decoration from Southampton was set with three amethysts, which comforted the body and soul, were an aid in the hunting field and cured a hangover. The Oxford ring was probably owned by one of the friars, for most ecclesiastics wore – and still wear – ceremonial rings. The Southampton one was found in an ordinary rubbish pit, and was presumably owned by a wealthy twelfth-century citizen.

There was a revival in secular interest in jewellery in the later Middle Ages, when many costly pieces were brought from France, and English jewellers imitated them. Delicate enamelling, finely-cut goldwork and carefully selected gems were used, and several recent finds have shown the quality of such work. One of the most interesting was a small hoard of finger-rings and coins dredged from the river near Thame, Oxon., in 1940 (Plate xxix). The latest of the coins dated to the 1460s, the probable date of the largest ring, a splendid gold *chef d'oeuvre*, its hoop set with amethysts, its bezel a rectangular casket for a relic, cut with an inscription of remembrance, and holding an amethyst worked into a Cross of Lorraine. There is a crucifixion engraved on the reverse of the bezel, and two quatre-foil knobs on its side can be turned to release the top plate, to give access to the relic. The hoard was probably jettisoned during the Wars of the Roses, like one found in Nottinghamshire.

Such finds justify the prices known to have been paid for jewellery – Lord Fanhope had two brooches worth £540, for instance. The country was rich enough to support such expenditure, even though it may have beggared some aristocratic families. Such display was to outshine rivals at court, perhaps an indication of the increased significance of London and of the central government in England's affairs in the late Middle Ages. The fashion for jewellery was mirrored in changing tastes in clothes. Close-fitting, tailored garments appeared for the first time, and fashion became an important social factor. Of dress archaeology has little to tell, though recent excavations on waterlogged sites, such as Oxford's castle moat, have provided enormous quantities of plain leather shoes and of other leather goods.

Tableware

The social demands which produce fashions in dress and ornament also affect people's entertaining, not only the food and drink that they serve to their guests but also the vessels in which their hospitality is offered. Just as inventories record precious jewels in late medieval households, so also there are records of expensive gold and silver plate. England's coinage usually had a higher weight of silver in it than continental currencies, and this is a reflection of precious metal's relative abundance in the island. Plate was another indication to contemporaries of England's wealth. Unfortunately there is little such plate surviving. Ecclesiastical vessels are known, and since many of them come from quite minor churches, their existence substantiates the evidence that gold and silver were liberally used. Slightly less expensive were the 'mazers', turned maplewood bowls with silver-gilt mounts, some of which can still be admired.

Wood was of course widely used for tableware, though little has survived. A twelfth-century well at Oxford produced a few fragments of small bowls and shallow dishes, from the very bottom where the contents had remained waterlogged. It is only in these conditions that such things can survive, although their condition is very different from what it was. The wealthy thirteenth-century burgess at Southampton had flat wooden dishes for his table, for some have been found in the pit from which came Richard of Southwick's seal.

That pit also contained a piece of pewter, another rare survival of what must once have been common. Lead and tin, its constituent metals, are both mined in the west of England and pewter was presumably relatively inexpensive. Again, its appearance in so many households impressed contemporaries.

On the other hand, England was at a disadvantage over glass vessels. There is little record of manufacture until the thirteenth century. Glass from Italy was an import to Southampton, and it is less uncommon in the port than elsewhere. At royal Ludgershall, a superb stemmed goblet has been found and another was recovered from a garderobe pit at Old Sarum castle. An exotic is a small fragment of a glass jug from the east Mediterranean, found at the deserted village site at Seacourt, a unique discovery in such a humble context. The beginning of English production is shown by a fourteenth-century jug top with pouring lip from a pit in the main street in Oxford, thought to have been an early product of the Weald.

Fifteenth-century glass vessels include fragments of 'alembic' from Selborne Priory, Hants., used in distilling. Urinals, bag-shaped vessels, were also used in this work, and by doctors and apothecaries when diagnosing a patient's illness. Winchester has produced in excavation a thirteenth-century glass pricket-lamp, with stem and shallow bowl, similar to some made in pottery, in which the wick floated in a pool of fat.

Pottery

Because pottery is usually common, and survives well in the ground, it is very important to archaeologists – much more important usually than it was to its owners, certainly after the end of the pagan tradition of burial with specially-made urns. People might do their cooking in pottery vessels, though metal cauldrons were often used, but on their tables they probably preferred to have vessels made in glass, precious or base metal, leather or wood, rather than those made in humble clay. Certainly there were periods, notably the thirteenth century, when some very elaborately decorated glazed jugs were available which were intended for display. But whether they would have been seen on the high table of the manor-house is a moot point. The social level reached by even the most costly jugs may not have been very high. Those found on palace sites may not have left the servants' quarters.

In the south of England, pottery does not seem to have been made by throwing it on a wheel until the tenth century, and similarly glazing was not practised until then. Much of the 'Mid Saxon' pottery was very crude. Simple cooking-pots, which had to have very thick walls and bases or the clay would have collapsed in making them, were fired in bonfires or clamps. All that is needed for a simple kiln is a pile of wood round the pots and a covering of turves: enough heat can be built up to 'fire' the pots to 700°– 800°, enough to harden them for use. No elaborate structure is necessary, and such kilns leave no trace in the ground for archaeologists to discover. Heat rises so even the soil immediately below the fire is only scorched, not baked, and after a year the site will have completely disappeared.

It is not only the kilns which may disappear, unfortunately. The sherds themselves are often not strong enough to survive in the ground without crumbling, and their tendency to disintegrate hampers the discovery of Saxon settlement sites. This is particularly true of pottery in which quantities of chopped grass or straw were mixed into the clay to stiffen it. Intensive field-work in Wiltshire, for instance, has recently begun to produce enough 'grass-tempered' pottery scatters to show that these wares, once thought a rarity, were in fact quite common.

Grass-tempered ware was certainly being made in the seventh century, but on the sites where it is found in eighth-century contexts it is possible that much is residual. Certainly it was obsolete by the ninth, although it is possible that it may still have been being made in a few places: it is reported from ninth-century contexts at Cheddar and Old Windsor. At Portchester it was probably not current after the mid eighth century. It is rare at Hamwic, which suggests also that it had ceased to be made by the early eighth century in Hampshire, but it is possible that Hamwic, being a town, might have favoured such simple pottery less than the countryside.

The Hamwic excavations have found large quantities of foreign, imported pottery, much of it from northern France. There were also large quantities of locally-made pots, some perhaps made in the town. This pottery was as crude as the grass-tempered, but probably more serviceable, for it used small grits of local stone instead of vegetable matter as a filler to improve the clay. Coarse wares were being made in many parts of southern England at least by the ninth century: in shape and style they varied little, the only detectable differences being in the temper used which changed according to the local geology. Their making was usually no more elaborate than that of the grass-tempered pots.

Only one group of Mid Saxon coarse pottery can be claimed as distinctive, and that only because it is decorated, with simple circles or squares stamped onto the pot with a bone tool. At least one such tool has been found at Hamwic, and some of the stamped wares were perhaps made there; they were probably made elsewhere also, though so far none has been found far from the Southampton–Portsmouth coastline. The excavator of Portchester, where stamped wares have been found, has suggested that they are a 'Solent group'.

Portchester has also produced the first domestic wheel-thrown pottery so far claimed in the south. It appears in the tenth century, and is much thinner than the coarse wares, using sand rather than stone as a temper for the clay. This change was partly for the potters' benefit, since it was uncomfortable to have hard lumps in the clay tearing against the skin of their hands as the pots spun on the turn-table. More important, however, was that the lumps would tear holes in the pot as they dragged against the potter's fingers. The use of sand in pottery is also a sign of better control of the firing.

'Portchester ware' has this title because it was first recognized there, not because it was made there; the production site is not known but it cannot have been far away, for so far it has not been found outside Hampshire. In the whole of the south of England only one kiln site of the late Saxon period has been located, at Michelmersh in Hampshire. Its products were also wheel-thrown, using sand-filled clays. Some of it has been found at

Portchester, and at other Hampshire sites where an eleventh-century date is probable. It was making cooking-pots, flat dishes – for cooking or for drinking – and spouted pitchers, the last often quite elaborately decorated, with applied strips of clay ornamented with stamps (*a* on Fig. 36). Whether the use of stamps was directly continued from the earlier 'Solent group' or is just a decoration that is always liable to be used on pottery is uncertain.

Applied strips with stamped decoration were also a feature of the earliest glazed pottery known to have been made in the south. It has been called 'Winchester ware' because it is common in that town, although so far no kiln site has been located. Geological analysis shows that it cannot have been far away: it is still possible that Michelmersh was the kiln, but no glazed sherds have been found there. Spouted pitchers were the most common vessels made in Winchester ware. They were often given rouletted decoration, as well as stamped, the potter running a notched wooden or possibly bone wheel over the pot to leave an impressed band in it. Rouletting was also used on some Portchester ware, and it is common on pots made in East Anglia, an area which seems to have been technically more advanced in its pot-making than the south. Both wheel-throwing and glazing appear to have started earlier there.

The East Anglian glazed pottery is called 'Stamford type' ware: kilns have been found in Stamford but it was probably also being made elsewhere. It is a smooth, thin, usually light-coloured pottery, which makes Winchester ware look rather crude in comparison. It was apparently more popular, for sherds of it have been found distributed over a wider area; pitchers were reaching Oxford, for instance, probably in some quantity (*b* on Fig. 36). But was this because they were valued as pottery, or because there was something inside them which was the real object of the trade – mead, butter or honey, for instance?

It is unfortunately very difficult to distinguish Winchester ware from twelfth-century glazed products in Oxford, and it may be that undecorated sherds have gone unrecognized. It may also be that there were kilns closer at hand than Stamford producing glazed pottery. Certainly Oxford had a large pot-producing centre nearby at Bladon, which is recorded in Domesday Book as worth 10*s.* a year, enough to suggest that several potters were working there. It is an unhappy irony that although many of us have searched for it, no trace of that industry has been found. Nor are the other two potteries named in the Survey, at Haresfield, Glos., and Westbury, Wilts., yet located. Michelmersh, the only kiln found, gets no mention, nor do others which must have existed (Fig. 37). These four places have in common that all are in the south and all are in the countryside. So far as we yet know, there is a difference between the south and the Danelaw areas,

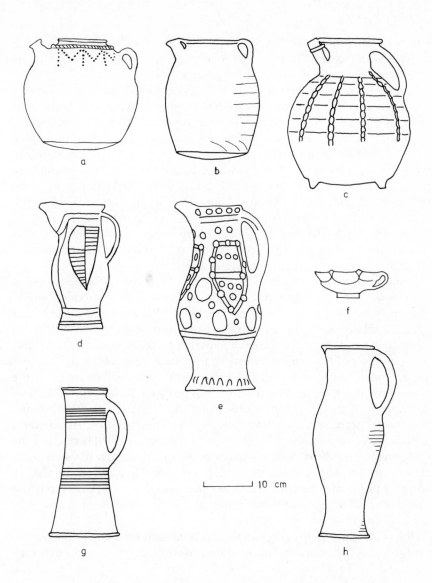

36 Some different types of medieval pottery: *a* – Michelmersh stamped pitcher; *b* – Stamford type pitcher (many Winchester type pitchers were very similar in shape); *c* – Oxford style of tripod pitcher; *d* – French Polychrome jug from Southampton; *e* – an English imitation made at Laverstock; *f* – lobed cup, many of which are 'Tudor Green'; *g* – the straight profile and the corrugations show that this jug copied a metal one; *h* – a 'baluster' jug.

for in the latter there were many kilns in such towns as Stamford, Thetford, Norwich and Northampton. In the rest of England, only Exeter and Gloucester seem to have evidence of urban kilns.

One very common type of 'Danelaw' pottery which was not so far as is yet known made in towns was 'St Neots type' ware, in which flakes of shell were used instead of sand as a temper (*a* on Fig. 38). During the tenth and eleventh centuries, pottery of this kind was prolific in Oxford and the district round, being much commoner than the glazed Stamford ware. Presumably it was being made in bonfire kilns at various different places, to produce cooking-pots and dishes. In the Bedford region it was used for jugs and, although none of these have been recognized, they were probably known in the Oxford area as jugs of the same shape made in coarse wares have been found. These coarse wares are sometimes referred to as being in 'Developed St Neots type' ware, but the term falsely implies an improvement process, and is better avoided.

It might have been expected that, if there was a real difference between the Danelaw and the south, it would be the former whose products would oust the latter, since most of them were 'better' in their glazing and their use of a wheel, and their industrial system was more 'advanced', being town-based and therefore closer to a market-linked distribution network. Yet this did not happen. Stamford ware ceased to penetrate the Thames valley after the eleventh century: urban kilns did not appear. Even the developments of the south coast were not pursued. Portchester ware, and derivatives of it, did not continue to improve but rather the opposite. Winchester ware seems to have ceased production and the glazed wares available were more crudely made tripod pitchers, so called because of the three small feet added to their convex bases so that they could stand on a flat surface (*c* on Fig. 36). Recent work has shown that a kiln centre making cooking-pots and tripod pitchers developed near Wareham, largely ousting coarse wares during the twelfth century. Yet its vessels were not as well made as Portchester ware.

Tripod pitchers were being supplied to Winchester at least by the eleventh century. They may not in fact post-date Winchester ware, although they outlasted it. They were glazed but they were less decorated and, more significantly, they were not thrown on a wheel. A turn-table was used to make them, as it was with the most coarse pottery, but the rotation was slow, perhaps no more than an occasional twist. No pivoted wheel was needed, for only a dished base was required: a broken pot sherd was enough, since placed on a flat surface it could be spun when required, and the clay could be built up using it as a stand. The process does not require such carefully prepared clay, although for glazed wares, such as the tripod pitchers, sandy rather than coarse wares were used. Often the upper part

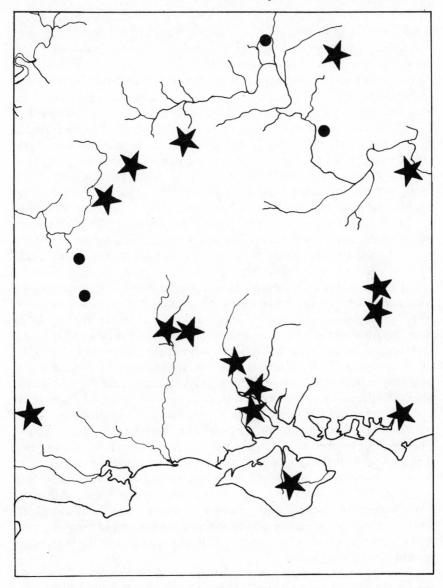

37 Distribution map of kilns known from archaeological evidence (stars) and documentary sources (spots).

of the pot would be separate strips of clay, luted in bands onto the body, the joins being smoothed over.

Tripod pitchers began production at a much earlier date along the south coast than elsewhere. They were probably being made in Wiltshire in the eleventh century and first appeared in Oxfordshire in about 1100, rapidly becoming prolific, and being effectively the only glazed vessels made there until the very end of the century. Tripod pitchers replaced Winchester ware, and ousted Stamford ware, in terms of method of production, of fabrics and of types of vessel. The predominant product of both Winchester and Stamford wares was a spouted pitcher, with small handles at the rim. These do not seem to have been made in the twelfth century, the larger tripods with bigger handles totally replacing them. Some spouted pitchers had been made at Michelmersh, and probably at a variety of other places, in coarse unglazed wares, presumably imitating the glazed ones, but these also ceased to be made. Was this merely fashion, or was it that the spouted pitchers had been containers for something for which trade demand altered in the twelfth century?

St Neots type jugs were copied in local coarse wares, but unglazed jugs were not really able to compete with glazed vessels as tableware. Coarse ware cooking-pots and dishes, however, were certainly still made in quantity. Most of the kilns producing tripod pitchers would also have been making cooking vessels in similar sandy fabrics, using a turn-table. Analysis of twelfth-century Wareham sherds has shown that both glazed and unglazed vessels were produced by the same pottery, and that the coarse wares and the sandy wares were not made in the same place, for the mineral contents were quite distinct. Were the coarse wares made by part-time potters, who supplied only the needs of their immediate neighbourhood? This could be assumed if the coarse wares were confined to rural areas, but they are found often enough in towns to suggest that they were taken there, presumably to sell. The sandy wares dominated certain markets, like Wareham, but were not economic if travel costs were too great, so that the less attractive but more cheaply sold coarse wares could under-cut them. Coarse wares were generally no less abundant at the end of the thirteenth century than they had been in the twelfth, certainly on rural sites, though possibly not in most towns.

Cooking-pots are both the most prolific and the least informative vessels found on medieval sites. A noticeable trend is the use of larger cooking-pots, perhaps as boilers for the constantly simmering stews that were blamed (in Chapter Four) for diet deficiencies. A few types are distinctive: there is one which has a rim narrower than its base, that seems only to be found in the Severn/Cotswolds/Upper Thames Valley area (*b* on Fig. 38). Another with oblique incised lines on the body is found mostly in the Chilterns (*c*). The south coast pots often have completely rounded bases, with no angle between side and base (*d*). They are also often noticeably cruder than contemporaries further north. 'Scratch-marked wares', which have the surfaces of the pots scored as though a bundle of twigs had been rubbed over them, occur in Wiltshire and along the south coast (*e*). Distribution maps of these different types of cooking-pot hint towards definitions of competing market zones, with only a few pots straying into other territories. How far this is valid requires more precise definition and mapping. Even then, it is difficult to know if such maps are a reflection of anything more than pottery distributions: were there any actual differences between regions to cause the different distributions, or were they caused simply by the market for pottery and nothing else? It would be absurd to say, for instance, that Oxford was 'cut off' from the Chilterns, simply because a certain type of cooking pottery known in the hills has not been found in the town twenty miles away. All it shows is that people bought their cooking wares locally, and that it was not economic for sellers to hawk them round over long distances. It is a record of a particular type of transaction.

The market for glazed wares was probably wider, and these were usually the products of quite large kiln sites, probably as early as the eleventh century judging from Winchester ware. Much work has been done recently on locating medieval kilns both from field-work and from documentary evidence, and it is clear that there were many more substantial 'factories'

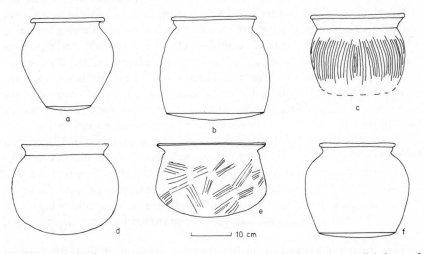

38   Some different types of medieval cooking-pot; *a* – the wheel-thrown 'olla' shape of St Neots type wares; *b* – Cotswold area cooking-pot; *c* – 'M40 ware', from the Chilterns area; *d* – round-based southern type; *e* – 'scratch-marked' pot, also found in the south; *f* – ubiquitous convex-based type, usually in a sandy ware.

than used to be thought. Unfortunately, kilns which are well known from documentary evidence, such as Crockerton, Wilts., or Woodstock, Oxon., have not been located: at the former, only a sixteenth-century kiln has been found, although the documents show that there were potters there by the 1230s, and probably in the late twelfth century. Those of us who have failed to find the thirteenth-century Woodstock kilns (which may have been on the same site as the Domesday industry recorded at Bladon) have cursed the eighteenth-century landscape gardener Capability Brown, as he may have flooded them in the Blenheim Lake.

Documentary studies indicate that the potters were close to the bottom of the social ladder. The rents that they paid were low, as were their tax assessments. When several were working in one place, their collective value was not inconsiderable, but individually few of them seem to have become at all wealthy, and those who did 'make good' bought land and gave up potting. There was therefore no reinvestment of capital which might have led to significant changes in the industry. No factories, in the capitalist sense of entrepreneurs with several men working for them, developed, although some working potters employed a few servants.

Most known medieval kilns are in the country. Is this because of fire regulations, or the difficulty of getting enough clay and fuel near a town, or because pot-making was an anti-social activity, with its smoke and fumes? Evidence of urban kilns in the later Middle Ages is growing: Chichester (admittedly in the suburbs), Salisbury and Southampton had potters, although those in the last are known only from finds of quantities of waster sherds. In Salisbury, the potters would presumably have been competing with those working a couple of miles away at Laverstock, and the latter had the advantage of being close to the royal palace of Clarendon, which they supplied in quantity (Fig. 39). There is even a record that in 1270 the Laverstock potters supplied 1000 vessels for the third year running to the royal household at Winchester, although the cost of carting the pots the twenty-mile journey may have contributed substantially to the price – 25s. There ought to be Laverstock pottery to be found in the Winchester excavations, but none has been recognized. The presumption is that the 1270 order was a special purchase, and that Winchester's market was not usually supplied by Laverstock potters, although it was not really far away. Yet Laverstock pottery is a common find in Southampton, where it is perhaps associated with the large-scale commerce between the port and Salisbury.

This caprice is typical of medieval pottery studies. The Brill kilns, for instance, are only a little closer to Oxford than is Laverstock to Winchester, about fifteen miles, but Brill pottery is extremely common there, and throughout the south Midlands, from at least the later thirteenth century.

Potters from Brill may have been the 'sellers of pots' who had a well-placed pitch in Oxford's High Street in the 1370s, or such sellers may have been middle-men, of whom there is a hint in the northern evidence. We do not know if those who had stalls in Salisbury's Pot Row were producers from nearby Laverstock, or regular tradesmen. Unfortunately these shreds of evidence do not give a coherent explanation of how pottery was generally distributed. It was, however, carried on carts and pack-horses, in the south at least, as none of the known kilns was on or close to a waterway. Furthermore, the only river which might have been used for carriage, the Thames, was not utilized either in the Saxon period for the spread of St Neots and other wares, or in the thirteenth and fourteenth centuries for Brill pottery, which hardly occurs downstream at Reading, for example.

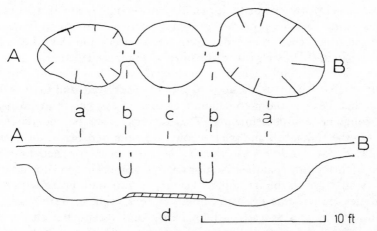

39   Plan and section through one of the thirteenth-century kilns at Laverstock: *a* – stokeholes; *b* – flues; *c* – oven (the pots would have been stacked in this, covered by a temporary roof during the firing) (after Musty).

Transport of pottery by sea is a different problem. So far as can be told from inadequate excavations, no southern English pottery has been found in France, the region on the continent where it would be expected if it was to be found at all. There may be pottery from Southampton to be found in Bordeaux and La Rochelle, just as quantities of south-western French pottery have been found in the English ports and at many other coastal sites. Much less imported pottery is recorded from inland, however, and there is nothing to show that even the very attractive Polychrome pottery (*d* on Fig. 36) was traded for sale, except possibly to a few cosmopolitan merchants in Southampton. It has also been found at many castles – a fine jug can be seen at Carisbrooke on the Isle of Wight, and it has been suggested that English soldiers who had seen overseas service might have acquired a taste for it.

Although there is not much of the Polychrome inland, it was certainly known. The potters at Laverstock were producing jugs which imitated its shapes and decoration (*e* on Fig. 36), and its influence can be seen as far from the coast as Oxford. Some of the most interesting recent discoveries have been of examples of Polychrome on kiln sites, such as the sherds of a lobed cup (*f* on Fig. 36) found at the Naish Hill kilns in Wiltshire, suggesting that English potters were using them as models for their own products. Is this an indication that the potters were aiming for a high quality market with their best vessels, or does it show that the peasantry would have been at least dimly aware of what was fashionable among people of rank and consequence? Was Polychrome almost the only pottery that would have been deemed worthy of a late thirteenth-century high table? If so, it might be surprising that the potters should have been so zealous to imitate it, since their own customers would only see it rarely. On the other hand, they also imitated vessels called aquamaniles, animal-shaped jugs in which water poured through a spout in the animal's head was used to wash the hands at table. Many bronze aquamaniles have survived, and there is little doubt that they were common enough to be in at least very many manorial and comparable establishments. The key may well be the difference between the high tables and the low, physically but not socially close, with metalwork for the diners at High Table and pottery for their inferiors. It was in this setting that the imitations would be most in demand and from them would spread the fashion, as visiting tenants took home with them memories of their entertainment, however brief, at the manorial hall.

However it was spread, fashion clearly did dictate the shapes and decoration of the most elaborate jugs. Great skill went into the use of different white or red clays to contrast with the body of the pot and create slip patterns, if the clay was painted thinly on, or patterns of applied strips, pads and stamps. The glaze was always lead-based, though copper filings might be added to it to produce flecks of dark green. The development of the potters' skill, from gradual initiatives in the late twelfth century to the splendid achievements of the late thirteenth, can be traced in the sequence of pottery from the Broad Street site at Oxford (*l* on Fig. 6). The bottoms of the medieval wells there were found to contain many vessels, a surprisingly large number of which could be pieced together.

It is easier to see the sequence than to give dates to it. There are very few fixed points which can be used to give precise dates to pottery: the material from below Norman castle sites like Oxford or Winchester is one such kind of fixed point, but these are few. Sometimes a coin may be found in a pit or well, which gives at least an 'earliest possible' date for the deposition of that pit's contents. But the coin might have been an old one, lost many years previously, which happened to stray into the pit, and be a century or more earlier than some of the associated pottery. Nor can dates established for one area be used safely in another, since potters did not all make changes in the same way or at the same time. The result is that the dating of the era of the most elaborate pottery could span the whole of a century, or only a couple of generations, especially if it was as susceptible to fashion changes as the Polychrome imitations suggest. These uncertainties limit the value of conclusions that can be drawn from the pottery: it would be interesting to demonstrate, for instance, that the elaborate pots ceased production in the middle of the fourteenth century, and to say that this was because it became too expensive to make them when labour became more costly after 1350. There is, however, some evidence that these pots were out of production well before the Black Death had its effect, and that therefore some other factor, such as declining peasant purchasing power, was the cause.

Those who believe that plainer pots were already ousting the more fantastic ones before the mid fourteenth century have to face the difficulty that most of the glazed wares available were types which varied very little over that long period. The later chronology reduces the time-interval between the introduction of jugs with little or no applied or coloured decoration, many of which clearly copied wooden, metal or leather vessels (*g* on Fig. 36), and the development of much thinner-walled pots using finer clays. On the other hand, baluster jugs, an elegant shape found in various forms in the south (*h*), certainly overlapped both the elaborately decorated pots when they began production, and the imitation-jugs before they stopped. This would favour the tighter chronology in the thirteenth/ early fourteenth centuries.

The evidence of kilns in the south is not good for the fourteenth and fifteenth centuries. Laverstock ceased production – perhaps because of competition from Salisbury – and many other sites have not been fully explored. Potting continued at Brill, the products being hard, thin sandy wares used for cooking-pots and plain jugs. A small fifteenth-century kiln on the Isle of Wight at Knighton has been excavated, its design no different from those at Laverstock two hundred years earlier. There is late fourteenth-century documentary evidence of kilns at Farnborough, Hants., presumably producing fine white wares, like kilns in Surrey supplying the London market. Clay from Farnborough was used by a tiler outside Winchester, and this was probably the white clay that he needed for his patterns.

Certainly by the fifteenth century, new types of pottery were becoming available. Stoneware from the Rhineland was the first imported pottery that can be said, from its wide distribution, to have been traded as a commodity for purchase by the lower social classes. In the north of the area, small 'Cistercian ware' cups became available, distinctive for their lustrous brown glazes over a thinly potted red clay. Similar cups became copied by local potters, and 'Black wares', with a thick black glaze, were made. 'Tudor Green' is the term used for fine white wares, with a more even and glossier green glaze than earlier medieval pots had had. It may have started production as early as the late fourteenth century. In general these new fabrics were used for smaller vessels than in the past, though cisterns with bung-holes near their bases, and very large shallow bowls, were being made at Knighton, and elsewhere (Fig. 40). The big jugs and cooking-pots fell into disuse, presumably because of the competition of the other materials whose shapes they had been imitating. This is almost certainly a sign of increased general prosperity in the late Middle Ages – for everyone except potters.

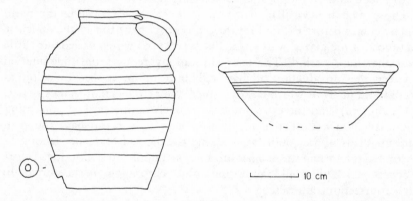

40   Two vessels from the late medieval kiln at Knighton, Isle of Wight: *left* – a cistern with bung-hole; *right* – large bowl.

Chapter 10

Archaeology and Medieval Society

Medieval archaeology is a very wide field, because so much physical evidence has survived intact, or can be recovered by excavation. I have tried to deal at least briefly with most aspects of the subject as far as they relate to a particular area, but there are still one or two which I have not covered. The useful study of village crosses, being completed by B. J. Marples, is one.

To many of those who are used to dealing with the data which is contained in documents, medieval archaeology seems a random, often haphazard, study, but it is still in many of its aspects at an experimental stage, and has not yet clarified its aims or acquired the experience of a fully-fledged academic discipline. I have tried to show what contributions have been made by archaeology to an understanding of medieval society in southern England, and to suggest some of the ways in which further observation can amplify the information now available to us, but it must be obvious that there are many aspects of the society which can only partly or inadequately be clarified by the physical evidence. Equally, however, a documentary study on its own cannot reveal all the ambitions and limitations by which the society was conditioned.

It is certainly easier to justify archaeology in the period up to 1100 than in the following four hundred years, when much more documentary evidence is available. Until some of the difficulties of dating physical survivals more closely are solved, archaeology's contribution is often going to be limited to observation of long-term trends, not of short-term fluctuations, and it is the latter which preoccupies the writing of most history. This can lead to the over-emphasis of a particular circumstance as a cause of some fundamental social change – the debate over the relative importance of the Black Death is a good example of this – whereas archaeology can give a better concept of the scope and pace of such change. It is, however, just as easy to over-emphasize a particular physical change and its importance – the introduction of the stirrup is one to which too much credit has been given. A society cannot act except within the constraints of its technology, but that technology may be more adaptable to meet society's needs than is usually appreciated. Nevertheless, the physical limitations of any society affect what it can, or can seek to, achieve.

Physical evidence is sometimes elusive, sometimes prolific, and its quantity does not proportionally increase its historical implications. Medieval pottery is found in vast amounts, but there are limits to the lessons that can be learnt from it which will not be widened merely by looking at more of it. Much of archaeology is involved with recognition – the fascination of being able to put a date and place of manufacture to a sherd – but mere recognition is not an historical end in itself. The aim of recognition is to place the object within a framework from which history can be deduced. Whereas a document may itself present a historical statement simply to be printed and edited, an artifact does not speak for itself but has to be explained and interpreted. It may be that it is this constant need by the archaeologist to interpret his data which causes consternation among some students of documents, to whom a hypothesis is the apotheosis of years of tedious transcription. An archaeologist is much more directly involved in interpretation than many who are similarly concerned with primary sources.

The study of primary sources is the nub of archaeology, for the physical evidence itself is nothing but a primary source. It is also one which can be recognized and collected by people who are not themselves trained historians or archaeologists. Only excavation, which is destructive, cannot be undertaken by those without experience. All other kinds of field-work are open to anyone with an observant eye and a certain amount of patience, and through their efforts and their collection and (accurate!) recording of physical data, more medieval history can eventually be written. Until the survivals of medieval England have been studied more thoroughly than they have yet been, the contribution that they can make to our understanding of medieval society cannot be properly assessed. I should like to think that this book will not only show what has been revealed, but also encourage its readers to get involved in the subject themselves.

Bibliography

An archaeologist interested in the Middle Ages has to have a grasp both of the range of contemporary documents and of the work of modern commentators, particularly those who write about social and economic history. The best starting-point for the latter is H. C. Darby, *A New Historical Geography of England* (1973), in which the contributors draw on detailed studies by M. M. Postan, E. Power, E. Carus-Wilson, H. L. Gray, E. M. Jope and others, whose own books and articles on the cloth, wool and other trades are basic sources. Good social histories are in the series published by Pelican Books, by D. M. Whitelock, D. M. Stenton, and A. R. Myers. The last can be supplemented now by K. B. McFarlane, *The Nobility of Late Medieval England* (1973), and by *The Decline of Serfdom in Medieval England* (1969), by R. H. Hilton.

It is always surprising to find that, despite the efforts of hundreds of scholars over the last three hundred years, there are still many medieval documents which are not available in printed editions. There is a pamphlet on how to find these by C. P. S. Platt, *Medieval Archaeology in England: a Guide to the Historical Sources* (1969), but most people will not need to have to go to such lengths. The multi-volume *English Historical Documents* is a compendium of selected texts, with information on other printed sources. These indicate the range of what is available: excellent studies on their use in practice are *History of the King's Works* (1963), edited by H. M. Colvin, and *Building in England down to 1540* (1952), by L. F. Salzman.

There is no single text-book on medieval archaeology, but there are many books and articles on particular aspects of its practice. The evolution of the landscape has been the subject of many general and local studies, stimulated by the eye-opening work of W. G. Hoskins, especially in his *Making of the English Landscape* (1955), which has led to several county studies, including one of *The Oxfordshire Landscape* (1974), by F. V. Emery, and an excellent one of *Dorset* (1970), by C. Taylor. The latter has also written *Fieldwork in Medieval Archaeology* (1974), which explains the techniques of the study, as does *Landscape Archaeology* (1974), by M. Aston and R. T. Rowley, which deals with some of the problems of urban topography as well. *Medieval England* (1958), by J. K. St Joseph and M. W. Beresford is a book of air photographs with explanatory texts and diagrams, showing how physical monuments can be interpreted, but it is unfortunately out of print.

The rest of this Bibliography will relate to the topics in individual chapters in the book, but the works mentioned above all contain material that is relevant to most of the themes. Other such general studies include the chapters by various writers in *Medieval England* (1958), edited by A. L. Poole, which are summaries of such subjects as coinage, trade, towns, religious organizations and costume. The essay by E. M. Jope in *Culture and Environment* (1963), edited by I. Ll. Foster and L. Alcock, is fundamental to the study of medieval archaeology.

I have avoided repetition of entries in this Bibliography as far as possible so that, for instance, sources for a particular town are only given where the town is first mentioned, unless later discussions of it have additional references.

Chapter One

Anyone studying pre-Conquest England starts with *Anglo-Saxon England* (Third edition, 1971), Sir Frank Stenton's magisterial survey. The social and economic background is explained by H. R. Loyn, *Anglo-Saxon England and the Norman Conquest* (1962), and a swift run through the archaeology is provided by D. M. Wilson in *The Anglo-Saxons* (1971 edition – the 1961 edition is out of date). R. I. Page, *Everyday Life in Anglo-Saxon England* (1970) is a well-illustrated survey. H. P. R. Finberg, in *The Agricultural History of England and Wales,* Vol. 1 (1972), summarized in his *Formation of England* (1974), deals with society and farming, although his interpretation of the status of the *ceorl* as a depressed person has been criticized.

Individual towns have a scattered literature. I like to think that *Saxon Southampton* (1975), a pamphlet published by the Southampton Archaeological Research Committee, is useful on Hamwic, and that R. Hodges and I will soon have published our excavation report on Wareham, in the Dorset Archaeological and Natural History Society's *Proceedings*. Winchester has seen ten years' intensive study by M. Biddle, now reaching fruition. He has summarized his findings in successive Interim Reports in the *Antiquaries Journal,* and in an essay in *Tenth-Century Studies* (1975), edited by D. Parsons. T. G. Hassall's work in Oxford has Interim Reports in *Oxoniensia* and there is a pamphlet *The City Beneath Your Feet* (1972): I hope soon to edit the report by B. G. Durham and T. G. Hassall on the St Aldate's site which produced eighth-century material. R. T. Rowley and R. Bradley are writing up their recent excavations at Dorchester-on-Thames; earlier work there by Professor S. S. Frere is reported in *Archaeological Journal,* CXIX (1964), and T. M. Dickinson considers its royal role in *Cuddesdon and Dorchester-on-Thames* (1974).

Rural sites include Chalton, reported in *Medieval Archaeology,* XVI (1972) and XVII (1973), Ufton Nervet, in *Berkshire Archaeological Journal,* 67 (1973–4) and

New Wintles, in *Oxoniensia,* xxxiv (1969). *Oxoniensia,* xxxviii (1973), contained reports on the M40 sites at Lewknor. The palaces at Old Windsor and Cheddar have as yet only a brief note for the former in *Medieval Archaeology,* ii (1958), and a longer Interim in the same journal, Volume vi–vii (1962–3), for the latter. *Shakenoak,* Vol. iii (1972), by A. C. C. Brodribb, A. R. Hands, and D. R. Walker, describes the Saxon finds there, though their interpretation is suspect – see reviews in *Britannia,* iii (1972), and *Medieval Archaeology,* xvii (1973).

Studies of church buildings begin with the two-volume gazetteer *Anglo-Saxon Architecture* (1965), by H. M. and J. Taylor. Still useful is A. W. Clapham, *English Romanesque Architecture before the Conquest* (1930), and there is a good discussion of minster churches by C. A. Ralegh Radford, in *Archaeological Journal,* lxxx (1973). These are amplified by work on Glastonbury, also by C. A. R. Radford, in an essay in *The Quest for Arthur's Britain* (1968), edited by G. Ashe; at Winchester by M. Biddle in *Tenth-Century Studies;* about Abingdon by M. Biddle, H. T. Lambrick and J. N. L. Myres in *Medieval Archaeology,* xii (1968); on the Wareham stones in *Dorset,* South-East volume, by the Royal Commission on Historical Monuments; at Titchfield by M. Hare, in *Proceedings of the Hampshire Field Club,* xxxii (1975); and at Bradford-on-Avon by H. M. Taylor in two model essays in *Archaeological Journal,* cxxix (1972) and cxxx (1973).

Finally on pre-Viking southern England, the coinage is dealt with by D. M. Metcalf in essays in *Oxoniensia,* xxxvii (1972), and in *Coins and the Archaeologist* (1974), edited by J. Casey and R. Reece. I have tried to discuss the gold and silver objects in a similar context in *Anglo-Saxon England,* 4 (1975), and many of the objects are described in detail by V. I. Evison, *Archaeologia,* 98 (1961), by D. M. Wilson in his *British Museum Catalogue of Anglo-Saxon Ornamental Metalwork* (1964), and by myself in the Ashmolean Museum's equivalent (1974).

Chapter Two

King Alfred has been the theme of many historical studies, the best recent biography being a short one by H. R. Loyn (1967). His first biographer, Asser, is a source called in question recently, but defended by D. M. Whitelock, *The Genuine Asser* (1968). The Burghal Hidage has been studied by D. Hill, in an important essay in *Medieval Archaeology,* xiii (1969), and in his discussions of individual *burhs* such as Hamtun (*Hants. Field Club,* xxiv (1967)). There have been other general studies of the *burhs* by C. A. R. Radford (*Medieval Archaeology,* xiv (1970)), and by N. Brooks (*Ibid.,* viii (1964)). The former has also written about excavations at Cricklade in *Wiltshire Archaeological Magazine,* lxvii (1972). C. Simpson has summarized *Wallingford* (1973), and B. W. Cunliffe's *Portchester Castle,* Vol. ii, will have appeared by the end of 1976. The defences at Wareham were sectioned by the Royal Commission – see *Medieval Archaeology,* iii (1959). What has been found at Saxon Bath will be described soon in a book edited by B. W. Cunliffe. Work at Chichester is appearing in volumes by A. Rule and others – two have so far been published.

Information on the churches is contained in the works already described. The Winchester wall-painting was described in *Antiquaries Journal*, XLVII (1967).

The Graveney Boat was first described in *Antiquity*, XLV (1971). Coinage and some of its problems are considered by S. Lyon, in articles in *British Numismatic Journal*, 36–8 (1967–9). He has references to many important specialized works by S. E. Rigold, M. Dolley, P. Grierson and other numismatists.

Another specialized topic is manuscripts. The tyro's best introduction is through M. Rickert, *Painting in Britain in the Middle Ages* (1954). Some Alfredian and later works are illustrated and described by J. J. G. Alexander, in a Bodleian Library pamphlet *Anglo-Saxon Illumination* (1970). The Alfredian period and its implications are described by F. Wormald in *England before the Conquest* (1971), edited by P. Clemoes and K. Hughes, by R. Deshman in *Art Bulletin*, LVI (1974), and by J. J. G. Alexander in *Tenth-Century Studies* (1975), edited by D. Parsons. The Alfred Jewel has attracted the attention of many writers, most recently D. R. Howlett in *Oxoniensia*, XXXXIX (1974). The Ashmolean *Catalogue* (1974) describes it (and the Abingdon sword), as does the museum's pamphlet *The Alfred and Minster Lovell Jewels* (1971), by J. R. Clarke and myself. The Trewhiddle hoard and its style were discussed by D. M. Wilson in *Archaeologia*, 98 (1961), the Fuller brooch and others by R. L. S. Bruce-Mitford in an essay in *Dark Age Britain* (1956), edited by D. B. Harden. *Sculpture in Britain in the Middle Ages* (1955), by L. Stone, introduces the Codford and Colerne crosses, and others. The theme is taken up by R. Cramp in a valuable article in *Tenth-Century Studies*.

Chapter Three

The stimulus to discussions about Saxon town lay-outs was provided by an article by M. Biddle and D. Hill, in *Antiquaries Journal*, LI (1971). Individual studies have mostly been referred to above, but E. M. Jope's work on Oxford in *Dark Age Britain* (1956), should be read because it is a seminal paper and a model study, although now augmented by the work of D. Hill and T. G. Hassall. The new site at Southampton has yet to be discussed in detail. Excavations at Old Sarum were published by P. Rahtz *et al.*, *Wiltshire Archaeological Magazine*, LIX (1964), and at South Cadbury by L. Alcock, *By South Cadbury is that Camelot* (1972). Coinage studies are being facilitated by the multi-volume *Sylloges of Coins of the British Isles*, as well as by studies of individual mints, e.g. by L. V. Grinsell on *The Bristol Mint* (1972) and on *The Bath Mint* (1973), and by C. E. Blunt and M. Dolley, *The Mints of Northampton and Southampton* in *Mints, Dies and Currency* (1971), edited by R. G.

Carson. M. Dolley's British Museum pamphlet *Anglo-Saxon Pennies* (1970) is a brief but basic source.

Chapter Four

Further works on church archaeology include studies on Thomas Wolvey by E. Roberts, *Archaeological Journal,* 129 (1972); on Henry Yevele by J. H. Harvey in a book of that title (1944), challenged by A. D. McLees in *Journal of the British Archaeological Association,* xxxvi (1973); on moulding by H. Forrester, *Medieval Gothic Mouldings* (1972); and on beak-head ornaments by A. Borg, *Journal of the British Archaeological Association,* xx (1967). A fundamental essay by H. M. Taylor in *Tenth-Century Studies* illuminates the tenth and eleventh centuries. The building at Potterne is described by N. Davey in *Wiltshire Archaeological Magazine,* lxix (1964). The distribution of churches and sculpture in relation to the quarrying industry was considered in *Medieval Archaeology,* viii (1964), by E. M. Jope.

To the works on manuscripts already cited, *The Benedictional of St Ethelwold* (1959), by F. Wormald, should be added, and the same author's *English Drawings of the Tenth and Eleventh Centuries* (1952). Frithstan's stole and maniple are fully described in *The Relics of St Cuthbert* (1956), edited by C. F. Battiscombe.

Death – or at least its statistics – has preliminary studies by B. K. Biddle in *World Archaeology,* vii (1975), for Winchester; by D. Brothwell and W. Kozanowski, in *Journal of Archaeological Science,* 1 (1974); and by I. Tattersall in *Man,* iii (1968). Sir Bartholomew Burghersh's figure is elucidated in *Archaeological Journal,* cxxv (1968); the Mackney family are in *Berkshire Archaeological Journal,* lxi (1963); and the Wharram Percy data is in M. W. Beresford and J. G. Hurst, *Deserted Medieval Villages* (1971). Charcoal burials are described in the Oxford and Winchester excavation Interims. Medieval effigies are used as archaeological evidence of the scope of the Purbeck quarries by R. Leach, *An Investigation into . . . Purbeck Marble in Medieval England* (n.d.). The Ashmolean's pamphlet *Notes on Brass-Rubbing* (1975), is an excellent introduction to the study of brasses.

Anyone interested in abbeys and monasteries will visit sites owned by the Department of the Environment, whose individual guidebooks set a very high standard. A book of air photographs and commentary, *Monastic Sites from the Air* (1952) by J. K. St Joseph and D. Knowles, provides a fine introduction, and serious students will become familiar with the latter author's *The Monastic Orders in England* (1966) and *The Religious Orders in England* (1959). I wrote up D. Watts' observations at Bicester Priory in *Oxoniensia,* xxxii (1968), and my excavation report is in the subsequent volume. The Reading report by C. F. Slade is in *Berkshire Archaeological Journal,* lxvi (1971–2). The abbots' houses are discussed by P. Faulkner, in *Archaeological Journal,* cxv (1958), and a description of the Titchfield barn has just appeared in *English Vernacular Houses* (1975), by E.

Mercer. Distilling vessels are described by S. Moorhouse in *Medieval Archaeology*, XVI (1972). Oxford University has been the subject of even more attention than the Alfred Jewel, the best recent history being by V. H. H. Green, *A History of Oxford University* (1974). On the architecture, there is my own Ashmolean pamphlet *Oxford Buildings* (1977), but anybody else would refer students to the magisterial *City of Oxford* (1939) by the Royal Commission on Historical Monuments, or to Professor Pevsner's *Oxfordshire* (1974). The interim reports on the friaries are in *Oxoniensia*, XXXIX (1974), and G. H. Lambrick and H. Woods have submitted their final report on the Blackfriars to me for Volume XLI (1976).

Chapter Five

M. W. Beresford and J. G. Hurst, *Deserted Medieval Villages* (1971) is the starting-point for any study of abandoned rural settlements. I have not myself gone into much detail of excavation findings, because of this excellent book. This chapter also relies heavily on the works on the landscape mentioned above. J. Wilson wrote on Woodperry in *Archaeological Journal*, III (1846), M. Robinson on Tetsworth in *Oxoniensia*, XXXVIII (1973), M. Biddle on Seacourt in the same journal, XXVI/XXVII (1961–2), B. W. Cunliffe and others on Chalton in *Medieval Archaeology*, XVI (1972) and XVII (1973), N. P. Thompson on Huish in *Wiltshire Archaeological Magazine*, LXVII (1972), C. Taylor on Whiteparish in *Ibid.*, LXII (1967) and LXIII (1968), P. Rahtz on Holworth in *Dorset Proceedings*, LXXXI (1959), and Hangleton is in *Sussex Archaeological Collections*, CI (1963) – by E. W. Holden – and CII (1964) – by D. G. and J. G. Hurst. The study of *Cuxham* (1965), is by P. D. A. Harvey. Hedgerow dating is discussed by M. Hooper in *Landscapes and Documents* (1974), edited by A. Rogers and R. T. Rowley. The potential of field-walking in East Anglia was revealed by P. Wade-Martins, in *Recent Work in Rural Archaeology* (1975), edited by P. J. Fowler. The Sadlers Wood excavation, *Oxoniensia*, XXXVIII (1973), was the work of R. A. Chambers. Site location was studied by A. Ellison and J. Harris in an essay in *Models in Archaeology* (1972), edited by D. L. Clarke.

Chapter Six

The best place to start when studying castles is with D. F. Renn, *Norman Castles in Britain* (Second edition, 1973), and with R. A. Brown, *English Medieval Castles* (new edition expected). The arguments between B. K. Davison and R. A. Brown about mottes can be followed in *Chateau-Gaillard*, III (1967), *Archaeological Journal*, CXXIV (1967) and CXXVI (1969), and in Brown's *Origins of English Feudalism* (1973). Davison's report on his Neroche excavations is in *Somerset Archaeological and Natural History Society Proceedings,* CXVI (1972). Some of the discoveries at Wallingford Castle are in *Berkshire Archaeological Journal,* LXII (1965–70). What is known about Southampton Castle is elucidated in C. Platt and R. Coleman-Smith, *Excavations in Medieval Southampton 1953–69* (1975). Ascott Doilly, excavated by E. M. Jope and R. I. Threlfall, is reported in *Antiquaries Journal,* XXXIX (1959), Middleton Stoney, by R. T. Rowley, in *Oxoniensia,* XXXVII (1972).

A most useful book on town walls by H. L. Turner, *Town Defences in England and Wales* (1971), can now be augmented by the Southampton excavation results, the walls there having already been studied in detail by B. H. St J. O'Neill in *Aspects of Archaeology in Britain and Beyond* (1951), edited by W. F. Grimes, and by D. F. Renn in *Medieval Archaeology,* VIII (1964). The Bargate is one of the buildings analysed by P. A. Faulkner in the Southampton Excavations volume, and the same writer's articles on late medieval planning in *Archaeological Journal,* CXV (1958), and CXX (1963), are important on later castles, calling in question a theory about the effect of bastard feudalism by W. D. Simpson in *Antiquaries Journal,* XXVI (1944). Preliminary reports on Ludgershall by P. V. Addyman are in *Chateau-Gaillard,* IV (1969) and VII (1975), and Banbury is soon to appear in *Oxoniensia,* XLI (1976), by K. Rodwell. Henry VIII's forts are introduced by A. Saunders' article in *Archaeological Journal,* CXXIII (1966).

Chapter Seven

There is a bibliography on works on buildings – *A Bibliography on Vernacular Architecture* (1972), by R. de Z. Hall. Books of general application include M. E. Wood, *The English Medieval House* (1965), M. W. Barley, *The English Farmhouse and Cottage* (1961), and E. Mercer, *English Vernacular Houses* (1975). Individual studies include those of the Southampton buildings by P. A. Faulkner in C. Platt and R. Coleman-Smith, *Excavations in Southampton,* Vol. 1 (1975), of the Oxford Wealden by J. Munby in *Oxoniensia,* XXXIX (1974), of the Yeovil one by L. C. Hayward and R. W. McDowall in *Somerset Proceedings,* CIX (1965), and of inns by W. A. Pantin in *Studies in Building History* (1961), edited by E. M. Jope.

North Berkshire has been surveyed by J. M. Fletcher – a synopsis is in *Oxoniensia,* XL (1975), the barns of north Oxfordshire by R. B. Wood-Jones, *Traditional Domestic Architecture of the Banbury Region* (1963), and priests' houses by W. A. Pantin in *Medieval Archaeology,* III (1959). Timber-framing techniques have many students, notably C. A. Hewett, *The Development of Carpentry* (1969), on jointing systems, a subject pursued by C. R. J. Currie in *Oxoniensia,* XXXVII (1972). Great Coxwell was described in detail in a monograph (1965) by W. Horn and E. Born. Roof trusses and related topics have provided a series of important articles by J. T. Smith, in *Archaeological Journal,* CXII (1955), CXV (1959), and CXXII (1965). The same author has an article in R. Berger (ed.), *Scientific Methods in Medieval*

Archaeology (1970), where the reader will also find more authoritative discussion of radio-carbon and dendrochronology than I can give. The cruck construction has fascinated many students: all discussion now starts with J. T. Smith in *Vernacular Architecture*, 6 (1975). The thirteenth-century Berkshire dates are in C. R. J. Currie and J. M. Fletcher, *Medieval Archaeology*, XVI (1972), and N. W. Alcock has a series of distribution maps in *A Catalogue of Cruck Buildings* (1973). The same author, with M. W. Barley, has done a survey of base-crucks, in *Antiquaries Journal*, LII (1972).

The study of floor-tiles is another with a long ancestry. E. S. Eames' British Museum booklet, *Medieval Tiles* (1968) is an admirable introduction, the same author's more detailed studies on the Clarendon tiles being in *Journal of the British Archaeological Association*, XX/XXI (1957-8), and XXXVI (1963). The Thames Valley tiles were studied by L. Haberly, *Medieval English Pavingtiles* (1937), the Penn industry by C. Hohler in *Records of Buckinghamshire*, XIV (1941-6), and William Tyelere's by E. C. Norton, *Hants. Field Club Proceedings*, XXX (1973). Ridge tiles were classified by E. M. Jope, *Oxoniensia*, XVI (1951), and roof furniture has been discussed in several of G. C. Dunning's works, notably in *Studies in Building History* (1961), edited by E. M. Jope, most recently in *Excavations in Medieval Southampton* (1975), Vol. II.

Chapter Eight

There are many works on the later history of towns, not all of them using archaeological information. A useful starting-point is C. Platt, *The English Medieval Town* (1976). Oxford excavation reports include those on Broad Street, *Oxoniensia*, IV (1939), by R. L. S. Bruce-Mitford; and in Cornmarket by E. M. Jope and W. A. Pantin, *Ibid.*, XXIII (1958), and by T. G. Hassall, *Ibid.*, XXXVI (1971). *Medieval Southampton* (1973) summarizes C. Platt's views, substantiated by his two-volume excavation report. Salisbury is one of the towns in the *Historic Towns Atlas*, Vol. I (1969), edited by M. Lobel; John Balle's house was described in the *Wiltshire Archaeological Magazine*, LXIX (1964). Information on Thame is in the Victoria County History, *Oxfordshire*, Vol. VII (1962), on Wimborne in the *Dorset Proceedings*, XCIV (1972), by N. Field. The planted towns are the subject of M. W. Beresford's fundamental *The New Towns of the Middle Ages* (1967), and several counties now have useful archaeological surveys of their new towns – Oxfordshire, by K. Rodwell; Hampshire, by M. F. Hughes; Wiltshire, by J. Haslam; and Dorset, by K. Penn.

The relative role of roads and rivers arises from a paper by R. H. C. Davis in *Oxoniensia*, XXXVIII (1973). The basic study of roads is by D. M. Stenton, *Economic History Review*, VII (1936), and *Transport and Communication 500–1100* (1972), by A. C. Leighton is useful, as is C. Cochrane, *Ancient Trackways of Wessex* (1969).

Bone reports are contained within excavation reports, e.g. by B. Noddle for Southampton, B. J. Marples for Oxford, M. Jope for Seacourt, and J. Pernetta and D. Bramwell for Tetsworth.

Chapter Nine

Sources for Saxon jewellery include the British and Ashmolean Museums' *Catalogues* cited above. I have tried to justify my ideas on treasure-giving in *Anglo-Saxon England*, 4 (1975). The qualities of stones are elaborated in *Medieval Lapidaries* (1924), edited by J. Evans and P. Studer. The Thame hoard was originally published by J. Evans *et al.* in *Antiquaries Journal*, xxi (1941), more recently by J. Cherry in *Archaeologia*, civ (1973).

Wooden bowls from Oxford were found by E. M. Jope (*Oxoniensia*, xv (1950)), from Southampton by C. Platt (*Excavations in Southampton*). Glass is reported in similar excavation reports.

Pottery has an enormous bibliography, but no synthesis. Much of our knowledge comes from the work of E. M. Jope, in articles already cited, and brought together in his essay in *Culture and Environment* (1963), edited by I. Ll. Foster and L. Alcock. Portchester ware and many other types are discussed in the relevant excavation reports. Essays in *Medieval Pottery from Excavations* (1974), were written as a tribute to Dr G. C. Dunning – whose own bibliography in that book is itself a basic source; they include B. Cunliffe on Saxon stamped ware, J. Musty on kilns, and M. Biddle and K. Barclay on Winchester ware. The Michelmersh kiln is briefly reported in *Medieval Archaeology*, xvi (1972). The Laverstock kiln report, by J. Musty *et al.*, is in *Archaeologia*, cii (1969). Polychrome pottery was studied by G. C. Dunning, *Archaeologia*, lxxxiii (1933), and more recently in *Archaeologia Cambrensis*, cxxiii (1974). The Knighton kiln was published by L. R. Fennelly, *Proceedings of the Hampshire Field Club*, xxvi (1969).

Broader studies include an important essay on the documentary sources by H. E. J. LePatourel in *Medieval Archaeology*, xii (1968). J. G. Hurst's introduction to B. Rackham, *Medieval English Pottery* (1969) is useful, though his commentary on the excellent photographs in the book is better. G. C. Dunning's work culminates in his essays on the pottery trade in *Dark Age Britain* (1956), edited by D. B. Harden, and in *Rotterdam Papers* (1968), edited by J. G. N. Renaud. A book of essays edited by D. Peacock, *Pottery and Economic Studies* (1977) should provide stimulating reviews! Least and very properly last, is my own Ashmolean pamphlet of photos of *Pottery of the Oxford Region* (1973).

Index